FIRST MILLION

5 STEPS TO FINANCIAL INDEPENDENCE

By Oliver Powers

Financial Disclaimer: I believe it is vitally important that you read and fully understand the following risks of investing.

INVESTMENT RISKS: All investments are highly speculative in nature and involve substantial risk of loss. I encourage all investors to invest very carefully. I also encourage investors to get personal advice from your professional investment advisor and to make independent investigations before acting on any information. Past performance is not necessarily indicative of future results. All investments carry significant risk and all investment decisions of an individual remain the specific responsibility of that individual. There is no guarantee that investments will result in profits or that they will not result in a full loss or losses All investors are advised to fully understand all risks associated with any kind of investing they choose to do. Do not enter any investment without fully understanding the worst-case scenarios of that investment.

FREE BONUS BOOK INSIDE

WIPEOUT!

5 DARING SCHEMES TO OVERCOME COLLEGE DEBT

By Oliver Powers

**Two personal finance books
for the price of one...**

For my wife, my treasure.

**"For where *your treasure* is,
there *your heart* will be also."**

—Matthew 6:21

1

PRECARIOUS

May / 30 Years Ago - A fleet of six black moving vans pulled into the driveway, as Betsy watched helplessly from the drapes of her living room window. Her chest was tight, and she struggled for breath, taking shallow, rapid gulps of air in a losing effort to stay calm. She had been expecting them.

Her eyes swept slowly across the contents of the room. Her new white couches, with light blue throw pillows, coffee table, and dining set were all purchased on credit from different furniture stores. The purchase of end tables, lamps and paintings were still camping on her credit card statements, with no plans to leave. For months Betsy struggled to make the minimum payments, hoping for a windfall that would never come.

Instead, the moving vans had come.

They had been circling her home for months, just waiting for her husband to leave. He was gone now, and they had come to take it all away. And Betsy with it.

The doorbell rang and she gasped, thinking of her son asleep in his bed. James knew about his dad, of course. But she had sheltered him from all the rest of it. And now they were at her door, ringing the bell.

She could barely breathe, and her legs were heavy, rooted to the floor. She looked down at her bathrobe and slippers. They were expensive, creamy white silk, perfectly matched, and she realized that she had also bought them on credit. She willed her slippers to move, to take a step, but she was frozen in place.

Could she just lock the door? Could she take James from his bed, buckle him safely into the leather interior of her new SUV, and make a run for it?

Before she could act, before she could move, the door swung open and the faceless moving men entered her home. They were each wearing black coveralls, black Ray-Ban sunglasses, and black tennis shoes. They filed into the room and kept coming, until hundreds of them had gathered. They were sitting at her dining room table, reclining on her couches, and flipping through her fashion magazines. She stared at them, thoroughly terrified, still unable to move.

The doorbell rang again. But before Betsy could answer it, the front door burst open as a giant wave crashed through her entry way and blasted into the back wall of her living room, carrying the furniture and moving men in its power. A collection of magazines, throw pillows and paintings swirled through the wave, as it crested back on itself, slamming the front door shut and blocking her only escape. The wave engulfed Betsy, along with her furniture and a tangle of swimming moving men. She desperately swam for the highest point of her ceiling, struggling through the legs of tables, chairs and kicking men. She reached the faux arch beam at the top of her ceiling, just ahead of the rising water. She took a last gulp of air, as a powerful current pulled her under...

"James!" Betsy gasped, sitting up in bed. She was reaching for the ceiling and her eyes were darting frantically. The sheets and blanket were tangled around her shoulders, wet with sweat. Her heart raced and she was panting, trying to catch her breath. She took a gulp of air, and then another, slowly calming herself. She fell back into her pillows. "What a nightmare."

Betsy closed her eyes and sighed deeply, slowly getting control of her breathing and her thoughts. Her room was dark, except for the red, neon display of her alarm clock. It was 3:27 Monday morning. And it was just a nightmare.

But Betsy knew that it was more than just a nightmare.

Her bed was so empty, so quiet. Her husband had been gone for several months, and she still wasn't used to the loneliness. It was a loneliness so real and present that it woke her from her sleep, almost every night.

She was wide awake now, and debated getting out of bed, putting on a pot of coffee, and getting some work done. But she was so tired. She rolled over and shut her eyes tightly, wishing for sleep, willing herself to pass out until the sun streamed through her windows. As the minutes threatened to stretch into hours, her thoughts rolled in her head like a marble in a cardboard shoe box, relentlessly searching for somewhere to rest. She wanted to pull the covers over her head and make her troubles disappear.

In that moment, tangled in her bed sheets, too exhausted to sleep, she realized that it was up to her now. She could either run from her troubles, or she could tackle them. And she wasn't helpless. She had good friends, loving parents, and an amazing son. She had her health, a good job, and a God who had a better plan for her life. She could handle this challenge, just as she had handled the other challenges in her life. And she wouldn't do it alone. She would ask for help.

"You must be joking!" Betsy exclaimed. "I need a million dollars?"

"I never joke about money," Julia Wright met Betsy's outburst with a cool, measured reply. Julia had that inner confidence that Betsy had always admired. She had straight, shoulder-length blonde hair and wore a crisp, blue business suit. Her nails were perfectly manicured, their color matching the light pink shade of her lipstick. Julia was always carefully put together and her calm presence made Betsy feel a little scattered.

They had known each other since third grade and had been close friends ever since. They backpacked through Europe together after college and were bridesmaids in each other's weddings. Even though the demands of life had pulled them apart over the years, Julia was the person Betsy reached out to when she was in trouble.

They sat in Julia's conference room at a long, polished wood table, lined with black leather chairs. The room was understated and professional, about what you would expect from a certified financial planner, with floor-to-ceiling glass walls and a view of a parking lot, surrounded by trees.

"Seriously? A million dollars? That might not be a lot of money for you, but it's an impossible fortune for someone like me," Betsy declared indignantly.

Julia shook her head slowly. "Let's skip the dramatics, Betsy. A million dollars seems like a lot of money today, but in 20 or 30 years from now, it won't be. It will really be just the minimum anyone needs for financial independence." She had this conversation every day, with every client. She was secure in the truth of her statement.

"And a million dollars is just the beginning, Betsy. Knowing your tastes, you're going to need more than that."

"But that's totally impossible," Betsy felt like crying.

Just a few months ago, Betsy Grant was living the dream. She had a beautiful home in an affluent neighborhood, a gleaming new SUV, a son who was crazy about baseball, and a devoted husband who loved her – or so she thought. Now she was in the middle of the most difficult year of her life. A single mom, deeply in debt, with nothing in savings, and divorce attorneys billing her at $150 an hour, as she fought to hang on to whatever was left. Betsy put her head in her hands, thoroughly defeated. "I am wiped out, Jules. I have nothing left but debts and bills."

"And you've got plenty of those," Julia agreed. She wasn't letting Betsy off the hook. It was truth serum time. "No charge for my help, by the way. I still owe you for that night in Venice. Remember that waiter?"

Betsy laughed, breaking the tension. They shared a lot of funny memories. "Thanks, Jules. That means a lot."

"I get it. You feel like the pilot of the Hindenburg right now. But this is right now," Julia leaned forward and took Betsy's hand. "You are still young. You have a good job with benefits. You have your health, an amazing son, and supportive parents. And you make the best chocolate cheesecake this side of the Atlantic. Betsy, I'm telling you, it's bleak right now, but you will get through this. You will rebuild your life. But I am suggesting that you do it differently this time."

"You mean, I shouldn't marry a childish, self-centered jerk?" Betsy laughed.

"That's a good start," Julia smiled, she was tempted to say more about Betsy's ex-husband, but she held back. "No, I am really talking about your finances. You need to handle your money in a completely new way. It's time to stop buying luxury items you can't afford just to impress your friends. You need to save your money, avoid all forms of debt, and stop pretending you're married to a rock star."

Betsy glared back at her and started to say something, but Julia spoke first.

"You need to grow up when it comes to money, Betsy. Seriously, you're like a sixth grader. OK, maybe a seventh grader. But your finances are still in middle school."

Betsy shook her head, surprised by her friend's directness. She glanced through the window at the trees, their shadows stretching across the parking lot. It was getting late and she needed to pick James up at practice. "Is this the tough love part?"

"Pretty much," Julia admitted. "We are long past Valentine's Day here. But I am not asking you to do anything that I don't expect from myself, or my clients. Face it, Betsy. You have a very reckless financial past. You lived in a house you couldn't afford, drove an expensive car you didn't really own, and wore clothes that cost double what you could get them for at a different store. And now you're broke. Big surprise, right?"

Betsy was stunned and ready to leave.

Julia held up a hand. "The games need to stop, Betsy. Your friends might think you're wealthy, but you and I know the truth. Your train is off the rails."

"That isn't true. We always paid our mortgage on time. We made our car payments. We could afford our lifestyle. We just didn't have anything left over at the end of the month…." Betsy's voice trailed off.

"That's what I'm talking about. You had a life you couldn't afford, living paycheck-to-paycheck. If the paychecks stopped, you were sunk," Julia explained. "It is time for you to take charge of your money and get it working for you. You need to make these changes now, so you can have that amazing life you've always wanted."

Betsy was quiet for a moment, soaking in her friend's words. They were hard to hear, but she knew they were true. She sighed deeply and finally said, "But I have no idea how to get there. I am in a hole so deep that I don't see any way out of it. I just feel like giving up."

"I get it. And I hear this every day, believe me. But it is not as bleak as you think. You still have a paddle and the waterfall isn't for another hundred yards or so. There are 5 steps I want you to follow. I am not saying they are easy, but they are not impossible either. They just take a little planning and a little discipline. And within a few months, you'll have that hole of yours filled in and you'll be building something special. It's called financial independence," Julia explained.

"You keep saying financial independence. What do you mean by that? I don't get money from my parents, or anything like that."

"No, I'm talking about saving money. Enough money so you don't need a job anymore. Financial independence means you don't live paycheck-to-paycheck. It means you don't have to rely on a salary from a job. It means that you have enough money saved up so you can take care of your family for the rest of your life, even if you don't work."

"That's crazy!" Betsy sputtered. "No one lives like that. Everyone works and spends the money they make, right? I mean, they might save a little bit, but not like what you are talking about."

"I am not talking about the majority of people, Betsy," Julia continued. "Most people are terrible with money. They spend every dollar they make. But they are living a lie. They can't really afford their lifestyles. As soon as they lose their job, they are in big trouble. That's a risky way to live. There is a better way. A simpler way. A happier way."

"And you're saying that you live like this, Jules?" Betsy asked.

"Of course, I do. I'm a financial planner. It comes with the job," Julia laughed. "I am not there yet, but I'm on my way."

"But you always look so elegant. And you drive a nice car."

"Thank you," Julia flipped her hair over her shoulder dramatically. "But I shop at discount stores. And my car is 8 years old with 135,000 miles on it."

"It looks new," Betsy said incredulously.

"Well, I do wash it. But I bought it used. I paid all cash. That's how I always buy my cars."

"Seriously? I thought everyone pretty much drives the nicest car they can afford."

"If they make car payments, they can't afford it. The bank really owns it."

Betsy signed and looked at her watch. "I gotta go, Jules. I think I understand what you're talking about, but I don't think this is for me. It sounds too…"

"Too radical?"

"Really radical. And totally crazy."

"Then it's time to be crazy. Look, Betsy, you need to listen very carefully. To be financially secure, you will need to save a million dollars. Even if you marry another Prince Charming, you will need to do this for your family. It is not a matter of whether it is right for you. It is something you must do. It's that simple."

"Why a million dollars? That seems like a lot of money," Betsy asked again.

"Don't you think it has a nice ring to it?" Julia shrugged.

"Yes, but..."

"Just kidding. Most financial experts agree that, in retirement, you can safely take an annual income of five percent from your savings or investment account. So, if you have a million dollars in about 30 years from now, you would have an income of about $50,000 a year. At five percent, you can take this $50,000 every year for the rest of your life, without the fear of reducing the amount of your savings. You would still have enough account growth to keep the balance steady at about a million dollars and be able to continue to receive that same $50,000 every year. This income from your investment account would probably be taken as a combination of dividend income and account appreciation," Julia explained. "$50,000 is roughly what the average American will make in 30 years from now. How much are you making now?"

"I make $25,000 a year," Betsy admitted.

"Right! You want to retire in comfort, with the ability to pay your bills, cover your taxes, outpace inflation, and maybe go see that waiter in Venice again. You want to enjoy your life after decades of hard work. To do that, you will need about the same income you have now, right? So, $25,000 of income today will be about the same as making $50,000 in thirty years from now. This means you will need to save a million dollars."

"30 years from now?" Betsy shook her head. "That seems so far away."

"Yeah, I wonder what the world will be like in 30 years from now?" Julia asked. "Flying cars and hover chairs?"

Betsy laughed. "I bet we'll just travel back and forth on a beam of light. Do you think Social Security will still be around by then?"

"I wouldn't count on it," Julia shook her head. "Sure, it might be there for you. But do you really want to trust your future to the politicians in Washington? If Social Security remains solvent, you would have that extra income. That, plus the $50,000 per year, would provide you with a pretty comfortable life. But Social Security is not designed to be your only source of income in retirement. You can't bank on it."

"So, instead of banking on Social Security and Prince Charming, I need to save a million dollars – on my own? But I don't make enough money to do that."

"Yes, you do. You don't need to earn a lot of money to save a million dollars. With an income of $25,000 a year, you can become a millionaire within your lifetime."

"I just don't see how that is possible. How do you turn an income of $25,000 a year into a million dollars?"

"It's not how much you earn, Betsy. It's how much you save. And the earlier you start, the faster you can get to a million dollars. Which is what you…"

"Which is what I need to be financially independent," Betsy finished her sentence.

"That's right," Julia beamed.

"This is a lot to think about," Betsy said, as she stood to leave. "I'm not sure I'm ready. You say it's easy, but I don't see it."

"No, it's not easy. But it isn't very hard either. Like I started to say, there are 5 steps you need to take to save your first million."

"My *first* million?" Betsy laughed.

"Yes, you'll see, Betsy. Once you save the first million, you can use the 5 Steps to save the next million and the million after that." Julia pulled a sheet of paper out of her padfolio and started writing.

"In fact, there is really no limit to how much net worth you can acquire by following these 5 Steps." She handed the sheet of paper to Betsy.

"This is it?" Betsy looked at the list. "Is this my prescription, Doctor?"

"Yes, and you're going to live. But I want you to do one more thing before you start cutting up your credit cards." Julia gave Betsy a conspiratorial smile. "There is a man that I want you to meet."

"Is he rich?" Betsy laughed.

"Very."

"By wisdom a house is built, and by understanding it is established; and by knowledge the rooms are filled with all precious and pleasant riches."

—Proverbs 24:3-4

2

BUDGET FIRST

June / 30 Years Ago - Betsy sat in her SUV outside of an old warehouse, near the airport. The parking lot was empty, except for a single, black pick-up truck parked in front of the huge, metal double doors. The parking lot was enclosed by a tall chain link fence, with a roll of razor wire along the top. Airplanes thundered overhead every few minutes as they descended to the runway a few blocks away. Betsy's ex-husband had her son, James, for the weekend, so she had agreed to meet Ernesto Sanchez at his office on this Saturday morning. Now she wished she hadn't.

By Julia's description, Ernesto was one of the wealthiest men in town. She must have given her the wrong address. This was not what she was expecting on her first step toward becoming a millionaire. She laughed nervously as she checked the address again.

Knuckles rapped on her car window and Betsy jumped. A man in his mid-fifties, wearing aviator sunglasses, a fleece-lined denim jacket, and a Caterpillar cap smiled at her from outside the driver-side window. His words were muffled. She rolled the window down halfway.

"Are you Betsy?" The man asked again with a wide smile, revealing perfectly even, white teeth under a carefully trimmed mustache.

"Mr. Sanchez?"

He smiled wider. "Please. Call me, Ernesto."

"Did you bring the 5 Steps?" Ernesto asked. They were sipping coffee at a plastic folding table in the middle of his warehouse. The cement floor was swept clean and the room was filled with natural light. It was a big space and it made Betsy feel like she could tackle big ideas. Pads of grid paper were neatly stacked in the center of the table, next to a coffee cup filled with mechanical pencils.

"Yes. I guess they're pretty important," Betsy said, pulling them from her purse.

"They are more than important," Ernesto replied with a knowing smile. "The 5 Steps are life-changing."

"I am sorry, Mr. Sanchez, but I…."

"Please. Call me Ernesto." He repeated.

"Ok, yes, Ernesto. I'm sorry, but you need to understand. I am new to all of this. And now I am sitting in a warehouse in a rough part of town with a total stranger talking about the life-changing properties of these 5 Steps. It all seems a little weird."

Ernesto chuckled. "You don't like my warehouse? My partner and I just bought it."

"No, I didn't mean that. It is a lovely warehouse…."

"And this part of town is going to change. This property will be worth a lot of money one day," Ernesto explained.

"Oh, I'm sure that it will...," Betsy was flustered. "It's just a strange place to meet, on a Saturday, you know..."

"I meet here every morning. This is one of our offices. We keep our trucks here for our construction projects. I have a team meeting with our crews here every morning, then send the trucks out. When the warehouse is empty, we are making money," Ernesto smiled. "But I understand where you are coming from. This is all new to you. But not to me."

"I feel like I am joining some kind of a secret club," Betsy laughed. "And you and Julia are trying to initiate me."

"I help a lot of Julia's friends. Most of them don't understand how the 5 Steps work. So, I try to show them. This isn't a secret club. But I guess it is an exclusive club. Membership is free, but most people don't want to join." Ernesto smiled and took a sip of his coffee. "Do you like my coffee?"

"Actually, yes, I do. This is one of the best cups of coffee I have ever had." And Betsy meant it.

"Thank you," Ernesto smiled with pride. He stood up and walked across the warehouse floor to a cabinet along the backwall, his voice echoed as he returned with a freshly ground bag of coffee in his hands. "We grind the beans ourselves. We invested in a little coffee plantation a couple of years ago and they fly our beans into the airport, right here. Super fresh. It's a passion for me and my wife."

Ernesto handed the bag of coffee to Betsy. "This is for you. I hope you enjoy it."

"I will. Thank you so much," Betsy studied the coffee before putting it on the table next to her purse. "It's very kind of you."

Ernesto smiled and took another sip. "So, what do you think of the 5 Steps?"

"They seem really simple," Betsy said. "I guess I expected something more complicated or earth-shattering."

"The concepts are simple. But hard work goes into implementing them," Ernesto leaned back in his chair. "Read them to me."

Betsy sighed and took up the sheet of paper that Julia had given her. She had read the list before, but nothing special had jumped off the page. "Let's see. Step One. Budget First."

"Do you have a budget?" Ernesto asked simply.

"Yes, sort of….. Well, maybe not. I mean, we always had a rough idea…"

"The budget is the most important thing you need to become a millionaire. Do not underestimate its power. What's the next one?"

Betsy continued.

"Step One: Budget First.

Step Two: Debt Free.

Step Three: Live Simply.

Step Four: Save and Reinvest.

Step Five: Work Hard."

"Got it?" Ernesto smiled.

"Yes, I get it. I just don't understand how these 5 Steps are so life changing.

"That's because you haven't taken them yet. You need to work through them in order, consistently, every day. And at the end of the year, your life will be very different than it is today," Ernesto explained. "I followed these 5 Steps when I was a young man, many years ago. And I am wealthy today as a result."

Betsy looked across the empty warehouse. The floor was spotless, and everything was neatly stored. She could tell that Ernesto took pride in his business and his success. But he was humble, too. "So, I start with a budget?"

"Yes, Step One: Budget First. Why don't you grab one of those pads and I will help you get started? You need to keep working on it until you have all of your expenses covered...."

"What if my expenses are more than my income? Ever since my divorce, I can't seem to get my head above water..."

"You need a budget that makes you cash positive, with at least a few dollars left over each month. You need to keep cutting expenses or expanding your income until you get there. But the income must be real. No dreaming," Ernesto insisted.

They went to work, listing Betsy's income and expenses. Betsy tried to use ballpark numbers, but Ernesto wouldn't have it. He asked for exact numbers, and every little expense. By the end of their session, Betsy had enjoyed three cups of coffee and had a stack of scratch paper and notes stacked next to her. She also had a budget, and it looked like this:

Betsy's Budget - Annual Household Income of $25,000.00

Monthly Income		
Salary Income (after taxes, social security, etc.):	$ 1,545.00	
Other Income: Child Support	$ 700.00	
Total Monthly Income:		**$ 2,245.00**
Monthly Fixed Expenses:		
Mortgage (Ex-Husband currently pays 50%)	$ 1,087.00	
Property Taxes (Ex-Husband currently pays 50%)	$ 108.00	
HOA Dues (Ex-Husband currently pays 50%)	$ 63.00	
Car Payment	$ 174.00	
Minimum Credit Card Payment	$ 75.00	
Water Utility	$ 33.00	
Cable (Ex-Husband currently pays 50%)	$ 42.00	
Home Phone	$ 29.00	
Electricity & Gas	$ 84.00	
Car Insurance	$ 63.00	
Life Insurance	$ 00.00	
Home Insurance (Ex-Husband currently pays 50%)	$ 31.00	
Total Fixed Monthly Expenses:		**$ 1,789.00**
Remaining Balance:		**$ 456.00**
Additional Expenses - Cash:		
Savings	$ 00.00	
Groceries	$ 250.00	
Meals & Entertainment	$ 50.00	
Vacation Fund	$ 00.00	
Christmas & Gift Fund	$ 25.00	
Gas for Car	$ 75.00	
Personal / Clothes Fund	$ 50.00	
Total Additional Expenses:		**$ 450.00**
Remaining Balance:		**$ 6.00**

"Now, you can see why I don't have a budget." Betsy slid the final budget over to Ernesto and sat back in her chair. "I have slashed my expenses down to nothing and I only have six dollars left over. And that's if I am super careful. I have no money for savings, a bunch of debt, and my ex-husband will only pay for his half of the house for a few more months. Then I will really be in trouble."

Ernesto studied her budget. "Yeah, but this is a good start. OK, now let's talk about your debt. Give it to me straight."

Betsy took another pad and started writing down her debts. The list was longer than she realized:

List of Betsy's Debts	
Credit Cards	$ 4,258.00
Department Store Credit Cards	$ 1,176.00
Car Loan	$ 26,525.00
Mortgage	$ 274,186.00
Lawyer's Fees	$ 2,106.00
Total Debt:	**$ 308,251.00**

"Pretty awful, isn't it?" Betsy felt like crying again.

"Oh, I've seen a lot worse," Ernesto said as he studied the list. He could tell she was upset. "I can see how you could get discouraged. But there is a way out of this debt and a way to start saving. But you need to make sure you are ready to start." Ernesto looked up from the list of debts and met her eyes. "You need to put savings aside first before you spend money on anything else. At least ten percent each month. But, in your case, I think you should save even more money, since you are a single mom."

"That seems totally impossible," Betsy protested.

"Americans like to spend everything they make. They buy the most expensive homes they can afford. They lease or take out big car loans so they can look cool in freeway traffic. Many of them are spending one hundred percent of what they make. And sometimes much more than that. Why? To impress their friends? Real friends don't need to be impressed. They are more likely to respect someone who is living within their means. You need to do things differently, Betsy. You need to live on eighty percent, seventy percent, or even sixty percent of what you earn. This is how you get ahead and save that first million."

Betsy considered Ernesto words. They made a lot of sense. She had been competing with her friends and neighbors in a game she couldn't win. It was time to play a new game. "What choice do I have?"

"You have many choices. But to see this through, you will need conviction. You will need to be determined. You will have to say no to a lot of fun opportunities and things that seem important. If you are not all in, you will never make it."

Ernesto studied her eyes carefully. "Are you all in?"

Betsy sighed and returned his gaze. "Yes, Ernesto. I am all in."

"Great. This is what you need to do…." Ernesto started marking up her budget with a red pencil, as Betsy looked on. "Sell my car?"

"Absolutely. And your house, too," Ernesto said in a gentle voice.

"Wait a minute…" Betsy protested.

"Betsy, you can't afford your house, or your car. They are keeping you on a debt hamster wheel. The best way to free up money to pay off debt and build your net worth is by cutting your expenses."

"But I love my house. It's the only home James has ever known."

"It's a thing, Betsy. And you're getting divorced. You will need to sell your house anyway."

"I was sort of hoping that I could keep it. You know, refinance the loan and cover all of the payments on my own..."

Ernesto shook his head slowly. "I am sorry, Betsy. It's just not in the cards."

"You weren't kidding when you said that these 5 Steps would change my life," Betsy shook her head in frustration, her eyes dropping to her list of debts.

"Julia wanted you to meet with me for two reasons. First, she knew I could tell you things that other people wouldn't dare say to you. But this is what you must do, Betsy. Otherwise, you will always be in debt."

"And the other reason?" Betsy looked up.

"Because I did it. And I can show you how."

They worked through the morning and well into the afternoon. Ernesto's wife, Rose, arrived at lunchtime with sandwiches. She joined them for lunch and added her ideas to Betsy's budget plan and the changes she needed to make in her life.

"A house is just wood, stucco and concrete," Rose said. "But a home has the heart that you create inside of it. It goes with you everywhere."

"So, you think I should sell my house, too?" Betsy asked, a little surprised.

"You must! The house you have now is too expensive. Find something nice that you can afford, with plenty of money left over. Don't let your pride tell you how to live."

"Wow. You really say it like it is, Rose."

"I want you to be happy. Live a simple life, with lots of money left over every month. That's how to be happy."

By mid-afternoon, Betsy and Ernesto had drafted a new budget. They cut her cable and reduced her expenses. They added life insurance and a tithe to her church. "Honor God, and He will bless you," Ernesto said simply.

By showing Betsy how she could sell her SUV and pay cash for a used car, they were able to eliminate her car payment. They also agreed to sell her house and, using some of the equity that would be left from her part of the sale, pay cash to buy her used car. Then, with a quick search through the Saturday real estate section of the paper that Rose had brought with her, Betsy was able to confirm that there were several nice townhomes and condominiums in the same school district that she could afford. They allocated the extra money to begin her savings campaign and pay off her debt. While the changes were radical, Betsy felt a huge weight lift from her shoulders. "I think I might like this better."

Betsy's Revised Budget - Annual Household Income of $25,000.00

Monthly Income		
Salary Income (after taxes, social security, etc.):	$ 1,545.00	
Other Income: Child Support	$ 700.00	
Total Monthly Income:		**$ 2,245.00**
Monthly Fixed Expenses:		
Tithe / Charity	$ 154.00	
New Estimated Mortgage	$ 650.00	
Property Taxes	$ 110.00	
HOA Dues	$ 66.00	
Car Payment	$ 00.00	
Minimum Credit Card Payment	$ below	
Water Utility	$ 25.00	
Cable	$ 00.00	
Home Phone	$ 65.00	
Electricity & Gas	$ 70.00	
Car Insurance	$ 42.00	
Life Insurance	$ 50.00	
Home Insurance	$ 25.00	
Total Fixed Monthly Expenses:		**$ 1,257.00**
Remaining Balance:		**$ 988.00**
Sell House and Car. Pay-off remaining debt of $7,540 @ $600 per month for 13 months, then begin saving in each of the categories below.		
Additional Expenses - Cash:		
James' College Fund	$ 50.00	
Next Car Fund	$ 50.00	
First Million Fund	$ 500.00	
Total Savings: (Once Debt is Paid-Off)		**$ 600.00**
Groceries	$ 200.00	
Meals & Entertainment	$ 20.00	
Vacation Fund	$ 50.00	

Christmas & Gift Fund	$ 10.00	
Gas for Car	$ 75.00	
Personal / Clothes Fund	$ 20.00	
Medical / Co-Pays	$ 10.00	
Total Additional Expenses:		**$ 385.00**
Remaining Balance:		**$ 3.00**

"This is amazing, Ernesto! I can't believe that I will be out of debt in just a year," Betsy exclaimed, seeing the magic of her budget for the first time.

Ernesto referred to her new budget. "And after that you will be saving $500 a month, plus putting money away for your son's college tuition and your next car. This will be the beginning of your financial independence."

Betsy studied the numbers. "So, I will save $50 per month for James' college… But I don't see how saving a $500 a month can grow into a million dollars."

"That's because your budget is only Step One," Ernesto explained. "You still need to take the other four steps."

"I almost forgot about the other four steps," she sighed, exhausted. "I don't know if I have the strength to take another step."

"Julia told me about your trip around to world," Ernesto replied, taking another sip of coffee.

"Europe," Betsy corrected. "Why do you bring that up?"

"Your trip through Europe must have taken a lot of planning. You had to map out your itinerary, buy airline tickets and rail passes, book hotels, plan out your expenses. Right?"

"Yes," Betsy smiled. "I did most of the planning. Julia had this impossible schedule as a senior in college, you know, always the over-achiever. So, I pretty much put the whole trip together by myself. I added a lot of twists and side trips to surprise her in different places. It was really fun."

"Julia said you did a great job," Ernesto agreed.

"Were you checking up on me, Ernesto?" Betsy's eyes narrowed.

"Of course. I didn't want to waste my time. Or yours. I needed to make sure that you could see the 5 Steps through."

"And Julia told you about our trip?"

"Yes, because she understands that financial planning is a lot like planning a vacation, or your adventure through Europe. You have to think things through, create a budget, consider the details and logistics," Ernesto explained.

"Yeah, I guess that's true," Betsy agreed.

"And you need to make sure that you don't get stuck in a foreign country, where you can't speak the language, with no money, no passport, and no idea where to go next."

"That sounds a little scary. Maybe that's why I planned the trip so carefully."

Ernesto nodded. "It's the same with money. You put careful plans together to make sure that you don't get stuck in a scary situation. And you can have a great adventure along the way."

"Planning a trip is a lot more fun than planning out your financial future," Betsy insisted.

"Is it?" Ernesto gave her a warm, knowing smile. "Really?"

"A good name is to be more desired than great wealth."

—Proverbs 22:1

3

DEBT FREE

September / 15 Years Later & 15 Years Ago - James Grant watched as the bartender pulled the tap and expertly filled an ice-cold mug to the brim with his favorite pilsner. The beer was chilled and foamy, just what he needed after a long, hot round of golf. He paid in cash and made his way through the 19th hole crowd looking for an open table. He found one by the window, overlooking the 18th green and the lake beyond it. Only one other person was sitting there.

"Mind if I join you?" James asked.

"Sure. Have a seat." The man stood up from some papers he was studying and gestured to the chair across from him. He was about James' age, with a confident smile. He was wearing a tailored blue suit, over a red polo shirt, with brown Italian loafers. His carefully trimmed, dark brown hair was combed back over his ears, making him look like he had stepped out of the summer edition of a Brooks Brothers catalog. James noticed that he was one of the only other twenty-somethings at the charity event.

"I'm Caden McBride." The young man thrust out his hand.

"James Grant," James replied, switching his beer glass into his left hand, so he could shake Caden's hand.

They both sat down and Caden referred to a chart he was working on. "You did alright out there. More pars than bogeys."

"Thanks," James said. "How do you know my score?"

"There are spies everywhere," Caden whispered, taking a sip of his chardonnay. His polo shirt was embroidered with the charity logo across his heart. "Actually, I was running the scorer's table. That's how I know your score. Mr. Sanchez asked our law firm to handle all of the event details for him."

"To discourage cheating?" James asked with a smile.

"Not much chance of that," Caden laughed. "It's all for charity."

"You never know..."

"True. If you are any indication, this is a pretty rough crowd. How are you connected with Bannister-Sanchez? Are you in accounting?" Caden asked.

"Do I look like an accountant?" James asked, a little surprised. He was tall and lanky, with dirty blonde hair, an easy smile, and eyes the color of Hersey's Kisses. He spoke slow and careful, like a reluctant hero from an old dime store novel.

"No, but most of the guys playing today are suppliers and sub-contractors to Bannister-Sanchez. I just figured you would be another professional like me, currying favor with Mr. Sanchez. Or playing your way through charity tournaments, until you hit the professional golfing circuit."

"Not likely," James laughed. "I'm one of his subs."

"Really? But you're like 20 years too young, and 40 pounds underweight," Caden observed with a laugh. "What kind of work?"

"Oh, I have a little plumbing business." James took a sip of his beer.

"You own it?" Caden was surprised again.

"Yup. And all the headaches that come with it," James replied, setting his beer on the napkin.

"Sounds like you really love it," Caden joked.

"I do actually. I've always wanted my own business."

"What got you into it?" Caden leaned forward, putting the elbows of his blazer on the table.

"I've been doing it since college. I wanted to pay my way through to help my mom out. So, I met with one of my professors, you know, from the entrepreneur program, about what kind of a business could work for me. He suggested that I find something highly profitable, highly scalable, and in high demand."

"Plumbing?" Caden asked, surprised for a third time.

"You'd be amazed at the margins in plumbing," James said simply.

Caden thought about it for a second. "You got a point there. But you don't strike me as the plumber-type. I can't picture you climbing under a sink, with your pants... Well, you know."

"I'm more of the accountant-type?" James smiled.

"No, you've proven that you're not an accountant. But I wouldn't peg you as a plumber, either."

"Well, I'm primarily a plumbing contractor for new construction homes and remodels. My projects are larger than the repair side of the business. I don't climb under many sinks."

"It didn't take you long to become a plumbing expert," Caden was impressed.

"Well, to tell you the truth, I am a rookie when it comes to plumbing. But I am learning fast. I have a great team of people. They're the plumbing geniuses. I just run the business and find the new projects."

"Smart." Caden nodded, as the picture came together for him. "And Bannister-Sanchez is one of your accounts?"

"Have been for a while. My mom introduced me to Ernesto Sanchez a few years back. He said once I got my business over the million-dollar mark, I should come and see him."

"A million dollars? In plumbing?" Caden was stunned.

"Yup," James smiled. "Well, that really motivated me. So, I set a goal to get to a million in revenue by the time I graduated. My grades suffered some, but I made it and Ernesto gave me a big project. Sort of a graduation gift."

"Really?" Caden leaned forward. "Which project?"

"Walden Glenn. You know, over by the movie theatre. Just west of the freeway."

"Three hundred homes," Caden knew the project well. The whole community did. "And you did all of the plumbing?"

"I had to earn it. Ernesto started me with just 10 homes and gave me targets. He said if I could hit them, and pass his inspection, he would give me more. I put my best guys on it and walked the site every day. We kept meeting the targets and he kept giving us more houses. Before we knew it, the project was finished."

"Amazing. And you just graduated a few years ago?"

"Yeah, long days but short years. You know how it goes."

"Sometimes the years are long, too," Caden observed, sipping his wine. "Where did you go to college?"

"State," James was growing uncomfortable under the questioning. "How about you? Did you always want to be a lawyer?"

"No," Caden laughed. "Growing up I wanted to be a rock star. I was in a garage band and we played high school gigs, and some corporate parties. I got pretty good."

"Why did you give it up?"

"To make money. The odds of making it big as a rock star were not in my favor. But I knew I would always be rich if I became a lawyer."

"And are you?" James enjoyed taking over the questions.

"What? Rich? Maybe, by some people's standards."

"So, you gave up the garage band and went off to college to be a lawyer? Sounds very practical. Except for the big tuition bills."

"Yes, plenty of those. I went to the Ivy league for undergraduate, then law school. I nearly accepted an offer from a big Manhattan law firm, but I decided to be a big fish in a smaller pond. I picked the biggest law firm in this little city and I have been working there ever since."

"You picked?" James took another sip of his beer.

"I had some choices. My grades were good, so I was courted by a few firms. Simple choice. I picked the firm that would allow me to make partner the fastest."

"And you're a partner now?" James asked.

"Well, no," Caden faltered. "I have a few more years to go. They have me on the fast-track, though. Which is a good thing. I need to stay ahead of my student debt…"

James stopped mid-sip. "Really? Did you take on a lot of student debt?"

"Sure. Everyone does," Caden declared.

"I never did," James said evenly. "The thought of a bunch of debt waiting for me after college terrified me. That's why I went to State. I could live at home and get my courses out of the way. Just paid as I went."

"You passed on the whole college experience? No keg parties? No cheerleaders?"

"I got a lot out of college. I just didn't live on campus or do the fraternity thing. But I learned a lot and earned a first-class education. That's what it's all about, right?"

"I suppose... but you missed some fun times."

"Sounds like I missed some expensive times," James corrected.

"And you're saying you have no student debt?" Caden was skeptical.

"No," James insisted. "I don't think Ernesto would have hired my company if I had exhibited carelessness with college debt. You know how he is."

"I don't actually know Mr. Sanchez personally," Caden admitted. "He works mostly through the senior partners."

"He's very sharp. And salt of the earth. But he is no nonsense when it comes to money."

"I hear he is worth a fortune," Caden lowered his voice.

"And you would never guess it. He lives a very simple life. He's had the same house for thirty years. Drives a truck like mine. You'd never guess he was worth hundreds of millions of dollars. For him, money is a tool, not something that you use to impress other people."

"He's crazy! If I had his wealth, I would live a big life. Cars, planes, houses all over the country."

James shook him off. "Ernesto is far from crazy. He's one of the best people I know."

"He's doing something right," Caden conceded. "I guess everyone has their own view of how to use money."

"Yeah, that's true. But Ernesto has the right one."

"Are you suggesting that I don't?" Caden shot back.

James was surprised by Caden's terse reply. "I'm not saying that. I don't know you, Caden. But willingly taking on a bunch of college debt has set you back financially. You're off to a tough start."

"Are you always this direct?" Caden said and picked up his wine glass. He just held it in his hand, not taking a sip.

"Only with the things I know about. And money is one of them. I learned a lot from my mom, and she learned a lot from Ernesto. I guess I'm carrying on their legacy."

"Legacy? I am not sure I follow...." Caden set his glass down again.

"I guess it's a way of life. You know, living debt free. A lot of people spend more money than they really have just to compete with other people. They get deep into debt and struggle to get ahead. But I live debt free and keep my expenses as low as possible. Frees up money to save, invest and grow my business. That's how Ernesto does it. It's how my mom does it. And now I am doing it the same way."

"Debt free?" Caden scoffed. "I don't see the advantages. Sometimes you need to borrow money to get where you want to go."

"I don't want to go there. It's very difficult to become financially independent if you owe money to banks and credit card companies."

"Why wait?" Caden corrected him. "I need to look the part of a successful attorney. It's no big deal if I take on a little debt. I'll pay it all off when I am making the big bucks."

"I'll grant you some of that is needed. I have nice looking trucks, and my guys wear professional uniforms. But I don't think it's worth going into debt to impress other people."

"That's your choice, I suppose," Caden was squirming a little and eager to leave. He picked up his wine glass. "But I like my choices."

James continued. "You're right. We all make our own money choices. You can invest your money or spend it. You can take on debt. Or save until you can afford to buy something. You can drive a luxury car, or a second-hand pick-up truck. Both are fine for getting you around. I didn't need to go to a fancy Ivy league. State was fine for me."

Caden put the wine glass down quickly, nearly spilling its contents. "I don't see it that way. I went to the best school I could get into. Same with law school. I knew I could get a good job when I graduated and pay the money back."

"No, I understand where you are coming from. I just don't believe in debt. I try to pay cash for everything."

"Everything?" Caden shook his head. "Come on. Some forms of debt are ok. What about buying a house?"

"Yeah, that's true. Borrowing money to buy a home can be a good investment. You build up positive equity over time and it's a great way to increase your net worth. It's better than paying rent. I just don't want to take on any debt. It's just not right for me..." James went quiet. The silence was unnerving for Caden.

"Do you own a home?" Caden was cross-examining him now.

"Yeah."

"Don't you have a mortgage?" The crowded bar was growing louder, and Caden nearly shouted the question.

"No. I lived at home, saved up my money, and paid cash. I bought a total fixer-upper in a part of town you probably wouldn't like. But it has a lot of potential. One day, it will be a great rental property. Then I'll buy my next house."

"Really? You paid all cash for your house?" Caden was skeptical.

"I don't usually talk about this kind of thing...."

"But what about your car? You didn't pay cash for that."

"Matter of fact, I did. But it's a truck. And I bought it used. I have a few of them. You know, for the business."

"No one does that, James!"

"Does what?" James spoke over the laughter of the crowd.

"Pays all cash for houses and cars," Caden insisted.

"I guess I do. It's the only way I know how. Why? How do you do it?"

"I lease a Mercedes. Nothing wrong with that. And I just bought a sweet, 3,500 square foot house. Brand new."

Caden was trying to brag, but James felt a little sorry for him. "But you have all that student loan debt. Why would you lease an expensive car and buy a big, new house? I'm sure they pay you pretty well, but you might want to rethink how you handle your money."

"How is it a problem to own a Mercedes and a big house?"

"That's just it. You don't own them. The bank does," James replied simply.

Caden grew quiet and James finished his beer. The silence between them became awkward.

"I better get back to help with the event," Caden stood. His face was ashen, the confident smile gone.

"I'm sorry if I made you feel badly. I usually shoot straight from the hip on money stuff. I guess it's part of my upbringing."

"No problem..." Caden forced a smile. "Nice to meet you."

"You sure about that?" James smiled.

Caden shrugged and disappeared into the crowd of golfers.

James went to get a second beer but thought the better of it and ordered a Coke, instead. The last few foursomes came into the bar, while Caden and his fellow lawyers took the stage and began to announce the awards. James got second for longest putt but gave his prize back to the charity.

Dinner was served and James sat with some of the other contractors at Ernesto Sanchez' table. After several stories and dessert, James excused himself and thanked Ernesto for his kind invitation. As he made his way out to his truck, Caden was walking across the parking lot to his Mercedes. It was parked in the spot next to James' truck.

"So, you're Grant Commercial Plumbing?" Caden said, as he reached his car and saw James unlock his pick-up.

"I am," James said. "Hey, I'm sorry if I offended you..."

"No, I'm not offended. Just surprised. I have never met anyone who lives like you do."

"I guess the Ivy League educates a different breed of cat," James observed.

"Absolutely." Caden laughed. "It's more of a status crowd."

First Million

"Look, I know what I said back there sounds pretty radical…"

"Or crazy," Caden interrupted.

"Or crazy," James admitted. "But it is something you really should consider."

"Maybe…" Caden said dismissively.

Despite Caden's rebuff, James felt moved to push a little harder. "Do you have time for a quick story?"

"Not really. I…."

This time it was James who interrupted. "It will just take a minute, and I think it explains what I am talking about."

Caden leaned against his Mercedes and shrugged. "Why not?"

"Many years ago, there were two sisters. When their grandmother died, she left each of them a million dollars and told them to use it as they wished. Her gift included a proviso that on the tenth anniversary of her death they would be contacted by her trustee and asked to give him an accounting of their finances."

"The older sister had a job in the fashion industry. She was talented in her field and had a flair for seeing the next big fashion trend. When she received her inheritance, she quit her job and started her own fashion label. She bought an expensive home, using every penny of the million dollars."

"That's the spirit," Caden replied. "I'm with you, Sister!"

James smiled and continued. "Of course, the purchase of the home was just the beginning. She needed to furnish and decorate it, in the contemporary and expensive tastes demanded of someone in her position. She promptly borrowed against the equity in her home to both furnish it and to furnish her fledgling fashion label with the working capital to fund her start-up."

"That sounds reasonable," Caden replied. "She's leveraging her capital, instead of letting it sit there in her home, unused. That's a sound financial strategy, right?"

James continued, undeterred by Caden's interruption. "The older sister's business grew and so did her reputation. She attended fashion events around the globe and her brand began to gain traction. But her success came at a price. She was in a hurry to grow. Rather than wait for her revenue to catch up to her spending, she continued to borrow against her home, while maintaining a lifestyle in keeping with a trend-setter. Expensive car, hip parties, and the latest fashions."

"Is this girl single?" Caden interrupted again.

"She's a lot older than you, Caden. This happened many years ago, remember?"

Caden was disappointed. "Ah, right."

"The younger sister also received her inheritance. She invested the money carefully and kept her job and her small, but affordable, apartment. She used the income from her new investment account to pay the tuition for graduate school at night and she completed her MBA and secured her series licenses."

"Boring," Caden said with a laugh. "I bet she didn't get many dates."

"She became a financial planner, deciding that she wanted to be up to the task of managing her wealth and living up to her grandmother's legacy. Once the younger sister completed her education, she joined a financial firm and began learning how to help others manage their money, while handling her own finances. She bought a cheap fixer-upper in an older, but quickly transforming part of town with $200,000 of the one million dollars and kept the remaining

$800,000 invested, allowing the interest to compound for the next eight years."

"During this time, the sisters grew apart. They had chosen decidedly different paths, and while they loved each other, they rarely got together. The years passed quickly and both sisters married and started families. On precisely the tenth anniversary of their grandmother's death, they received phone calls from her trustee. They agreed to meet at the older sister's home to give him an accounting of their finances."

"The trustee had been directed by their grandmother to award the trusteeship of her remaining estate to the granddaughter who had best managed her million dollars. Whichever sister had accumulated the greatest net worth would be placed in charge of administering her remaining $20 million trust, to be shared equally by both sisters. The trustee knew that, while equal beneficiaries, the sister who controlled the trust would receive a generous annual stipend for its administration and make all of the financial decisions until each girl reached the age of 45."

"When the trustee pulled into the older sister's driveway, he was impressed with her large and beautiful house, and with her sportscar parked nearby. He entered her home and noted her fine furniture and talent for decorating. He thought, surely this is the sister who has been most successful with her inheritance. She will be the new trustee."

"They sat at a fine dining room table, as lovely music filled the room. The trustee asked each of them to present their finances, as he had detailed in his letter that had arrived the same day of his phone call."

"The older sister went first. She spent quite a bit of time discussing her fine home and fashions and explained that in her business these luxury items were required. She explained the status of her business, still in growth mode and nearing a point where it would turn a profit. Her presentation was professional and well-reasoned, but when she showed her financial position to the trustee, he was shocked. The older sister had not only spent the one million dollars but had amassed huge debts. While she had a fine home, it was really owned by the bank, and her net worth was a large, negative number."

"Stunned, the trustee moved on to the younger sister. Her presentation was direct and to the point. She explained how she used her money to secure her MBA and series licenses while keeping her job. She had invested $200,000 into her fixer-upper home in an up-and-coming neighborhood, and it had increased in value by 50%. She had invested the remaining $800,000 and allowed the interest to compound over the next 8 years. Additionally, she had faithfully saved $500 per month, every month, for the past eight years, adding it to her portfolio. Her resulting portfolio was worth over $1.7 million dollars. With the increased value of her home factored in, the younger sister had built a net worth of over $2 million dollars, doubling her inheritance."

"The trustee awarded the younger sister with the trusteeship and responsibility for the $20 million trust. Additionally, she would receive a generous annual stipend for its administration. They thanked the trustee for his stewardship over the years and he left. The older sister was shocked and ashamed. But her younger sister sat down with her and they talked about her fashion business, its potential and its current needs. The younger sister became managing director and handled the business' finances, leaving her sister free to be creative and lead the next new trends of the fashion industry. The label became enormously profitable with the older sister's creative spirit and the younger sister's careful and steady management of their finances."

"The End?" Caden asked.

"The End."

"Wow. That sounds like a Disney movie, or one of the parables from the Bible," Caden said, absorbing the story.

"Actually, the story is true."

"Seriously?"

"Yeah, the younger sister is a close friend of my mom's. She helped her get on her feet after my parents divorced. She was the one who introduced my mom to Ernesto."

"That's a good story," Caden admitted.

"I am glad you liked it," James replied.

"Oh, I didn't like it at all," Caden said flatly. "But you have given me a lot to think about."

"Well, if you ever want to talk money, just let me know," James offered. "Part of the deal is that we need to share the knowledge with other people."

"Is that from Ernesto? Part of the legacy?"

"Yeah. Someone helps you and you help someone else. Ernesto really helped my mom. And she has been a big help to me." James handed Caden a business card.

Caden took the business card but didn't look at it. "Thanks, James. I appreciate your offer. But I don't think I need your help."

James nodded. "Well, then, it was nice to meet you." The two young men climbed into their cars and drove off in different directions.

March / 5 Years Later & 10 Years Ago - Several years later, James' phone rang on a Saturday afternoon.

"You may not remember me, James. This is Caden McBride. We met at a Bannister-Sanchez charity golf tournament a few years ago…"

"Are you the lawyer?" James asked.

"You have a good memory," Caden was impressed. And a little nervous. "I kept your business card…"

"How can I help you?" James replied. "Got a plumbing job?"

They met at a coffee shop out by the interstate the next Saturday. Both were married now, with kids and greater responsibilities.

Caden still looked like someone who stepped out of a Brooks Brother catalog, even on a Saturday. He wore a polo shirt, tucked into his khaki shorts, with a belt that matched a pair of expensive tasseled loafers. James was wearing a simple t-shirt and jeans.

They ordered their coffees and took a table by the window. "You sure about this?" James asked once they both sat down.

"Not at all," Caden replied, his coffee was still too hot to drink. "I am not sure about anything right now."

"Lay it out for me," James said simply.

Caden handed James three carefully typed pages, detailing his income, budget, debts, and assets. He spoke for the next 30 minutes, detailing his expensive lifestyle. He described his current mortgage, his vacation home, leased cars, country club dues, their continuing student debt, and their credit card debt. Caden had recently made partner and earned a very impressive salary, but he was deeply in debt with little relief in sight.

"I thought once I made partner, everything would be taken care of. I could pay all of our debts and finally start saving."

"You still can, Caden," James replied. "It's not too late. But you need to change your lifestyle and focus on getting out of debt. Once you pay off your debts, you can start saving toward that first million." James explained the concept of the first million and shared the 5 Steps to financial independence. He grabbed a sheet of paper and wrote them down for Caden.

"Step One: Budget First.

Step Two: Debt Free.

Step Three: Live Simply.

Step Four: Save and Reinvest.

Step Five: Work Hard."

"Sarah and I just put together a pretty good budget," Caden indicated one of the sheets that he had prepared for James. He started reading over the 5 Steps.

"How about Step 2. Debt Free?" James asked. "You have a lot of debt. You need to eliminate it, as fast as possible, so you can start saving. Look at your balance sheet. Expensive home, vacation condo, foreign cars, and lots of debt. If you lost your job tomorrow, your debt would wipe you out," James pointed out.

"When we had our second child, I realized it wasn't just about me anymore. I am responsible for my family. I need to do a better job of building our net worth and leaving a legacy for our kids. We look pretty good to the outside world, but on paper we're broke."

"That's true for a lot of people. It's time to get started on Step 2 and get out of debt as quickly as possible. You won't believe the freedom of being debt free. I never worry about money."

"Never?"

"Nope. I don't owe anyone anything. I could stop working tomorrow and last several years without ever having to draw another paycheck. When the economy heads south again, and it will, I am in very good shape financially."

"That must be a great feeling," Caden sighed.

"It is," James agreed. "It's so much better than driving a fancy car or living in a huge house. It's better than traveling around the world or belonging to some impressive country club. I sleep well at night knowing that I own everything that I have. No debt. No bank loans. No worries."

"I can't imagine living like that," Caden held up his debt sheet. "I feel like we are too far gone."

"But you're not. You already have your budget. Now you just need to wipe out those debts. With your high salary, you can do that in a couple of years."

"Really? Show me." Caden leaned forward as James started tackling his numbers, just as Ernesto had for his mom so many years before.

On paper, James sold Caden's vacation home immediately. "Save up and pay cash for your next vacation. This extra house is bleeding you dry. The property taxes alone can cover a nice two-week vacation every year, not to mention saving the mortgage payment, maintenance and homeowner's fees."

"I could turn it into a full-time rental," Caden suggested.

"Sell it. Pay down your debts. Buy a rental property later, once you are financially solid," James replied simply. He then suggested selling Caden's current home and gave him a budget $385,000 for a new, smaller mortgage. With a quick internet search, James showed Caden available homes in the same area, at significantly lower prices.

"They are so much smaller," Caden complained.

"Face it, Caden. In that big house of yours, you mostly gather around the kitchen and the television set. You have a couple of rooms you don't even use. Get rid of them. Get out of debt."

He unraveled the leases for the expensive cars, too. Then showed Caden how he could buy two very nice, used cars for a fraction of the cost. "I buy my cars only a few years old, with maybe 20,000 miles on them. I like to let someone else pay for the depreciation. A car that age still has plenty of years left, at a fraction of the cost of a new car."

They eliminated the country club membership and researched neighborhood gyms and in-home work-out equipment, instead. They reduced the budgets for clothing, meals out, groceries, and kid's activities. The only item that he increased was their tithe. "Honor God and He will honor you," James said, repeating Ernesto's words.

The resulting cuts generated $4,000 dollars of savings each month. James used the captured savings to pay down Caden's debt. He showed him that in just over 3 years, they would eliminate his credit card and student loan debt, and then start paying off their new house.

"We would own our home outright in just 11 more years," Caden said carefully.

"Not ideal, I know. But, yes, in 11 years you can pay-off all of your credit cards, eliminate the student loans, and pay-off your mortgage."

"Can I get there faster?" Caden asked. "Like you did?"

"It's much easier before you have kids, but you can do it. Let's take another stab at your monthly budget." Twenty minutes later and Caden had a budget that would allow him to save $6,000 per month and pay off his credit cards and student loans in just two years, and the house in another 6 years.

"Debt free in eight years..." Caden reflected. "That's not too bad."

"And when you get raises and other financial windfalls, don't spend them. Just keep paying off your debt. Once that's done, you can start saving and investing that same money each month. With compounded interest on your investments, you should save your first million in about nine years, after your house is paid for. And that doesn't count the equity in your home, which should be well over $400,000 by then, depending on the real estate market."

"I would have a net worth of about $1.5 million in just 17 years. I won't even be 50 yet."

"Right. But more than that, you will be financially independent. You will own your home outright, you will have no debt, and you could live on the $50,000 per year that your investments would pay you."

"Not to be greedy, but I think I want more than that," Caden replied.

"Well then…" James grabbed his calculator and showed Caden his new total. "Keep saving at the same rate and you will have $2.5 million in just 23 years from today. Plus, the equity in your home."

"So, I will own my home, and have $2.5 million. So, I could count on annual income from that of…" Caden started doing the math in his head, but James was well ahead of him.

"$125,000 per year."

"That's more like it. And I will be just 54 years old."

"Exactly. It will look something like this, "James grabbed a sheet of paper and made some notes.

"Next Two Years: Pay Off Credit Card & Student Loan Debt: $150,000

Next Six Years: Pay Off House: $385,000

Next Fifteen Years: Save for Financial Independence: $2.5 million"

"Now we're talking," Caden declared. "This is great."

"You will love living debt free," James agreed.

Caden took a deep breath and let it go slowly. "I am so tired of owing money, worried about what I would do to support my family if I lost my job. This will be so much better." Caden went quiet for a moment. James left him to refill his coffee cup.

"What's on your mind?" James asked, as he came back to their table.

"Well…." Caden pulled his thoughts together. "I have a pretty high salary. So, I can make these adjustments, pay off my debts, and be very strong financially in just a few years. What about the family who earns less than I do?"

"They can be debt free, too. You can always lower your expenses and devote the extra money to paying off debt. You can pay cash for a less expensive car, move to a more affordable state, live in a less expensive home, and tighten your budget to eliminate the unnecessary excesses. For entertainment you can visit the parks, beaches and libraries – all of which are free. Skip dinners out and barbeque at home. Most people likely wouldn't need $125,000 per year to retire comfortably. They can do it on $50,000 a year, or less, if they manage their expenses and eliminate their mortgage. That's how my mom did it. She makes a lot less money than you do, but she was able to save her first million when she was still young and reach financial independence. It's all relative."

Caden's face brightened. "I am glad to hear about your mom. She sounds pretty cool."

James considered that for a moment. "She's super cool. But what she has done with her money can be accomplished by anyone with the will do to it."

**"Do not wear yourself out to get rich; have the
wisdom to show restraint.**

Cast but a glance at riches, and they are gone,

For they will surely sprout wings

And fly off to the sky like an eagle.

—Proverbs 23: 4-5

4

LIVE SIMPLY

July / Present Day - "This traffic is unbelievable," Sarah McBride said for the third time.

"Do you wish we were in Europe, instead?" Caden asked, growing weary of the complaining. He had been behind the wheel for the last two hours, crawling behind long lines of semi-trucks and cars, as they inched forward on the 101 freeway. It was a Friday night in central California and Caden was exhausted.

Sarah sighed. "No, this has been a great trip. The kids needed to see more of California at some point. Europe would have been fun, but it was so expensive. I just wish the traffic would cooperate."

"And are you still ok with our simple life?" Caden asked. Several years had passed since he last met with James Grant and they had implemented the Simple Life. Their student loan debt was long gone, and they had just paid off their mortgage. They were now putting money into their First Million fund and adding monthly to their kid's 529 college funds. Their lifestyle had changed dramatically.

"Do you mean family car vacations and cheap hotel rooms, instead of luxury European travel?"

"And a smaller house. And public school for the kids. And older cars. And no more country club membership…" Caden went on. "But I really like my used Ford Explorer with 45,000 miles on it…. And no lease or car payment."

"And no more credit cards. Just paying cash for groceries and clothes, and making my own coffee at home…"

"I like your coffee better."

"I do, too. And the price is right. I can't believe how much money we would spend each month to get our caffeine fix," Sarah replied.

"You mean our status fix?"

"Yeah, I guess it was a sort of affordable luxury."

"That became unaffordable," Caden agreed.

"We made a lot of changes in our lives over the past 10 years," Sarah sighed.

"And?" Caden asked, not completely certain of her answer.

"I absolutely love it," Sarah declared. "No more student loan debt. No more mortgage payments. No more huge credit card bills. A smaller house that is much easier to clean. Yes, I love it."

Caden sighed deeply. When he first sat down with Sarah to talk over their new way of life, she was surprised. She immediately asked if he had lost his job. But when he gave her the big picture and showed her what their lives would be like in just a few years, she agreed to try. They worked as a team and stuck to their plan.

"I love it, too," Caden agreed. "I am sleeping so much better. Work is more fun because I am off the paycheck-to-paycheck treadmill. If the law firm melted down next week, I am not super worried. I would need to find another job, but we would be ok. If we were still spending like we were a decade ago, we'd be trapped."

"Would you rather have eight solid hours of sleep every night for the rest of your life, or a million dollars?" Sarah asked.

"No question. I'll take the sleep."

Sarah looked at her kids sleeping in the back seat. "They've been out for a while."

"I know. I am getting really tired. I'd like to join them."

"Need a coffee?"

They were approaching an offramp that advertised several fast-food restaurants. Caden pulled off, bought a large coffee to go, stretched his legs for a few minutes, and merged back on to the freeway.

"Speaking of the law firm…" Caden began.

"Everything ok?"

"Yes, everything is fine. But I don't see myself staying there for the rest of my life. I'd like to go out on my own at some point."

"And give up being a partner? You worked so hard for that. We all did."

"Tons of sacrifices, no doubt about it. But now that we are completely debt free, I feel like the horizon has cleared. Like anything is possible. I think I would rather have my own practice, bill my own hours, and choose my own clients. Plus, there would be huge tax advantages. I think we would actually keep more money." Caden took a welcome sip of the hot coffee.

"If you said this 10 years ago, I would have sent you to a psychiatrist to help you through your mid-life crisis. But now I am totally fine with it. I'd rather have a simple life and be happy," Sarah replied taking a sip from Caden's coffee. She handed it back to him and he took another sip.

"That's where I am, too. Maybe in a couple more years...." A truck cut directly in front of Caden's car and he slammed on the breaks. He missed the truck by inches, but his coffee exploded and spilled down his shirt, scalding him. "Aaaaah!"

"Are you ok? I'll grab the wheel. Get that shirt off!"

The kids were startled awake. "What's wrong with Dad?"

"That truck nearly hit us. And dad spilled his coffee. Are you ok?"

"I'm fine." Caden tore off his shirt, while Sarah held the wheel. "That's it! This road trip is over. At least for tonight." Caden pulled off the freeway. "I'm exhausted, anyway."

"I think we all are," Sarah agreed. "Where are we?"

"San Luis Obispo," Caden reported, as he pulled to the curb of a quiet street. "I hear this is a cool little town. Danny, can you please grab me a shirt from one of the suitcases?" Caden tossed his ruined shirt over the seat to his 14-year old son.

"Sure." Danny grabbed a t-shirt from his own bag and threw it forward at Caden, hitting him in the head.

"Thanks, Pal," Caden pulled it over his head, without looking at it.

Sarah dialed a number into her cell. "I'll cancel our reservation for tonight in San Francisco. We never would have made it, anyway."

While she spoke, Caden talked to himself as he turned onto one of the main streets. "Friday night.... Cute town..... middle of summer..... I hope we find a place to stay tonight."

"We can always camp!" Danny called from the back seat.

Trisha yawned and rubbed her eyes. "No way. I need a hot shower. Dad, you gotta find something with a hot shower."

"Working on it..." Caden drove along the busy street, eyeing the no vacancy signs on each motel. He finally pulled over at a place where the vacancy sign was illuminated. The parking lot was packed, so he pulled in front of the lobby and let the car idle.

Caden opened the front door and stepped into an airconditioned lobby. Before he could reach the front desk, a large, black man in his late sixties, wearing a greying mustache and western shirt, boomed, "Sold out, Fella."

"But your sign..."

"Is broken." His smile was friendly if his answer was not.

"Got it," Caden replied, reaching the front counter. "Listen, I've got a car full of tired family. What would you do if you were me?"

"Check out The Ranch," The desk manager said, without hesitation.

"Is it far from here?"

"It's not close. Most people don't want to drive that far into the country at night. The road is curvy and narrow. A lot of people get lost."

"It sounds like you recommend it often."

"I do. But no one ever takes me up on it. But you will," he announced.

"Why's that?"

"Because my shift is over. And I live out that way. Come on, you follow me. That way you won't get lost."

"And it's a good place?"

"Yes, sir." He smiled broadly. "Better than this place. I put my visiting family up there all the time."

"Do you think they have vacancies?"

"They should. And it's a big place. Like I said, no one likes to drive out that way. You might get lucky. If not, you can sleep in my barn."

"Really?"

"Sure. Got plenty of space out there. It's remodeled. Nicer than most houses. But let's find you a hotel room at The Ranch, first."

Caden returned his infectious grin. "What's your name?"

"I'm Cal." He announced in his deep baritone.

"Caden."

"Nice to meet you." They shook hands and Caden's hand disappeared in Cal's massive grip.

"Are you always this nice to total strangers?"

"Sure. You look like a nice family, judging by what I see in your car." Caden turned to see his family smiling and waving.

Caden laughed. "I think they are sucking up, so you'll give us a room. They're exhausted."

"No problem. I'm happy to help."

As Cal logged out of his computer, Caden noticed several bottles along the back-shelf, behind the counter. "SLO Sauce? What's that?"

Cal beamed. "My own recipe. Best barbeque sauce in Central California. I sell it to all of the restaurants round here."

"Really?" Caden studied the labels, many of them with flames printed on the sides. "How many flavors do you have?"

"Six. Working on number seven right now. But it's not ready for prime time."

"I'll take one of each," Caden said, pulling several bills from his wallet.

"You're in for a treat," Cal said, putting six bottles into a paper bag.

"Now, I just have to find a barbeque."

"Plenty of those in this area. It's a local passion," Cal explained.

"That's what I've heard."

"Let me turn the counter over to the late-night shift and I'll pull my truck up front. You just follow me. Stay close, though. You don't want to lose me out there at night. Sure to get lost."

Caden shook his giant hand again, overwhelmed by his kindness and went out to wait in the car. He opened the door and sat behind the steering wheel.

"Did you get a room?"

"Sort of. And I got some great barbeque sauce," Caden handed the bag to Sarah.

"Doesn't sound like a hot shower, Dad," Trisha whined.

"Super nice guy. He is getting off work. The whole town is booked up. But he says there is a good place east of here, but no one likes to drive that way at night, because it's easy to get lost. He said we could follow him to it."

"What if they are booked, too?" Sarah asked.

"He said we could sleep in his barn."

"Wait! Seriously?" Danny said.

"Does his barn have a hot shower?" Trisha asked.

"It will work out. Plus, what choice do we have? I don't want to go back to the freeway and fight traffic," Caden replied, taking a deep, satisfying breath. He was beginning to unwind. Friday night. Vacation road trip. Friendly little town. He was just going with it.

A white F-150 pulled alongside their car and Cal waved at them. He was wearing a cowboy hat now. The family waved back, and he pulled ahead. Caden followed him closely as he led them out of town. They wound through the foothills east of San Luis Obispo. They passed wineries and ranches, and very few lights.

"This is amazing," Sarah said. "We might need to spend a few days visiting these wineries."

"Ok by me…" Caden said and followed Cal deeper into the night. The road became narrower, with trees and horse fences squeezing them into the center of the road. They followed close behind the pick-up truck for several twisting miles. Cal finally signaled and turned his truck under a log-pole gate with a hanging, wrought iron sign that said *The Ranch*. They followed the paved drive up to a brightly lit white house, with several little cabins spread out behind it.

"Thank you, Cal," Caden said, shaking his big hand again. He was quickly echoed by his family. "There is no way we would have found this place on our own."

"No problem. I'll wait here. You give me the thumbs up when you have your room and I will drive off. No room? Then follow me to my barn."

"I think you're the nicest man we've ever met," Sarah declared and shook Cal's hand. His smile spread wide under his mustache.

Caden left his family talking with Cal and walked up the pathway to the main house, cheered by the lights. The house glittered like a wedding cake. Caden entered the lobby to the smell of cinnamon and fresh brewed coffee. A teenage girl was waiting expectantly for him behind the counter. "You found us ok?"

"With a little help. This place is great."

"I'm glad you like it," She replied, typing into her computer. "We think you're great. You *are* one of the Deranged Prophets, right?"

"I am definitely deranged," Caden agreed.

"I saw your t-shirt, but you look a little old to be a Prophet," she said skeptically. "I didn't expect you for a few more hours. I just need to confirm that you are one of them."

Caden was tired and didn't fully understand what she was saying. He had forgotten that he was wearing Danny's t-shirt. If he had remembered, he may have noticed that it was a tour shirt from the Deranged Prophets. But he went with it. "If it will get us a room, then I confess to be one of the most deranged people you will ever meet."

"Yeah?" She was trying to be polite, just in case his story was true. But she wasn't convinced. "What instrument do you play?"

"Instrument? Bass. Why? Is that important?"

"Just making sure. I don't want to give you the wrong room."

"Well, I used to play bass. But I'm a lawyer now," Caden explained with a yawn.

"I get it. You're in management. So, you left early?"

"Not early enough."

"That makes sense," she said with a suddenly eager-to-please smile.

"I'm glad it makes sense to you, because I'm starting to get a little confused."

"You're a riot! I just love you guys."

"It's cool to know we have fans all over the country," Caden said off-handedly.

She laughed again and handed Caden the key. "Room 106. Just behind the main house. The rest of the crew are in the other cabins. You booked up the whole place. And we really appreciate your business."

"Thank you. We really appreciate the hotel room." Caden left the well-lit lobby and the smells of cinnamon and coffee. He stepped out on the wooden porch and waved. Cal waved back, hugged Sarah, high-fived the kids, climbed into his truck, and drove down the driveway.

The little cabin room was spacious and beautiful, with two queen beds and a pull-out couch. The room was also hot and stuffy, and apparently did not have air conditioning. They were too exhausted to care. They opened the windows and propped open the door with the little desk chair. Hot showers followed for all of them and they quickly dove into bed and fell asleep. Danny had promised to close the door after reading his book, but he fell asleep after one paragraph and the door remained open for the next few hours, cooling the room, and letting in the occasional mosquito.

The hotel parking lot became a hive of activity just after 2:00 A.M.. The bus for the Deranged Prophets pulled in and keys were handed out to each member of the band, as well as the road crew. They gathered around the pool, popping cold beers, and playing their instruments, under a warm, starlit sky.

Music entered the open door and filled the McBride's room, followed by a tall skinny man with an extremely long beard. He was wearing black jeans, cowboy boots, and a red sport coat, with no shirt underneath. He slipped through the open door, past the chair, walked across the room, dropped an overnight bag on the floor, and went into the bathroom, locking the door behind him. Caden woke to the sound of the music from around the pool and someone singing in his shower in a deep, husky voice.

"Danny?"

"Yeah, Dad?" Danny said from the fold-out couch, still asleep.

"Is that you in the shower?"

"How could I be in the shower? I'm asleep."

The music became louder and people were laughing and singing around the pool. There were loud splashes and several people started to yell. Sarah and Trisha were wide awake now. "What's going on?"

Caden stood up and looked outside. "There is a big crowd around the pool. It looks like a pretty rocking party."

"At 2:30 in the morning?" Sarah said, looking at her phone.

At that moment, the shower stopped, but the man inside the bathroom kept singing. Trisha screamed. "Who's in our bathroom!"

The door opened. Light and steam poured into their room as a tall, lanky man wrapped in a towel stepped out and looked around. He surveyed the room, seeing Caden and his wife first, then the kids. He had obviously entered the wrong room but was completely unfazed. "Hey, you guys got any barbeque sauce?"

Over a hundred people had gathered around the pool, including the hotel staff. They had fired up the grill by the pool and an assortment of meat and fish was in various stages of sizzling. The fact that they had forgotten barbeque sauce did not diminish the wonderful smell of the food at 2:30 in the morning. Several of the band members had assembled with their instruments at the deep end of the pool, where they had pulled chairs into a semi-circle and were jamming impromptu, sipping beer, and eating their late dinner between chords.

Caden, Sarah, Danny and Trisha McBride were half-dressed in pajamas and bathing suits and enjoying the food and music. They had received an invitation to the party, if not an apology for the break-in, from Otter, the towel-wearing bass player for the Deranged Prophets. The selection of barbeque sauces Caden had purchased from Cal were passed out across the party, with everyone sampling the different flavors. As they pulled up pool chairs and watched the musicians shred, a stocky, balding man with a thick black beard and friendly smile joined them.

"I'm TJ!" The lead singer said, as he sat on an ice chest.

Caden and Sarah shook his hand and introduced their family. His kids were too stunned to speak. TJ Russell was a super-star with an international following. His summer tour was packing stadiums around the country and here he was talking to the McBride family.

"And that's Tiny, Sid, Alberto, Tom, and Retro." Each band member waved or nodded as the introductions were made. "And, of course, you've met Otter."

Otter hooted as he carried a giant swan floatie to the shallow end of the pool.

"It's great to meet all of you. Thanks for letting us join the party."

"Seriously. Were you at the concert tonight?" TJ asked.

"No, we got here a few hours ago. All the hotels in town were booked and a super friendly local recommended this place. We had no idea you guys were staying here. I'm sorry if we took one of your rooms."

"Don't worry about it. Seriously. Otter can bunk with me. We're glad to meet you."

"That's very kind of you..." Sarah started to say.

"We're indebted to you. Otter forgot the barbeque sauce and you are bailing us out. Can't have a party without barbeque sauce. It was seriously meant to be."

"So, you guys are the Deranged Prophets?" Sarah asked.

"Yeah, that's us. Did you meet the rest of our traveling family?"

Caden looked across the pool at the crowd of rockers, roadies, and family members. Some of them waved back or raised their beers. "No. There's a lot of you."

"This road trip stuff is complicated. Seriously. And expensive. We have over a hundred people in our caravan. And we are not the easiest house guests. So, it's seriously awesome when we can stay in a place like this, out in the country, where we can book the whole place, and sort of turn it into a party. We'll rest here tomorrow and then head to LA the next day for three shows."

"That's amazing," Caden replied. "So, you're in the middle of your concert tour?"

"Started in Boston back in late April and we play until the first week of November. We wrap it up at home in Texas."

"That's lot of travel." Caden was impressed.

"Seriously. But we take breaks. Fly home for a few days. That sort of thing. But, yes, it's a grind," TJ said with a sigh, then grabbed his guitar and started jamming. "No place I'd rather beeeeee. Seriousleeee," He crooned. The kids sat in awe, busy posting photos for their friends and basking in their amazed and jealous comments.

"And we have no choice," TJ continued.

"What do you mean?" Caden asked.

"We owe serious money. To launch this band and cover our tours, I had to borrow heavily. I produced the last album myself, and we owe millions and carry some serious interest that we have to cover. If we aren't careful, we'll be playing our next tour from bankruptcy."

"Really?"

"Seriously..." TJ sighed.

"But you guys are so talented. That just doesn't seem right," Sarah empathized.

"Talent has nothing to do with it. This band plays on our stomachs. And I need to feed the beast. Super beastly, Man."

"TJ! Toss me a beer!" Otter shouted from his swan floatie in the middle of the pool. He had a plate of food and wore a cowboy hat and a water-logged pair of boots. He had a large flashlight in his hand, and he was panning the crowd looking for beer. The beam was focused on the cooler that TJ was sitting on.

"Otter is a little unusual," TJ admitted. "But he seriously shreds on bass."

"I think he's sweet," Sarah said.

"Sweet like a little child," TJ agree as he stood up, pulled an ice-cold long neck from the cooler and closed the lid. He tossed the beer to Otter in a high arc, but Otter's attention was diverted. He was swinging his flashlight around the pool looking for cheesecake. The beer tumbled out of the dark sky and crashed into the metal handle of the flashlight, busting into a shatter of glass and suds. Shards of glass sliced deeply into Otter's hand and blood flowed immediately, mixing with the chorine of the pool. Otter held up a mangled hand, "TJ!"

"We got this, TJ!" Caden leaped up and ran to the hotel room, while Sarah pulled Otter to the edge of the pool and used a towel to apply pressure to the wound. Since they were in the middle of nowhere and didn't know the area, the receptionist jumped in their car with Otter and shouted directions as they raced him to the emergency room.

5 hours and 17 stitches later, the sun was up and the McBrides, the receptionist, and Otter returned to the hotel, where the Deranged Prophets were sitting in the hotel lobby drinking coffee, worried for their friend and the future of their tour.

"Seriously? How are you?" TJ leaped up from the couch. It was clear that he hadn't slept all night.

"It's pretty bad, TJ. I'm done for at least three weeks." Otter was grey and exhausted. He held up his hand, showing a carefully wrapped bandage from his fingers to his elbow.

"The doctor did a great job," Sarah reported. "No long-term issues for Otter. He was really lucky. But those stitches need to stay in place. He can't play until…When Otter?"

"Albuquerque," Otter replied miserably.

"Albuquerque!" TJ collapsed into the couch. "Seriously? We have seven shows between now and then and three of them in LA. This is where we finally make a little money. We are totally sunk."

"What about calling Sam to fill in? Or Jayce?"

"It's summer. They're both touring. Sam's in British Columbia. And Jayce is in the Carolina's, I think. We already tried calling them. And I don't want to add anything more to the payroll."

"We're going to LA. Let's pull in some guest talent. Gotta be some guys around. Studio musicians and the like."

"What if we just cover for him?" Sid asked. "I can switch over on the key songs."

"In LA? We need to give them the complete show. I guess some of that could work, but we would still be short-handed for most of our stuff." TJ shook his head and studied the carpet for inspiration.

Sarah McBride spoke up. "Wait? Are you guys looking for someone to play bass?"

"You're kidding, right?" TJ said, he had heard this before from hundreds of fans and followers.

"No, TJ, my Dad totally shreds," Danny suddenly spoke up.

"I'm alright," Caden shrugged.

"He would really need to shred to take Otter's place," Retro said from the corner of the couch. He was wearing sunglasses and sipping coffee from two different cups.

"One way to find out," Otter said. With his unbandaged left hand, he pulled a bass guitar out of Sid's hands and handed it to Caden.

"I don't know, guys. I'm a little rusty," Caden admitted.

"Do you know any of our songs?" Sid asked, leaning forward.

"That one I hear on the radio all the time…" Caden said, taking the bass guitar.

"*Concussion?*"

"No, the other one. *Stupefied.*"

"Want us to fill in? Or do you want to show off solo?" TJ asked skeptically.

"I think I got it," Caden said. He started tuning the guitar and then went through some simple progressions, getting the feel for Otter's instrument. He pulled in some classic covers, to show his versatility, then went into a riff for *Stupefied*. He dragged the notes out slowly at first, then chopped them down for a faster rhythm. As he played, his fatigue fell away, and his nervousness vanished. Soon he was back in high school, chilling with his old garage band. He disappeared into the music and forgot about the crowd around him.

But they were all sitting up now, leaning forward. Sid grabbed his guitar and Retro pulled sticks from his jacket pocket and kept the beat on the coffee table.

"Damn," Otter said. "This dude can play."

"Seriously." TJ smiled for the first time all morning. "Caden, you want to play a little with us and see if we can make this work? Just until Otter can play again?"

"Seriously? I mean, really? You guys want me to play with the Deranged Prophets?"

"Yeah, Dad!" Danny shouted.

"Go for it!" Trisha agreed.

The rest of the band shouted their encouragement. "Otter can sit with you and give suggestions and we can bring you along. We have all day. If you can play *Stupefied*, you should be able to hang with the rest."

"But what about our vacation?" Caden protested. "We're supposed to go to San Francisco and Big Sur. What about Yosemite?"

"Next year!" Danny shouted.

"Yeah, let's travel with the band!" Trisha echoed.

"You guys sure?" Sarah asked the kids.

"Yes!" They replied unanimously.

"But are you guys sure?" Caden asked the Deranged Prophets.

"Let's see how it goes. We can keep trying to find someone, but I don't know if they would be any better than you are. Plus, we have a day to practice together before LA." TJ reasoned.

Caden looked over to Sarah and the kids. "Family? You sure?"

"Seriously!" They shouted in unison.

"Alright, Otter. TJ. Guys. We are in," Caden nodded and continued warming his fingers up on the bass.

They practiced together all morning and knocked off for naps in the middle of the day. That night they jammed around the pool and worked Caden into the sets. The McBrides agreed to travel with them to Los Angeles, Denver and Phoenix, and Otter would step back in by Albuquerque. Caden called the office and got the extra time off that he needed. The kids were thrilled. And Caden was living his rock star dreams, if only for a few weeks.

Caden sat by the pool with Otter, practicing the songs for each set. TJ came up to them with a big smile. "Seriously. This is a real trip."

"For me, too," Caden said, continuing to play.

"And I will pay you," TJ continued.

"No need," Caden said. "You're already covering our travel costs, just playing with you is payment enough."

"Man, I wish everyone in our traveling family was like you. I have no idea if I can keep the band together with all the overhead we've taken on. A day of reckoning is coming. Seriously."

"Serious…. I mean, really?" Caden asked and stopped playing. "You guys are sold out, right? You must be making a fortune."

"Oh yeah, we're making millions. But we're spending millions, too. And I still owe millions. I need to get a handle on this. We are racking up major debts. Stage crew, lighting, pyrotechnics, food, travel, lodging, taxes, gate split…. It's seriously overwhelming."

"Why not make it simple?" Caden asked, channeling his new approach to life and money.

"What do you mean?"

"What if you get rid of all of the bells and whistles? Reduce your crew. Eliminate the special effects. Just play your music and let the crowd do the rest."

"No, our fans expect a big show. Especially in places like LA."

"Are you sure? What if you gave it a try? Strip it down to the basics and let the crowd in. Just like the barbeque we had last night. That was super cool."

"Seriously? I don't know…"

Otter weighed in. "Hey, TJ. I think he's on to something. We need to cash in while we're hot. There's no guarantee that we will ever be this big again. Let's strip it down to the studs and bank some money. Didn't we lose money last year?"

"Yeah, and I am still paying for it. We have major overhead on this tour. If I'm not careful, I might lose my house. Which is cool, I guess, since I'm never there. And don't get me started on my bank. They charge a premium for working with a crazy rock band. And they are always on me to make payments. We are rocking. But almost on the rocks."

"You need to work from a debt free model," Caden explained. "Everything you do should be profitable, or you don't do it."

"That sounds good. But we're a rock band. We have a reputation to maintain. We gotta destroy hotel rooms and crash our Ferraris," TJ joked.

"Look, TJ, I am a rookie at money stuff, but I am learning fast. I used to spend money like there was no tomorrow. My wife and I racked up huge debts. But then we started on this Live Simply program. We sold our big house, cut our costs, got rid of the bells and whistles, and made our lives profitable. We don't have any debt. We pay cash for everything, as we go. And you know what?"

"What? Seriously."

"We have never been happier."

"Debt free sounds totally awesome. But what about our commitments? We've signed contracts for most of this stuff."

"Do you have copies of them?" Caden asked.

"Copies of what?"

"Your contracts?"

"What are you? An accountant?"

"I'm a lawyer. I write and enforce contracts for a living. Let me know what you've got and I'll see if we can settle some of this for you."

Caden spent the evening reviewing their contracts. He pointed out how TJ could settle with some and rewrite others. They started making phone calls and each of the suppliers was understanding and fair, eager to please the Deranged Prophets. By the time they were done, the tour was stripped down to its essentials and the traveling party was cut back to its core. They paid termination bonuses to their crew members who traveled home early, grateful to be with their families again and happy for the break.

"Are you sure about this, Caden?" TJ asked, reviewing their modified list of expenses for the rest of the tour. The new numbers eliminated all debt and showed a profit of several million dollars by the time they reached Texas. "I feel naked without the elements of a big show."

"But what's it all about? You are on tour to make money. Yeah, you love your fans and your music, but cutting back your expenses is the right move. Any loud rock band can have a big, crazy show, but you need to feature your talent. Sometimes you need to zig when the world zags. Take a new path and make it more about the music and the fans. You are inviting them in. And at the end of the tour you will be very wealthy."

"And I can pay off my debts?"

"Yes. And you need to be debt free. There are too many people relying on you."

"Seriously. You got that right. I am always worrying about them. I feel like I am the big daddy to a couple hundred people."

"And you are. So, you need to change the way you live your life and handle your money. You need to run Deranged Prophets like a business. A highly profitable business. With proper margins and returns on your investments. The fly-by-the-seat-of-your-pants, big debt model is going to crush you."

TJ was silent for a moment. Caden picked up his bass and began to play through the progressions of sets.

"You're going to rock, Caden. You totally have it down. I've never seen anyone take to our stuff so fast."

Caden smiled. "I'm a big fan.... Actually, I didn't know who you were, but I knew some of your songs. But I am a big fan now."

"And I am your fan, Caden. Seriously. Why don't you come and work for the Deranged Prophets? You can handle our contracts, keep our expenses under control, and help me take care of all of these families."

"You're kidding, right? Don't you already have a business manager?"

"Yeah, Dave Roscoe. He's already in LA. He's more of a music guy. You know, connections within the industry and such. He discovered Will Keys back in the day. Ever heard of him?"

"Doesn't ring a bell," Caden admitted.

"Well, anyway, Dave Roscoe has been our manager from the drop. He's pretty good with numbers, but I think he would love it if you stepped in. Then he could focus on what he's best at."

"TJ, are you serious?"

"Totally serious," TJ insisted. "I think this was meant to be. What are the chances that we would bump into you, and you can randomly fill in and cover bass for Otter? You even had barbeque sauce when we needed it most. I think God put you in our path for a reason. We need your help to keep this show profitable. And a little back up bass. What do you think?"

"I think you're crazy."

TJ held up a hand. "Please. I prefer the term Deranged."

Caden quit his law firm and joined the Deranged Prophets. They rebranded their tour the Simple Tour and went into LA, Denver and

Phoenix unplugged with their finances tightly under control. Otter took over at bass, once his hand healed in Albuquerque, and Caden flew home to wrap up his job at the law firm and get the kids plugged into school.

Caden then set up his own business and created a command center in his home office, continuing to shape the band's expenses and transform the Deranged Prophets into a simple, highly profitable, and debt free business. The summer tour was a big financial success, and critics applauded their unique, simple, music-focused experience. Caden worked with TJ to pay off the band's debts, and then set about the work of designing the next tour to be even more profitable.

"The most powerful force in the universe is compound interest."

—Albert Einstein

5

SAVE AND REINVEST

October / Present Day - The plane to Dallas was completely booked, so Oliver Powers dropped into the first available aisle seat, joining an elderly couple in the cramped row. He smiled but said nothing to them. He had raced through the airport to catch his flight and didn't want to forget to tip his rideshare driver. He slipped off his suit jacket, loosened his tie, and opened the app on his phone. After posting a generous tip for his driver, he relaxed and settled in for the flight.

Oliver Powers was in his late twenties, with wavy, light brown hair, and a habit of sweeping it out of his eyes to reveal a warm smile and blue eyes. He also had a sincere face that made people want to trust him immediately.

Oliver had only been at his new job for a few months, so he was burning the midnight oil to prove myself. He gave into his exhaustion and closed his eyes, promising himself that he would fire up his laptop before the plane touched down.

"Something to drink?" The flight attendant asked, waking him from his brief nap.

"Coffee, please," Oliver managed, pretending to be fully awake. He brushed the hair out of his eyes and looked around, realizing that the elderly couple had already placed their orders. He passed them their steaming cups of coffee and accepted his own.

"You must be exhausted," the elderly woman ventured from the window seat. She had genuine concern in her face and reminded Oliver of his grandmother. He warmed up to her instantly.

"Yes, I think I am," he admitted and took a welcome sip of coffee. "I think I fell asleep."

"You did," she replied with a gentle laugh. Her blue eyes bright with joy. Oliver could tell that she had been a real beauty just a few decades ago.

"Business trip?" Her husband asked from the middle seat. He had a deep rolling voice, like distant thunder. Oliver knew immediately that he was sitting next to someone of substance and experience.

"Yes, I'm going to a conference."

"What's your industry?" The old man asked. He was well past seventy, but trim and tanned. His grey hair was carefully combed, and he wore a black, fleece pullover.

"Hotels. It's a marketing conference. I need to get caught up with the latest trends for my industry. Everything is so internet focused, and it changes all the time," Oliver explained, but wondered if the old guy was tracking.

He was. "Yours is a cut-throat field. I imagine no one pays full price anymore."

"You're right about that. Everyone wants a deal. But it works out. We have so many tools now to fill our empty rooms. We just need to figure out how to raise our margins."

The old man nodded and sipped his coffee. They talked for a while longer about Oliver's new job, the hotel industry, their hometowns, and where they went to college. They were separated by several decades, but the conversation was easy. Oliver became convinced that this older couple sharing his row were the most relaxed people on the early morning flight.

Between sips of coffee, they learned a lot about each other. However, they never gave their names, in observance of one of those weird marvels of air travel where people speak openly about their faith and family, careers and hometowns, and even their politics, but names are rarely exchanged, somehow keeping the acquaintance safer.

Oliver finished his coffee and was ready to get some work done, so he waited for a break in the conversation and reached for his laptop bag, pulling the computer onto the tray table. As his computer came to life, the old man held up his paperback. "Ever read this book?"

"*The Richest Man in Babylon*", Oliver said, reading the title. "I don't think so. Is it any good?"

"It's better than good. It's life changing," the old man replied a little mystically. He had established his credibility and wisdom during their brief chat, so Oliver listened to his recommendation with more care than he usually would.

"Really?" Oliver was impressed. "How exactly?"

His wife leaned in over the armrest again. "It's a good thing you're wearing your seatbelt, young man. My husband can talk for hours about that book."

The old man's laugh rolled through the little row of seats. "She's right about that. I read this book at least once a year. More than any other book...."

"Except the Bible," she interrupted.

"Well, yes, except for the Bible. I read that every day. But this book is also a treasure..." He said warmly, holding it up for Oliver to see.

"What's it about?"

"How to save money and invest," she replied from the window.

"How to become wealthy," he added.

"It sounds like a good book," Oliver exclaimed, interested in both subjects.

"Here. Take this copy," the old man offered his book to Oliver.

"I couldn't possibly...." Oliver protested.

"Please, I insist. I give these away a lot," the old man said kindly.

"That's very nice of you, but..."

"You must know that my husband will keep insisting until you take it. And if you refuse, he will probably slip it into your bag when you aren't looking," his wife explained.

"She's right. I believe strongly in the wisdom of this book. It truly is life changing. I have several copies. Please do me the honor of accepting this one."

Oliver accepted the book with a shrug, "Thank you. You must really believe in this book."

"It's a simple book, but the lessons in it are essential for becoming wealthy. Don't let the strange Babylonian stories and phrases throw you. Stay with it, and it will change your life."

"How exactly?" Oliver turned the book in his hand, noting he had never heard of the author, George S. Clason.

"When I was your age, someone gave me this same book. They told me it contained the secret to becoming wealthy," he explained. "They were right."

"And what's the secret?"

"It's in the book. You'll have to read it yourself. But the core if it is this: save ten percent of everything you make. No matter what. Then invest it carefully and reinvest the earnings, and you will become wealthy. My wife and I were flat-broke at the time and it seemed impossible that we could ever become wealthy. But we read the book, worked hard, tightened our belts, and stayed with it. And today we are multi-millionaires."

"Really?" Oliver asked, studying the older couple who were flying coach on a discount airline to Dallas.

"We're loaded," his wife said with a warm smile, leaning over his armrest.

"I would never guess it," Oliver admitted, just a little dubious.

"We don't look wealthy," the old man replied. "We dress simply, fly coach, drive regular cars. Our house is pretty nice, though."

"We have a ranch outside of Dallas. It's pretty cool," she admitted.

"We learned a long time ago that you can't become wealthy if you always look like you're wealthy," the old man explained. "We might not look very impressive to you, but our net worth is."

Oliver studied the book awkwardly. The woman guessed his thoughts. "You will have to excuse my husband," she said quietly. "He is not trying to brag. He just wants to help you. You're young, with your whole life in front of you. You are precisely the person who will benefit the most from this book and the financial advice my husband is giving you."

"I don't mean to pry, either. Your life is none of my business. But someone shared these secrets with me when I was a young man just getting started," the old man explained.

"And you just want to pass it along," Oliver finished his sentence for him.

The rental car agency had a line out the door and had lost his reservation, so Oliver arrived at the hotel a few hours later than planned. He dropped his suitcase at the front desk, straightened his tie and went immediately to the conference kick-off reception on the top floor of the downtown hotel. He found the pool patio surrounded by hundreds of faux candles, heat lamps and black-tie waiters serving mini-sliders and salmon skewers. A crowd was gathered around the open bar and people were drinking and swapping hotel stories. Other attendees were hugging, and high-fiving, and Oliver quickly realized that he was a rookie in a conference filled with seasoned professionals.

He shouldered his way through the crowd and managed to order a beer. Tucking some bills into the bartender's glass, he made his way back through the crowd to the relative quiet of the pool's edge.

"This your first time?"

Oliver turned to find an attractive woman in her early sixties, wearing a black evening dress and high heels.

"Is it that obvious?" Oliver asked.

"You're the only person wearing a name badge," she observed. "We all know each other, so it's easy to spot the newcomers."

"Not much I can do about that," he admitted. "I'm Oliver Powers."

"Betsy Grant." They shook hands and Oliver was impressed by the strength of her grip.

"What property are you with?" Oliver asked, trying to fit in.

"None," Betsy replied. "I'm a consultant. I'm running a few workshops on marketing."

"Oh, you're *that* Betsy Grant. I read your profile in the meeting program. You really know your stuff," Oliver said, grateful that he had researched Betsy and signed up for all of her sessions.

"Kind of you to say," Betsy replied, sipping from her sparkling water. "I've been doing this for a while. How about you?"

"I'm brand new to the hotel industry. My last job was at a search engine optimization company," Oliver explained.

"SEO is a critical part of hotel marketing. I think your company made a good hire," Betsy said warmly. "What are you hoping to learn while you're here?"

She indicated a table and chairs at the edge of the pool area, overlooking the Dallas skyline. They made their way through the crowd, with the blue light of the pool illuminating their drinks and faces. As they sat down, Oliver's copy of *The Richest Man in Babylon* fell out of his suit pocket and landed at his feet. He reached down to pick it up, but Betsy picked it up first.

"Do you carry a copy with you everywhere?" She asked, studying the title.

Oliver was a little embarrassed. This was not the first impression he was hoping to make. "No. Someone on the plane gave it to me. I forgot I had it with me."

"So, you haven't read it yet?" Betsy asked, and handed it back to him.

Oliver took the book and tucked it more securely into his jacket pocket. "Nope. But I hear it's a good one."

"It's life changing," Betsy replied simply and took a sip of her drink.

"Really? You're the third person to tell me that today," Oliver laughed, looking at the Dallas skyline. "I guess I really am late to the party."

Betsy smiled and studied Oliver for a moment. "No, you're right on time. Are you interested in becoming wealthy?"

"Who isn't?" Oliver asked, taking a sip of his beer.

"You'd be surprised. I agree that everyone wants to be wealthy, but very few people are interested in doing what's necessary to make it happen."

"And you are?" Oliver asked abruptly, then stammered. "Sorry."

"None taken…"

"Thanks. It's been a long day," Oliver sighed.

Betsy waived him off, putting him at ease. "To answer your question, yes. A few good friends took me aside several years ago, at a time when I really needed their help. I had just gotten divorced and was deeply in debt. I was a single mom and a financial train wreck, spending money I just didn't have. They shared the concepts for building wealth with me. I can honestly say they changed my life."

"The guy who gave me this book said the same thing," Oliver admitted, patting his jacket pocket.

Betsy took a sip of her sparkling water and placed her drink on the table. "So, are you more interested in learning about building wealth or hotel marketing?"

"Do you offer seminars for both topics?" Oliver replied with a smile.

Betsy nodded. The band had started playing and the crowd was grabbing their drinks and heading to the dance floor. Betsy raised her voice to be heard. "I will. If you're certain it's something you are really interested in."

The band played set after set and waiters visited their table and brought a continuous stream of food, while they talked through the 5 Steps and the concept of the First Million. Oliver was sharp and had a good handle on the concepts. He already had a detailed budget, no debt, and was living well below his means. He was also saving a good portion of his earnings, by maximizing the employer match for his 401K.

"You're really doing it right, Oliver. But you need to save more than just your 401K contribution, if you're going to get to your first million," Betsy shouted over the familiar cover song. "If you run the calculations, you will see that you will be short."

"And you think putting an extra ten percent aside will get it done?" Oliver tried to keep his voice even, not wanting to shout his financial questions.

"What?"

Oliver shook his head, leaned in, and shouted. "And you think putting an extra ten percent aside will get it done?"

Betsy nodded. "Yes, but more is better, if you can manage it."

"Is that what you did?" Oliver shouted, then worried that he had pushed too far. "Sorry. I don't mean to ask about your personal finances."

"Not at all," Betsy replied, leaning in to be heard. "I decided a long time ago that I would help other people become financially independent, just like others have done for me. To do that, I need to be pretty open about my finances."

Oliver was relieved. He didn't want to burn his first real contact in the hotel industry. "Well, thank you. And did you make it? I mean, are you financially independent?"

"I am," Betsy nodded, and bit the last shrimp from her skewer and put it on her plate. "I have been for several years. But it didn't happen overnight. I had a lot of trial and error. When my friends taught me the 5 Steps, I jumped in and started following them almost immediately."

She wiped her fingers on her napkin and continued, "I created a budget, with their help. I sold my big, expensive house and bought something I could afford. I traded my expensive car in for a more affordable used one. I paid off my debts and started to save. After a while, I was earning a nice income from my savings. But that's where I went wrong."

"What do you mean?" Oliver asked.

Betsy sighed and picked up her glass. "Let's move away from the band. I need to introduce you to my mentor."

* * *

June / 29 Years Ago - After their first budget meeting, Ernesto made Betsy promise to meet him a year later, to see how she was coming along on her first million. By the time they met 12 months later, Betsy was debt free and had just started to save. They met in his office trailer on a Bannister-Sanchez construction site, where he was building a neighborhood of new homes.

"It's so amazing, Ernesto. I can't believe it. I am debt free!" Betsy was overjoyed, as she gave him a hug and took the chair in front of his desk.

Ernesto beamed and remained standing. "I knew you could do it. And you have started saving?"

"Yes, I just started. I opened a brokerage account with low fees, and I am now putting aside $600 a month, with $500 going into my First Million account, and the rest going to my car fund and college fund for James."

"That's excellent," Ernesto opened the cabinet behind his desk and retrieved a large box. He placed it in front of her. "I have some new coffee flavors for you."

Betsy opened the box and was immediately hit with the aroma of several different blends of rich coffee. She went through the coffee flavors and read the exotic names from around the world. "This is too much, Ernesto. I can't accept all of this."

"Please. I want you to have it. I am so happy for you getting out of debt and beginning your savings. You deserve it."

"Well, thank you. I do love your coffee."

"Everyone does," Ernesto agreed simply. "Now, let's talk about your investments." They discussed her planned investments for an hour and scheduled their next meeting.

* * *

August / 28 Years Ago - A year later they met again, in a new warehouse that Ernesto had purchased. It was next to a self-storage warehouse. "I have a feeling they will want to expand, and this is the only available land for them to buy. One day they will make me an offer. Until then, I will use it to store my trucks," he said, as he sat down at the plastic folding table that was set up in the middle of the cement warehouse floor. There was a single stack of grid paper, and a coffee mug filled with pens.

Betsy took a metal folding chair and joined him, wondering where the coffee pot was. "Do you still have your other warehouse? Where we met the first time, by the airport?"

"Oh, yes. I rent it to another company. They are in the aviation business. It has become a nice money maker for me."

"I can image," Betsy said, proud of her mentor's ability to make money. She was hoping this meeting would include some of his gourmet coffee, but he didn't have his iconic mug, and she couldn't smell anything brewing. She tried not to show her disappointment.

"So, tell me about your investments. Are you still putting the same amount of money aside every month?" Ernesto asked. He was all business today, and Betsy grew nervous.

"Yes, I am." Betsy shared a spreadsheet with Ernesto, and he could see that she had saved $6,310 in her investment account since their last meeting.

"I see," Ernesto frowned as he studied her balance.

"Is something wrong?"

"You are not following Step 4," he explained.

"Saving? Of course, I am." She was surprised at his disappointment. She had worked hard to put aside the $6,310 and had denied herself many things that she felt she needed.

"I agree that you are saving. But what are you doing with the income from your savings?" Ernesto asked.

"You mean the growth and dividends?" She replied haltingly.

Ernesto nodded, studying the spreadsheet.

"Well, I used it this summer for our vacation," she explained.

"I can see that," Ernesto sighed, putting the spreadsheet aside and looking her in the eye. "You have murdered the miracle."

"Excuse me?" Betsy was surprised by his unusual abruptness. "Murdered the what?"

"The miracle. Of compound interest. It is one of the most powerful forces in the universe and you are not letting it work for you," Ernesto explained.

"I'm sorry, Ernesto, but I don't follow you..."

"You are taking the profits from your investments and squandering them on travel, rather than rolling them back into your savings. You are disrupting the miracle of compound interest. It allows your money to grow exponentially."

Betsy was visibly frustrated, her face flush. "Look, Ernesto, I have made a lot of sacrifices to save that $6,000. Now, you're saying I need to save more?"

"Yes, that is exactly what I am saying. To earn your first million, you must use the power of compound interest. I addition to your annual savings plan, you must reinvest the growth and income. This allows your money to grow and grow. It is the only way to reach your first million. Too many people make the mistake of spending the dividends and growth of their investment accounts. They also spend the equity of their homes as the values increase. They will never become wealthy by doing this. You don't want to make those same mistakes. You need to wait until you reach your first million. Let me show you the difference."

Ernesto took the pad of grid paper and pulled a red pencil out of the coffee cup. He started jotting notes. "This is what you will save in 30 years if you continue to spend the income from your investments."

Betsy looked at the table Ernesto had created:

30 Years of Savings – Without Compound Interest:

Years:	Annual Savings:	Interest Rate:	Accumulated Savings:
5	$6,000	N/A	$30,000
10	$6,000	N/A	$60,000
15	$6,000	N/A	$90,000
20	$6,000	N/A	$120,000
25	$6,000	N/A	$150,000
30	$6,000	N/A	$180,000

"$180,000. That's pretty good." Betsy declared.

"But it is not a million dollars. And that's what you will need, as we have discussed before," Ernesto explained carefully, and then asked. "If you keep saving in this way, how long will it take you to earn your first million?"

Betsy borrowed his calculator and punched in the numbers. "About 165 years? I'll never make it."

"But you will. You just need to follow the 5 Steps." Ernesto scribbled more numbers on the pad. "Here is an example of how much money you will save if you compound the interest at 10% for 30 years."

30 Years of Savings – With Compound Interest:

Years:	Annual Savings:	Interest Rate:	Accumulated Savings:
5	$6,000	10%	$37,435
10	$6,000	10%	$96,921
15	$6,000	10%	$192,723
20	$6,000	10%	$347,013
25	$6,000	10%	$595,499
30	$6,000	10%	$995,688

Betsy looked at Ernesto's calculations. "That's a million dollars."

"Exactly."

"So, it is costing me over $800,000 to spend the interest and growth from my investments? That's crazy."

"And you're not crazy," Ernesto agreed. "And a 10% rate of return could be modest. You could expect more like 12%, which would be closer to $1.4 million."

Betsy took a deep breath. "Wow. This saving stuff is not easy. I finally paid off my debts and saved more than I ever thought I could, so I decide to celebrate with a nice trip for me and my son. And you are saying this is wrong?"

"No, I think taking a trip with your son is an excellent idea. It is how you pay for it that I am taking issue with. The money in your investment account must continue to grow until you reach your goal of the first million. And longer if you want to save more. If you want to take a vacation, then you must save for it in another way."

"How?" Betsy closed her eyes tightly, completely exasperated.

Ernesto waited a minute and then replied patiently, "You are debt free and a consistent saver. You will find a way. Eliminate some other expenses and focus those savings on your vacation fund. But never touch the principle of your savings account and never touch the growth and income."

"But, Ernesto, you've seen my budget. There is nothing left at the end of the month. I am putting all of my extra money in my investment account."

"If you can't reduce your spending, then you'll have to increase your income," Ernesto said simply.

"You make it sound so easy. I thought I was increasing my income with the dividends from my portfolio," Betsy sighed deeply and sunk into her chair.

"To have a vacation fund, you will need to generate money from other sources," Ernesto replied.

"You mean like a second job?"

"Yes, that's one way to do it. You could work on the weekends when you don't have custody of your son."

"Yeah, I guess I could…" Betsy agreed reluctantly.

"Or you could work smarter," Ernesto said cryptically.

"What do you mean, Ernesto?" Betsy asked. "How can I work smarter?"

"What is your largest expense?" He picked up the pad and began writing something Betsy couldn't see.

"My mortgage?" Betsy asked.

"I don't think so."

"Well, what then?"

Ernesto flipped the pad over. He had written TAXES in bold letters. "As an employee, you pay a big percentage of your income in taxes," Ernesto explained.

"But that doesn't count. They are taken out of my paycheck before I even receive it. There is nothing I can do about that."

"Then you must work smarter," Ernesto said. He leaned back in his chair with his eyes fixed on something outside.

"You are trying to make a point," Betsy said, looking through the front roll door of the warehouse at his trucks parked in the lot, each marked with the Bannister-Sanchez logo. "So, you are saying that I should work smarter by no longer being an employee? You think I should start my own business?"

"That is exactly what I am saying. Taxes work against the saving power of every employee. As you say, they are taken out of your paycheck and you can't do anything about it. But as a business owner, you can take charge of your expenses and there is a lot that you can do to eliminate your tax burden."

"But starting a business is risky," Betsy protested, a little shaken.

"People always say that owning a business is riskier than having a job. But I have never understood that. When you have a job, you only have one source of income. You can be let go at any time. Employees are always at risk. But when you own a business, you can anticipate trouble and do something about it. Most businesses have hundreds of customers. And each customer is another source of income. When you lose a customer, you still have several other customers that will provide you with income. And you can always go out and find more and more customers until you reach your income goals."

"That's true. The more customers you have, the more money you make."

"But when you work for someone else, you are relying on a single paycheck. It is usually your only source of income. If you lose your job, you lose your income. To me, that is far riskier than owning your own business."

"I see what you mean," Betsy agreed.

"When you have a job, you are a passenger on a bus. But when you own your own business you are the driver. You can steer a new course and find new business opportunities," Ernesto explained.

"Yeah, that makes sense. And I hate paying taxes, everyone does. But what kind of business?"

"I would suggest that you do what you are good at, Betsy. Do some brainstorming, put together a business plan and call me when you are ready to share it."

* * *

Back to Present Day - As Betsy recounted her story from several years before, Oliver listened from a sleek, light green couch next to a huge potted palm. They had moved to the lobby where they could hear each other better. Betsy sat in a highbacked chair, with a water feature pouring in steady sheets behind her. They were just a few feet away from a check-in table for the hotel marketing conference, anchored by two young women wearing lanyards with name badges.

Late arrivals were stopping by to register and get their event packets. Several of them stopped to greet Betsy on their way to the elevators. She was clearly very popular. Oliver was introduced to each of them, and he could tell that his stock was rising because of his personal meeting with Betsy Grant.

"I think I know where this is going," Oliver said, as a hotel owner from Cleveland left them to join the party upstairs.

"I didn't at the time," Betsy admitted, as she looked out over the lobby and waved at two women who had just entered the hotel, pulling their black rolling travel bags after them. "So, I continued working at my marketing job for the hotel, but in my free time I worked on business ideas. I looked at businesses to buy. Went to franchise shows. Drafted out ideas for my own start up. It was really fun."

"Nothing really appealed to me, so I took Ernesto's advice. I started a business in a market that I understood. I used my experience and contacts and started my own hotel marketing consulting business."

"And here you are," Oliver said with a sweep of his hand.

"And here I am," Betsy smiled, then stood and greeted the two women with suitcases, giving them hugs and introducing Oliver.

They headed for the elevators, while Oliver and Betsy sat down again. "So, you are really doing the same thing that you always did. Just in a different way. Are the taxes really that much lower?"

"Oh, my gosh. Absolutely. And my income is much higher. When I want to make more money, I just need to find a new client. The combination of lower taxes and higher income is what allowed me to save my first million. And my second."

"Really?" Oliver was impressed. "Can you explain how your business works?"

"So, I pitched my current employer on the benefit of hiring me as a consultant, rather than as a full-time employee. They paid me almost as much money, but they no longer had to cover my benefits, social security, insurance and other employer expenses. It represented a huge savings to them. I did all the work that they needed me to do, plus I had a flexible schedule and was able to add more clients. I knew a lot of people in the hotel industry, from events like this one. I soon had five other clients. So, rather than having income from a single employer, I had income from six different sources."

Oliver shook his head. "But how do you have the time for six different clients, or six different jobs?"

"It's amazing how much time is wasted as an employee. I am so much more efficient as a business owner. I meet with each client and we define the most critical tasks. They only pay me for those. The other, less important responsibilities are covered by other employees. Trust me, the model works, and it is more affordable for the company. And, most importantly, I make a lot more money. And now I am a conference speaker, which is another source of income for me."

"And your taxes are lower, too?"

"Yes, as a percentage, they are about half of what I was paying before, by the time you factor in the write-offs and business expenses."

"But what about health insurance and benefits?" Oliver asked.

"I pay them myself. I am earning more, and paying lower taxes, so I can afford to do this. The tax savings more than covers my insurance costs. And I get to select my own insurance plan."

"That sounds pretty good," Oliver admitted. "But no 401K?"

"No, but I have a SEP-IRA. I contribute to it every year and I let the interest compound by reinvesting the earnings. It's the power of compound interest I was telling you about. And I get to run my SEP-IRA anyway I want. I buy my own stocks, bonds, mutual funds and ETFs through my SEP-IRA. I love the flexibility."

"And the compound interest," Oliver echoed her enthusiasm.

"Yes, compound interest is the real force behind the 5 Steps. The other 4 steps are super important, too. But they all lead us to compound interest. That's where the power is. It is the force that can take an average earner and make them a millionaire."

"And it really began for you when you started your own business?" Oliver asked.

"Yes, that's when my earning power took off. But I could have made it as an employee, too. I had my plan in place and I was following it. I would have made it in 30 years. Owning my own business just got me there faster."

"So, I can still make it as an employee?"

"Definitely," Betsy said, and stood to greet another conference attendee. She promised to see them at the reception soon, and rejoined Oliver. "Can you see yourself as a business owner, Oliver?"

"Maybe. It sounds a little complicated," Oliver sighed, watching the relentless sheet of water tumbling from the fountain over Betsy's shoulder.

"I guess it is, at first. But then it becomes like anything else; familiar. I don't think I could ever work as an employee again," Betsy explained. "I guess I like to drive the bus."

Oliver was quiet for a minute. "I am not sure I'm ready for such a radical change. I just got this job, and I am still learning the industry."

"You don't have to do what I am doing, Oliver. Just be open to the possibilities. Excel in what you are doing now, but always be looking for new opportunities. One of the greatest benefits of owning your own business is that you decide how to invest your time. You can pursue other opportunities to make money. Ever since I started my own business, I have been contacted by people with business and investment opportunities."

"Give me an example," Oliver leaned forward, soaking in her experience.

"Well, a few years after I started my own consulting business, a former client approached me to start an ad agency. I continued with my consulting business, but I became a part owner in the new agency, too. I helped find some new clients, acted as an account executive, and helped to grow the business."

"You owned an ad agency and a marketing consulting company? At the same time?" Oliver asked, clearly surprised that a single mom had the bandwidth to handle both.

"Yes, one was 100% mine, and the other was a partnership. It gave me another source of income."

"But how did you manage your time? That sounds impossible." Oliver marveled.

"It wasn't easy. But when you own your own business you naturally become more efficient with your time. You find time in the margins..."

"Under the couch cushions?"

"Exactly. And you can always hire staff to help you grow your business. Once you do this, the sky is the limit."

"And this Ernesto guy taught you all of this?" Oliver asked.

"Pretty much. My business model is unique to me. But he showed me the concept. Ernesto is fearless when it comes to business. He sees something he wants, and he goes for it. And then he works really hard to make it happen."

"And you were fearless when you started your business?"

"No, I was terrified," Betsy laughed. "But the fear of not having enough money was greater. Fear drove me to own my own business.

And the fear of failure still drives me now. But I have become financially independent because of it. I guess I don't need to be afraid anymore. But I keep working."

"Stay hungry, right?" Oliver said, noticing that Betsy was waving at a woman about her age, who had just entered the lobby. He waited while they hugged and was introduced again. They were close friends, so Oliver went through emails on his phone while they caught up. After a few minutes, Betsy promised to see her upstairs and sat back down.

"You were saying that you keep working, partly out of fear," Oliver said as she joined him again.

"I guess so," Betsy agreed. "Ernesto is now in his eighties and he is still working. I don't know anyone who works harder. I plan to be the same way."

"So, you love it?"

"I do. Absolutely," Betsy confided.

"We should get you back to the party. Your public is waiting."

Betsy laughed and took a mock bow.

"I just met you. And you really don't know me," Oliver ventured. "But would you be willing to mentor me? The same way Ernesto helped you?"

A year passed. Oliver met Betsy at the next hotel marketing conference in Orlando. He was still working at his marketing job, and he was beginning to discover the power of compound interest. They were in the hotel cabana restaurant, out by the pool, under dark wood fans that spun in lazy circles. The wait staff wore Hawaiian shirts and served colorful drinks in large glasses. A song by the Deranged Prophets began playing and Betsy laughed.

"What's funny?" Oliver asked.

"Oh, this song makes me laugh," Betsy said, humming along.

"The Deranged Prophets?"

"Yes, their manager is a friend of my son's. I've met him a few times."

"Let me guess," Oliver said as he opened his menu. "He is a disciple of the 5 Steps, and on his way to earning his first million."

"Yes, and he's got the whole band on board, too." Betsy took a sip of her Pellegrino. "And how about you? Are you on the bandwagon, Oliver?"

"I'm all in," he said, putting the menu down without deciding what he wanted.

"So, you are saving each month, in addition to what you are putting in your 401K?"

"Yes, I'm contributing the maximum amount to my 401K, and I am saving in my own investment account. I love saving my own money. I feel like my 401K has too many strings attached, and I can't use the money until I retire."

"Exactly. And the money you are investing on your own really belongs to you."

"Yeah. I can use it anytime that I want to. In case of an emergency."

"Or for a business opportunity."

"Totally. I don't plan to use it, but it is great to know that it's there. It gives me a feeling of freedom."

"It's more than a feeling, Oliver." Betsy smiled.

"That's a song from another band," Oliver chimed in. "And I am beginning to realize that. Soon, I can lose my job and I have enough money to find another one. Or start my own business. Or buy a rental property. Or fund a comfortable retirement. It's a great feeling."

Betsy nodded. "I remember the feeling of first being debt free. I was lighter than a feather. But it was the savings I was putting aside that really made me soar."

"I love it," Oliver stated with a broad smile and leaned forward, "And it has inspired me to do something about it…"

"To start your own business?"

"Not quite. But I have an idea that I want to run by you," Oliver said seriously.

Betsy leaned in too, she could tell that he had spent a lot of time thinking through this conversation.

"I read the *Richest Man in Babylon*. And it's a really great book…," Oliver began.

"I think it is the best book written on personal finances," Betsy agreed.

"Probably so. But I really struggled to read through it. I started and stopped several times, before getting the hang of it. It finally clicked and I read through it another couple of times…"

"I had the same experience," Betsy admitted.

"But when I recommend it to friends, they start reading it…"

"And give up?" Betsy nodded. "I know what you mean. That old English language and the strange characters can be a little hard to relate to."

"Getting debt free and saving money is hard enough, but when you are given that book as the guide to do it, it seems even harder," Oliver declared, building up to his idea.

"Good point," Betsy looked up as the waiter approached. "We'll need just another minute."

After the waiter left, Oliver continued. "So, I was thinking that maybe I would write a new book. I could share the 5 steps and the concept of the First Million. I would keep the book simple and easy to read. That way, more people will read it and be able to participate in the life changing benefits of the 5 steps."

"I think it's a great idea," Betsy nodded. "I think a lot of people would benefit from it."

"So, you won't mind? I would be using your ideas."

"They're not my ideas, Oliver. And they don't belong to Ernesto Sanchez or George S Clason. They would both be quick to say so. The concepts for saving money and becoming financially independent don't belong to anyone. They are as old as time and come from common sense. They are free to everyone."

Oliver shrugged. "I guess I just want your blessing to turn these ideas into a book."

"Of course. You've got it. I learned these ideas from Ernesto and my friend Julia. And they learned them from other people, who learned them from someone else. I think it's great that you want to write a book to share them with thousands more."

"And you think Ernesto would agree?" Oliver was hopeful.

"I do. But if you're going to write this book, you should meet him in person."

**"Whatever you do,
work at it with all your heart."**

—Colossians 3:23

**"The soul of a lazy person desires
and has nothing; But the soul of the
diligent shall be made rich."**

—Proverbs 13:4

6

WORK HARD

Present Day - The sun was just rising over the foothills as
Ernesto Sanchez drove up to the construction site in his Chevy
pick-up. Many of his men were arriving, too. They streamed across
the dusty expanse of stacked dry wall, lumber, and concrete bags,
toward the skeletons of framed houses that stretched down the newly
paved street for a thousand yards. His men wore dusty work boots
and hard hats and carried their hot coffee in steel travel mugs. They
all waved and smiled as Ernesto climbed out of his truck and went
over to each of them to shake their hands and ask about their families. He knew each man. He knew their dreams and he knew
their troubles.

He once had the same troubles, which was one of the reasons he woke up so early each morning to arrive when his men did. Well into his eighties, Ernesto Sanchez was a constant presence on his job sites. He greeted his men each morning and worked alongside them, driving nails, reviewing plans, sweeping the work site, and getting as dirty and sweaty as each of his men. And they loved him for it.

Bannister-Sanchez was one of the most profitable home builders in the western United States. They had a reputation for running the tightest projects in the industry. Their work sites were spotless, without fast food trash or beer cans. They finished their projects on schedule and on budget. Ernesto Sanchez was the main reason for this. By his example, his men worked hard. They were always respectful, always on-time, and never swore on the job site. Ernesto Sanchez ran his company differently than most of his competitors. He regarded his work as a higher calling and personally trained each of his men in how to do it properly.

Ernesto walked the job site with his three project managers, discussing their progress for each phase of the build. Each of his men were in their middle fifties and had worked for Ernesto for a long time. Each man had also accumulated enough wealth to retire years earlier. But they still came to work every day, in their simple pick-up trucks, dressed in work boots, hard hats, jeans, and proudly wearing the same, simple dark blue Bannister-Sanchez logo shirts that Ernesto wore every day.

"Let me refill your coffee, Ernesto," Ed Rollins said as they headed back to the trailer after their morning site inspection. Ed was tall and wore black framed glasses. He was a graduate of Michigan State with an MBA from UCLA. His personal net worth was north of $4 million but he came to work every day for Ernesto Sanchez.

"Thanks, Ed," Ernesto smiled at his foreman's daily offer. "I'll get my own coffee." His men chuckled. They loved to hear their boss say those simple words. They had all worked their way up through the company and adopted Ernesto's work-ethic. They were proud of what they had built together and had emulated Ernesto's dedication for the past several decades.

"By the way, Henry's grandson will be working with us today," Ernesto mentioned as he poured the imported black coffee into his mug. He took a sip and ran his thick, coarse hands through his grey hair, still streaked with strands of the black that once filled his head.

"Yes, Ernesto. His name is on your schedule," Frank Menendez replied. He was a huge specimen of a man, with giant hands and an even bigger smile. He was Ernesto's closest friend and had worked with him from the early days of his construction business. He winked at the other men and they smiled back, knowingly. Ernesto emailed a detailed agenda every night to his three foremen, which they shared with each of their men, so they all knew exactly what the project list and priorities were for the next day. He had included Max Bannister on his agenda and had been talking of Max's arrival for some time now.

"Can we put him through your boot camp, Ernesto?" Sam West said with his big New York laugh. He was lean and wiry from the 10 miles he ran every morning before work, as he trained for the marathons he signed up for all around the world. He had a quick wit and sharp tongue. But the men who reported to him knew his heart was huge.

They all laughed. Sam was tough and the new workers were a little afraid of him. He kept the schedules and made sure every project was completed on time.

"I don't want to scare him away on his first day," Ernesto laughed. "I've been trying to get this kid here for a couple of years now."

"He's soft, Ernesto. It's not going to work. His dad spoiled him."

"I think you're right about that, Frank. But I want to do this for Henry. I owe my old partner a lot. We all do. If it wasn't for him, none of us would be here right now."

"Ernesto, you would have been successful with or without Henry Bannister," Sam said sharply. "But don't worry, we get it. We all miss Henry and want to help his family. I just can't believe Henry's son blew through his money so quickly. He's only been gone for 15 years and $200 million is a lot of dough."

"It's not all gone," Ernesto sighed. "They still have some in the trust."

"Thanks to you," Ed replied. "You stepped in just in time to help them out. And you even put in some of your own money."

Ernesto shrugged. "I just did what Henry would want. No big deal. Now the grandchildren need to get jobs and earn a decent living, until their trust kicks in when they're older."

"And you think Max Bannister, with his fancy degree from Boston College and his ridiculous car, will be willing to work for us?" Sam shook his head.

"I need to try," Ernesto replied simply. Then his eyes twinkled as he pointed at the huge Bannister-Sanchez Construction sign at the entrance of the work site. "His name is on the sign."

Max Bannister drove up to the work site after 10:00 am. He parked his bright orange Lotus next to Ernesto's Chevy pickup and slowly climbed out of the car. He wore leather loafers, faded jeans, a white button-down shirt, and a tie. He wore a dark jacket with a light plaid and dark, expensive sunglasses. His hair was full and slicked back and he carried a leather attaché case. Ernesto watched him climb the metal stairs of the trailer and open the door. He stood and greeted his old partner's grandson.

"Max!" He beamed. "I am so glad you came."

"Sorry, Ernesto. I meant to be here sooner, but there was this girl….." Max shrugged.

Ernesto shook his head. "There is always a girl with you, Maxito. In that way, you were very much like your grandfather…. Until he met Helen, of course."

"Yeah, that's what I heard, Ernesto. But unfortunately, the similarities stop there." Max took a chair in front of Ernesto's desk.

"No, Max. You have your grandfather's quick intelligence. I've seen it," Ernesto corrected.

"Yeah, I guess I'm book smart, like him. But my dad and I didn't inherit his gift for making money. How he became so wealthy is a mystery to us. And hanging onto money is even harder. Our family blew through it so quickly."

"Money is a funny thing, Max," Ernesto explained. "If you don't respect it, it will leave you for someone who does."

"Oh, come on," Max was incredulous. "It can't be that simple."

"No, not simple. But it's not complicated either," Ernesto explained. He stood up and went over to the coffee pot. When he had refilled his cup, he noticed Max had his brown leather loafers on his desk. He calmly put his coffee cup down and pushed his feet off the desk. "Don't you ever look lazy while you are on the work site, Max,"

Ernesto demanded. "I won't have it. My men work hard out there, and I won't ever allow you to disrespect them by looking lazy."

"Easy, Ernesto. I got it." Max stood and walked around the trailer. "I understand I need to fit in. But I'm not sure that this is the right gig for me. You know, college educated and all that."

"That doesn't make you special. Most of my men have college degrees, or they are on their way to earning them. What makes you special is what you do with it."

"My point exactly. I'm not sure that I'm cut out for this kind of work. Coming to the job site every day, wearing work boots, breathing dust, and working in the sun. Ernesto, you don't need to do this. You are worth a fortune. One of the richest men in the state. Why do you wake up so early, show up to this crummy trailer, and work alongside your men in the hot sun all day? You could be on the golf course, hitting the day spa, watching TV and chilling. Man, if I had your wealth...." Max cleared his throat and paused.

"If you had my wealth, what?" Ernesto asked, his face stern and searching.

"I'd be in Aspen right now. Or the South of France sipping wine. I'd fly a corporate jet all around the world, go on safari... Oh, and the women. Maybe I'd have my own island..."

Ernesto laughed. "None of that has any interest to me. Sure, I travel a little. It's good to see the world. But my place is here. With my work."

"Work! Work! Work!" Max sat down again, frustrated. "Work gets in the way of everything. I have to work now, since the money is gone. I will be working for the rest of my life. All day, 5 days a week, slogging away like a slave..."

"First of all, the money is not gone. There is a trust waiting for you and your sisters…"

"Yeah, I know, when we are forty. Thank you again for setting all of that up for my grandmother. At least we will have a little something to keep us from starving when we're older."

"It's a lot of money to most people. You just need to rein in your spending. Your life-style has to change now."

"It's what I know, Ernesto."

"But it's not what you can afford. Not anymore. Like that car…"

"It's an investment," Max declared defensively. "They only made 500 cars like mine. I'm going to take really good care of it and sell it for a fortune one day. Anyway, we were talking about work. I don't understand why you work so hard, Ernesto. You are super-rich, and yet here you are, every day, on a work site like this one, building homes, and drinking your gourmet coffee."

Ernesto paused. How could he get through to this pompous, lazy kid? Ernesto was on the brink of doing something radical to get the boy's attention.

Should he go there? What would his grandfather, Henry Bannister, say? Then he smiled. He knew just what Henry Bannister would say. He took a deep breath and smiled. "You've got a point there, Max. My coffee is brewed from some of the highest quality beans in the world. It's definitely gourmet, and a lot better than the crap I drank in prison."

"Prison!" Max's jaw dropped. "What are you talking about, Ernesto? When were you in prison?"

"Many years ago, Max. Another lifetime, really. But my time in prison made me what I am today. It taught me that hard work was my best friend. Work is not something to be avoided. It is something to be embraced. You need to lean into it and give it everything you have. Everything I have is a result of hard work. It got me out of trouble." He paused and looked out the window, watching his men work together to carry a heavy, pre-framed section through the site.

"Trouble so deep, I thought I would never escape it. And it keeps me out of trouble today. That's why I work every day. First, because I love it. Work is my best friend. It fills my soul with purpose and I really love what I do. And, sure, I could buy a jet and live a lifestyle of the rich and famous. But that would ruin me. I need to stay close to my roots and not forget who I am, something else I learned from my time in prison."

"I still can't believe you were in prison. You're practically a billionaire!"

"Money doesn't make you anything special, Max. It's your character that counts. Now, I will tell you my story if you promise to listen carefully. But we can't do it here. I don't want my men to see us sitting on our asses all day. Let's take a drive."

"Where are we going?"

"To our new project site. I want to show you what we will be building next." Ernesto grabbed the keys to his truck and lead Max down the metal trailer stairs to the parking lot. "And, I guess, take you back in time...."

"Can't wait to hear it. But let's take my car," Max said, as they walked across the dusty parking lot.

Ernesto didn't even look up. "Max, get in my truck."

As they took a highway east, past the foothills and toward the unincorporated parts of the east county, Max Bannister marveled at Ernesto's truck. "Ernesto, your truck is like a million years old. Come on. You can afford to drive anything. Why do you still haul around in this old thing?"

"I love my truck. It's only eight years old. It's in great shape. I'm good."

"So, this is just your work truck, right? You must use it for the job site and then drive a sweet Mercedes or Bentley on the weekends?"

"No. This is my truck. It's the only car I drive. My Valerie has her own car though. We got that for her a few years ago."

"Something nice, I hope," Max said, his discouragement growing deeper.

"Oh, yes. It's one of the best cars ever made. A Ford Taurus."

Max sighed and rolled his eyes. "Really, Ernesto? You don't own any fine cars? No foreign sports cars? No luxury sedans? Come on. You're pulling my leg."

"Max," the old man smiled. "I drive what I like. To me, a car is totally unimportant. My men work hard. They are simple men, who are putting their kids through school and saving for the future. What kind of message would it send if I drove some fancy car? They wouldn't respect me."

They drove in silence for a few minutes, as Ernesto's words sunk in. "Plus, they wouldn't recognize me. I'm the guy who built a company by working hard alongside his men. So, I drive what they drive. I want them to recognize me, Max. And more important than that, I need to recognize myself."

"What are you trying to say?" Max replied defensively. "That because I drive my Lotus, I don't know who I am?"

"I think you are young and trying to figure it out. Until you do, you are driving what you think the world wants you to drive. You need to be true to yourself. You can't let other people define who you are."

"Man, you sound like a Hallmark card, Ernesto."

They switched lanes and merged onto a southbound freeway. "I had a lot of time to think in prison, Max. Three years of thinking. It changes a man, and it certainly changed me. When I was young like you, I had a big chip on my shoulder. No one could tell me anything. My parents wanted me to study to become an engineer in Mexico City. I wanted to be a musician because that's what my friends were doing. It didn't matter to me that I didn't have any talent. But everything changed when my father died. He left my mom with big debts to some very dangerous people. My other brothers were already married and supporting their own families. So, I filed the paperwork to become a US citizen. It was a little different in those days. The application process wasn't so crazy and not as many people were trying to get to America from Mexico. I knew we needed to leave Mexico, it just wasn't safe for us. Fortunately, they accepted our application and we moved here and lived with my Aunt Maria. My mom worked as a cook in a restaurant and I went to community college to start my degree. I struggled in school because English was not my first language. My grades suffered and I stopped trying. I eventually dropped out and started helping on construction sites. It wasn't an engineering degree, but I was building houses and I thought it was a good start. But that's where my trouble began."

"There were some guys on the construction site who always seemed to have money. They drove new cars and were always going out at night to nice places. They told a lot of wild stories while we were working, and I decided that I wanted to be like them. They paid the foreman a little something on the side to get the easy jobs on the site, and many days they didn't show up at all. I couldn't understand how they were doing it. Until one day, one of them, Ramon Diaz, took me aside and spoke to me in Spanish."

Max sat quietly and listened. He lost track of where they were headed and which freeway they were taking.

"Ernesto," Ramon said to me. "You want to make some extra cash?"

"Maybe?" I said. "Who doesn't?"

"We have a job tonight and we could use your help. You do this little job for us and we will cut you in for 10 percent."

"What's the job?"

"No, Ernesto. That's more than you need to know. This is a no questions asked thing. Are you in or not?"

"Ten percent of what?"

"We don't know until the job is done. Are you in or not? I can always ask Barnes. He doesn't ask so many questions."

"No, I'll do it. I need the money."

"I went back to work and thought about it all day long. What was the son of my father about to do? After work, we all got in a truck and headed south to the border. We stopped on the US side and picked up a white van in a neighborhood I had never visited before. We left Ramon and this guy named Tomas with the truck we took from work, and me and two other guys went across the border in the van."

"We headed into Mexico and stopped at a little ranchero up in the hills. You could tell the owner was living well. Nice place. He had a barn on his property, and we pulled up in front of it. The doors of the barn slide open and there were about six guys, all with guns. Some of the meanest looking guys you ever saw. They didn't even talk to us. They loaded the van with packages. I didn't ask what was in them, I knew they were drugs. They packed them tightly on the bottom of the van, and then put rolls of carpet on top of them, stacked them to the ceiling. The rolls were heavy and awkward, just the kind of thing the border patrol agents wouldn't want to hassle with. They slapped some magnetic signs on the side of the van for American Carpet Company, like the factories they had in that area. They handed me the keys and explained that I was going to drive the van across the border into the US. They would hold my two friends until they knew I made it across and dropped off the van at an address they made me memorize."

"If I didn't show up as planned, they would kill my friends. Just like that. I was in way over my head. The guys I showed up with smiled nervously at me and said I better stick to the plan. I was told to go through a certain line at the border, at a certain time. Under no circumstances was I to use another line or drive through at a different time. Row three, 8:45 pm. Or my friends would be killed."

"So, I drove the van. I was worried that I would get lost, or go to the wrong border crossing, because I didn't know that border town very well. But it went smoothly. No problems. I drove up to the agent at the crossing and he waved me right through. Simple. I found the house and Ramon and Tomas were waiting there, playing pool, and drinking beer like it was just another night."

"Another guy took the van and drove it off into the night. We hopped back into our truck and picked up the other two guys at a McDonald's near the border. They were fine and we all had a good laugh about the risk they took with a stranger like me. But they were happy that they could trust me."

"We were paid in cash the next day, at a fast-food place a few miles from the work site. We went through the drive through, ordered some ice cream and there was $10,000 in a white paper bag. I was paid $1,000 for just driving a van. Easy money, Max. That was a lot of money in those days. In Mexico, I would work for over a year to save that kind of money. But here, in America, the land of opportunity, I made it in a single night. Doing almost nothing."

"I had a lot of fun with that $1,000. I bought my mom some new clothes and lied to her that it was from my earnings at the construction site. Then I blew the rest on beer and wild times. I was broke again. So, when Ramon told me we had another job, I didn't hesitate. Same plan, same van, but more packages this time. I did everything the same. Same time, same line, but this time it was a different border agent. They pulled the van over and searched it. They removed the carpet and found the packages. It turned out to be marijuana. It wasn't legal like it is today, and they arrested me on the US side of the border. The two guys I left behind in that barn were killed, I guess. And I never saw Tomas or Ramon again. I was found guilty and thrown into a maximum-security prison."

"So, you went to prison for dealing drugs?" Max was shocked.

"Not for dealing. I was just a mule. But it is a federal crime, and they take it very seriously. I was given 10 years and I deserved every one of them. I was so ashamed of what had become of my father's son. I was helping to bring dangerous drugs into the United States. Drugs that would be sold to kids, addicts, mothers, and fathers. People might die or ruin their lives for what I had done. I deserved those ten years."

"But if it wasn't you, someone else would have done it," Max reasoned.

First Million

"But it was me. People follow the examples of others. If I had stood by my morals and handled my life the way my father had taught me, I never would have helped Ramon. Maybe they would have seen something in me that was different and given them a reason to quit. Now my friends were dead, and I was going to prison."

"They sent me to a prison in Texas. It was maximum security. Lots of really bad guys. Murder, armed robbery, drugs, rape... You name it, I shared a cell with them. My first night, I was put into a cell with three other guys. It was late at night when we arrived in the prison and they were planning to process us in the morning. So, we weren't in the full prison yet, but we could hear what was going on. I heard men crying, screaming, laughing. It was like hell on earth, Max."

"Sounds awful," Max replied, hanging on every word.

"None of us could sleep, so we started talking. Mel was a nice-looking black man. He was a small business owner. He had a family and a couple of convenience stores in Oregon. He was really proud of what he had built, and we were all really impressed with him."

"So, you're a rich guy?" I asked.

"Not yet, but I'm on my way," Mel told me.

"Then how come you couldn't just hire a flash attorney and get out of this?" One of the others asked.

"I did. I had my sentenced reduced. I will only be here for 5 years."

"Damn, what did you do?" I asked him.

"I was working late at my Frontier Street store. That's my best store. It's on a busy street and I get a lot of walk-in traffic. The cash register is always full, and I usually have a line two or three deep throughout the day. Lunch time is crazy. It's a great location, until the sun goes down. Then it becomes a dangerous neighborhood. I usually lock up early and get out of there, but we had a super big day, and I was reconciling my cash drawer. My manager had just left, and this guy came walking in."

"We're closed," I told him.

"That's good," he said and pulled out a gun and held it against my forehead. Man, when that steel barrel is against your head, you really get to thinking. I just wanted to survive, you know?"

"Take it all, my friend," I told him, and I started piling the cash into a paper bag for him. Must have been $8,000. I thought by being cool he might, you know, let me live. But I could tell he wasn't going to let that happen. He had a beany cap pulled low, but I could see his eyes. They were cold and I could feel in the pit of my stomach that as soon as I gave him the cash, he was going to pull that trigger. So, I started talking to him."

"You came at the right time, Man. I had a big day. But this is only part of it. Most of it is in the back. I just took it there a few minutes ago."

"Why are you telling me this?" He asked.

"Help yourself. I got insurance. I just want to live, Man. Let's go get that other cash and you be on your way." I was bargaining for my life, but I knew he wasn't having it."

"Let's go. But try something and I'll slam a bullet into your head."

"So, I led him into the storage room. I keep an extra safe on this high metal shelf, you know. And right above it, I have my gun. It's up high, out of view, and I knew just where it was. So, I reached up to the shelf, it's kinds dark back there, I got my hand around the gun, put my finger on the trigger and just turned and shot him before he knew what I was doing. His gun went off, too, but the bullet went high and buried itself into a beam, just a few feet above my head. I got him in the chest, nothing fancy. And I knew I had him. But after he took a shot at me, I pulled the trigger a couple more times and finished him off. That's what really did me in. It became more than self-defense. And they sent me away. I thought the jury would understand. I was just trying to protect my family, my business. Man, I know that guy would have killed me. But the fact that I led him into the back room and shot him a couple more times.... Well, that was too much for them."

Ernesto and Max took another freeway and continued driving east. As the traffic thinned out, they left the main highway and took a two lane into the hills.

"We were all quiet for a while. Just thinking about this hard-working family man with a couple of businesses. Here he was, sitting in jail with us low-lifes."

"None of us could sleep. The first night in prison is a real shock to the system. After a while, we went around and told our stories. Biker, he never told us his real name, just said he killed a guy in a bar fight. He had tattoos all over his arms and a long beard. He was one tough hombre."

"And then there was Nathan. A little skinny white guy. He was a fraudster. He wrote false checks, stole people's social security numbers, set up fake credit cards, that kind of thing. He was working hard to be lazy. Just stealing money where he could."

"Mel, the business owner who killed that robber, said to us, "We all have a choice for how to get out of prison. We can melt into the prison culture, join the gangs, and try to stay alive. But I have a plan.

I'm going to do what I have always done. I am going to *work* my way out of here."

"Work? No way, Man," Nathan said. "I just going to chill. We're here to do our time, not to work."

"You take that attitude, and you will serve your whole sentence," Mel told us. "Listen to me, my friends. Stay clean, listen to the guards, and become known as someone who can be trusted. You will get your sentence reduced and get to walk sooner."

"The guards?" Biker cursed. "They touch me, and I'll kill them. No one's going to mess with me."

"I feared for Biker then. I had an uneasy feeling that he would be in the middle of some terrible fights in prison."

"The other two disagreed with Mel, but I listened to what he said. He sounded a lot like my father. And if I had just listened to my Padre, I wouldn't be in this prison. So, I spoke with him."

"Ernesto, make hard work your best friend, as I have. Everything I have ever earned, my family, my businesses, my wealth... Everything has come from hard work. Do the same, and you will see. Keep your cell clean, listen to the guards, stand up tall when they talk to you. Say, "Yes, Sir!" Eat your meals with me, work in the kitchen, and volunteer for work duties. Give yourself a purpose and they will let you out of here much faster."

"So, I listened to Mel. When they processed us, we were careful to do what they said, and they could see that we were going to be cooperative. They gave us a better cell and put us together in a softer block. Mel and I volunteered for everything we could. We worked in the library sorting books, volunteered for the laundry and the kitchen. We went to every church service and did exactly what the guards told us. And it worked. Mel was released in just 18 months.

And I had my sentence reduced from ten to three years. It was hard work that saved me."

"It wasn't the same for Biker. He got into fights all the time. He was strong, but stubborn and after so many fights he was moved to another prison in Arkansas. I heard he was killed in a gang fight."

"And Nathan never changed. He just sat in his cell and did his time. Never volunteered. Never put in the work and I heard he served his whole sentence. I got out many years before he did."

"When I got out of prison, I went to work on the construction sites again. I saved my money and earned my contractor's license. I learned the concrete business and did little remodels and home improvement projects for whoever would hire me. I worked hard, all the time, and always did my best work for every customer. I got a reputation as a contractor who showed up on time, worked hard, and delivered a project on budget. I wasn't making much money, but I was out of prison and building a career."

"Then one day, I did a little concrete patio project for an apartment building remodel that your grandfather was working on. He saw that I arrived early every morning and worked all day to make the deadline. He watched me work and liked what he saw. He asked around and heard I was a hard worker. After I finished that project, he offered me a job."

"I could tell that Henry Bannister was going places and I wanted to go with him. I took the job and I made hard work my best friend. I was always on the site first, always the last to leave, never had a sick day. Your grandfather was building his business and he needed people he could rely on. He liked my work-ethic and kept promoting me, site manager, project manager, and then he asked if I would like to be his partner. He explained that if I worked that hard all the time, every project would be a success."

"We built the company together and Bannister–Sanchez became something special. So, hard work saved me. I am not about to stop now. I must be true to myself and keep working hard," Ernesto concluded. Then repeated, "Hard work is my best friend."

They reached the site and Ernesto turned off the main highway onto a dirt frontage road. A large plot of land, dotted with scrub brush, rolled away from the two-lane highway. They followed the bumpy, unpaved road away from the highway and up a small rise. As the hill became steeper, the road narrowed to a path. They parked the truck and got out. Max followed Ernesto through the sage brush and up a winding path to the top of a hill.

When Max reached the top, he was a little out of breath, and looked over to see how Ernesto was handling the climb. If he was tired, Ernesto certainly showed no sign of it. Max shook his head in admiration and looked out over the little valley, bordered on the far side by a small, basin lake. They stood there for a moment, letting the wind weave through them, while a red tail hawk circled high above.

"The city is moving this way, Max. We are a few years early, so the land is cheap and the permitting process a little easier. I hope to break ground in a couple of years." Ernesto sighed, "I love it out here."

Max nodded, saying nothing.

"There is a lot of work to do," Ernesto continued. "I'd like you to help me build it. But you will need to work hard, start at the bottom, and move your way up slowly, just like I did."

Max studied the land and immediately saw the wisdom of Ernesto's plan. "Why are you helping me like this, Ernesto?"

"Because your grandfather helped me," Ernesto said simply.

Max considered this for a moment. "I'm in, Ernesto."

Ernesto walked quietly across the ridge, as Max trailed behind him. He finally stopped and looked back toward the frontage road, where his truck was parked. He didn't reply.

"I mean, I am all in," Max continued. "On this project. Working hard. Doing it right. And starting at the bottom."

Ernesto smiled and looked back at Max. "Your grandfather would be so proud of you."

It was dark the next morning when Ernesto pulled into the parking lot. There was a used Ford F-150 parked next to his trailer. The spotlights were on and he could see a man in the shadows of the framed house across the street, sweeping the concrete floor.

Ernesto went into the trailer and poured two cups of coffee. He clanked down the metal steps of the trailer into the cold morning air, with the steam from the coffee trailing behind him. He crossed the street and walked into the early morning shadows of the framed house.

"I like your truck," Ernesto said, handing Max one of the mugs.

Max accepted it and smiled, holding onto the broom. "Thanks! I do, too. That Lotus just wasn't me."

A few hours later, Oliver Powers arrived at the job site for his 9:00 am appointment with Ernesto Sanchez. They met in the trailer and Ernesto offered him a cup of coffee. It was delicious.

"Betsy told me about you," Ernesto said after his first sip. "She said you were alright. You followed the 5 Steps and saved a lot of money. I'm happy for you."

"Betsy is terrific," Oliver declared. "And she credits you with everything she knows about money."

Ernesto warmed his hands on the steaming mug. "It was my partner, Henry Bannister, who taught me the 5 Steps. He helped me save my first million. And someone else taught him."

"Are you ok with me writing a book about it?" Oliver asked. The coffee really was delicious.

"The 5 Steps belong to everyone. I think it's a really good idea."

"Thank you," Oliver replied gratefully. "I really appreciate your willingness to share."

Ernesto shrugged, "So many people shared with me. Everything I know was taught to me by someone else. I am here only through the kindness others. The 5 steps changed my life. I am happy to pass them along."

Ernesto began telling Oliver about his conversation with Max from the day before. He repeated the story of his drug arrest and time in prison. He shared how he learned to make hard work his best friend.

Then he stood up and pointed through the window to Max working on the job site. He was loading a wheelbarrow with scrap wood and sweating profusely. "I shared some of what I learned with Max yesterday. I think his life may have changed, too."

Oliver watched Max working and sipped Ernesto's gourmet coffee, enjoying the transformation. "So," he asked. "Where should we start?"

"With Step One," Ernesto said simply.

"Therefore, everyone who hears these words of mine and puts them into practice is like a wise person who built their house on the rock."

—Matthew 7:24

7

REFERRAL

James Grant looked down the unforgiving 18th fairway. The curving pitch followed a narrow stream bed, filled with boulders, and dotted with scrub pines, which formed its eastern boundary in a shallow dogleg right. A stand of palm trees and a treacherous rough bordered the west shoulder, with a few tricky bunker placements that forced a careful, straight drive along the right side, cutting the edge of the dogleg.

James steadied his ball on the tee and took some relaxed practice swings. He gauged the slight cross breeze, considered the narrow fairway, and double-checked the position of the bunkers. Satisfied, James carefully set his feet, took a deep calming breath, and pulled his driver back in a slow, gentle backstroke. Then, with careful force, he drove his ball straight down the right edge of the fairway. The ball touched down on the edge, just a few yards from the stream bed, and rolled to rest in the middle of the fairway, just where it began to angle right.

"Nice ball. That should help your cause," Miranda Flores said from behind the wheel of the golf cart. Miranda's observation came from experience. A past collegiate athlete, she continued to play local golf tournaments and was currently beating James by a few strokes in their annual golf outing.

"I need a miracle to catch to you," James said, as he slid his driver into his bag and joined Miranda in the golf cart.

"Or a solid approach shot. This isn't over," Miranda replied with a gentle smile. She was in her late thirties, with short dark hair and eyes the shade of almonds. Wearing a black visor and matching long sleeve polo, Miranda could still pass as a college player.

"You said that last year," James replied, far from upset. He was happy to be within a few strokes of one of the best golfers he knew. "I'm not expecting a surprise finish. Just hoping for respectability."

Miranda drove the cart forward along the path, curving past the raised tee. She left the path and the cart's wheels went silent as they glided over the manicured fairway and rolled steadily toward her ball. James' drive was several yards ahead of Miranda's, but he knew she would crush him in the short game.

"Speaking of surprises…" Miranda began. "Before we have our annual tax lunch, is there anything I need to know?"

In addition to a competitive golfing friend, Miranda Flores served as the outside accountant for Grant Commercial Plumbing. She had been doing James' taxes for a few years, providing advice for both his corporation and his personal finances. In addition to meeting a few times each year to review his corporate tax plans, James and Miranda put their busy schedules aside to play an annual round of golf. And Miranda always won.

"You're trying to distract me," James said politely, as the cart glided down the fairway. "It's not going to work."

"Nothing like that. Just curious about your business."

"Right." James admired Miranda's competitive spirit. "You'll see soon enough. Nothing to worry about. The numbers keep growing. Both revenue and expenses."

Miranda pulled even with her ball and got out of the cart, while James waited. She selected an eight iron and strolled confidently up to the ball. She studied the approach and took a few easy practice strokes. She was just about to settle in when James commented, "The surprise I have for you isn't really about the business."

Miranda looked up from her shot and stared back at James, who smiled innocently from the golf cart. She looked back to her ball, erasing James and his comment from her mind. While she was a natural athlete, Miranda's real talent was her focus and intensity. She carefully centered herself, studied the green some 130 years away, took note of the bunkers, and watched the flag flutter slightly. She shifted her gentle backstroke into a powerful forward swing that launched her ball in a high arch. Her ball sailed straight for the green, landing just past the pin, then spun backwards slightly to rest a few yards away.

"Beautiful shot, Miranda," James clapped. "Just a few feet away from another birdie."

"We'll see," Miranda strolled back to the cart, slid her club into her bag, and hopped behind the wheel. She drove the golf cart forward several yards, pulling even with James' ball. James climbed out, selected his 9 iron, and joined his ball in the middle of the fairway.

"What's the surprise?" Miranda asked casually, as he studied the green from 110 yards away. James smiled but did not reply. He knew the match was over, but he wanted to finish strong. He took a full practice stroke, set his feet, and followed through with a cautious stroke that soared high over the fairway and landed on the green. His ball hit with a lot of forward momentum and bounced across the green, settling a few feet off the fringe.

"Good shot!" Miranda shouted politely from the cart.

"Not good enough. It looks like you're going to widen your lead by another stroke," James said without malice. He climbed into the cart still holding his 9 iron and Miranda pulled forward.

"I'm featured in a new book about personal finances," James finally confessed.

"Really?" Miranda was impressed, but not surprised. She knew James actively shared advice on personal finances with other business owners, friends, and acquaintances. He referred a lot of business to Miranda and each new client spoke highly of his helpful advice. "Who wrote the book?"

"A guy named Oliver Powers. He's a friend of my mom's," James explained. "He's turning Ernesto's five steps into a book."

Although they had never met in person, Miranda was familiar with the legendary Ernesto Sanchez and his five steps for financial independence. She drove the cart off the fairway and rejoined the path. The cart followed a gentle curve around the green and came to a stop just in front of the waiting clubhouse. "Will you give me a signed copy?"

"Are you sure one is enough?" James asked, as he hopped out of the cart and pulled his putter from his bag.

"A putter?" Miranda asked.

"Yeah, I think the green is too fast for a wedge," James replied quickly. "I plan to tap this in from the fringe and then order lunch."

"I like your confidence," Miranda replied.

"Well, I might need to tap it a few times to finish," James admitted.

"You think I should order multiple copies?" Miranda asked, as she climbed out of the cart and took her putter from her bag.

"Maybe. Read it first," James suggested. "But if the book is helpful, you could give it to your clients as a gift. You know, a tool to help them get their finances under control."

"Good idea," Miranda agreed, as she walked up the slope to the green. "I'm interested in anything that will help my clients."

James followed behind her. He traced the fringe of the green to his ball as Miranda removed the flag. "Looks like I'm away."

"Want me to mark?" Miranda asked, as she stepped back from the hole.

"I'm good." James studied the lie and tapped his ball gently. It rolled straight down the mild slope, following the contour of the green. It gained speed as it approached the cup and ringed around the lip, stopping a few feet away.

"Almost!" Miranda shouted in encouragement.

James walked up to his ball and tapped it easily into the cup. "No shame in finishing with a par."

"None at all," Miranda agreed. She laid the flag down behind her and came in from behind her ball. She crouched low and judged the subtle angle of the green. Then she stepped up to her ball, lined up her putt, and dropped the ball in from a few feet away. Miranda secured her birdie and another match win.

James strode over to Miranda and high-fived her. "Nice round."

"Maybe next year?" Miranda asked.

"Maybe. But I'll need to play a lot to beat you," James said evenly. "It's cool. I'm happy with the way I played. Just keep my taxes as low as possible and you are welcome to beat me every year."

"I'll do my best," Miranda promised. They picked up their balls, replaced the flag, and crossed the green to their cart. "So, when does this book come out?"

"Not sure," James said as he slid his putter into his bag. "But I'll send you a copy once it's published."

"And it's about all of those things we talk about? Creating a budget? Living simply?"

"Saving money. Investing. Working hard," James continued the list as he climbed into the cart. "Yeah, that's what it sounds like."

"I will need extra copies," Miranda agreed. "I can think of a few clients who need a book like that."

Kayla Rios slipped her iPhone into her Prada bag and settled in for her annual tax appointment. With the demands of her office out of sight, Kayla was free to focus on her taxes.

Her black bag was carefully selected to match her shoes and simple, chic business outfit. Clothes had always been a priority for Kayla, with each accessory added to harmonize her wardrobe. She didn't realize that her expensive clothes would clash with her annual tax appointment.

Her file was open, and Miranda Flores leaned over her numbers, making notes with a red pencil. "You got another raise?"

"A couple of them last year," Kayla said proudly, as she studied her newly manicured nails.

"That's awesome, Kayla," Miranda replied, without looking up from the file. She billed by the hour and her clients rarely welcomed a chatty conversation. "What about savings?"

"You mean my 401K?"

"Yes, I don't see that you made any contributions last year," Miranda said, flipping a form over and trying to determine what Kayla had been up to.

"That's because I didn't make any," Kayla confessed.

Miranda looked up and met her eyes. Kayla was in her late twenties, working for one of the region's fastest growing high-tech companies, and fearlessly climbing the corporate ladder. But Miranda could sense fear in the dark, bright eyes of the attractive Latina woman who sat across from her.

"Wait. Doesn't your employer match dollar for dollar?" Miranda probed further, holding Kayla's eyes.

Kayla avoided her gaze by sweeping her long hair over her shoulder and looking out the window at the traffic zipping by. She didn't reply.

"But, Kayla, that's like giving money away. You could be saving up to $57,000 a year," Miranda pressed, knowing she was hitting a pain point.

"I know! I know!" Kayla met Miranda's eyes again. "But I am investing in a different way."

"You're investing outside of your 401K?" Miranda pursued further.

"Yeah, in my new house," Kayla announced defiantly.

"Are you paying down the principle?" Miranda asked, not letting her off the hook.

"No, but I am making my payments…" Kayla avoided her eyes again, focusing on her nails.

"And how much are they?" Miranda continued.

"About six," Kayla replied.

"Six thousand? A month?"

"What's wrong with that?"

"Nothing, Kayla." Miranda took a deep breath. "Except that I know how much money you make. And I can see that you are not taking advantage of a generous dollar for dollar retirement matching plan from your employer. You are spending too much money on your home."

"But it's a good investment, right?" Kayla replied softly.

"It can be. But if you are just making the interest payments and not saving for the future, you are really hurting yourself."

"I thought you would be proud of me," Kayla said defensively, eager to change the subject.

"We both know that isn't true," Miranda countered directly. "We talk every year about the importance of maximizing your employer contributions. It's found money, Kayla. This should be your number one priority."

Kayla felt ashamed. She had purchased her dream house in a posh neighborhood just a few years ago with a teaser loan. However, the low interest term was over and the higher monthly mortgage payments were sweeping in. Despite her raises, she was reeling from the home-owners dues, property taxes, water and electric bills, insurance costs, and higher mortgage payments. After her house expenses, Kayla had little money remaining to pay the rest of her bills.

"I can't contribute to my 401K right now. My mortgage payments just went higher, and I need the money."

"Do you have any credit card debt?" Miranda asked. Judging by Kayla's fashion choices, she already knew the answer.

Kayla sighed.

"How bad is it?" Miranda continued.

"Not terrible. About $8,000."

Miranda took a deep breath. "So, you're making minimum payments of about $320 a month on your credit card? Money that could be set aside for your 401K?"

"I don't know what else to do, Miranda. I'm trying the best I can." Kayla studied her nails again, wishing the appointment would end.

"You need to do more than try, Kayla. You need to make some big changes in your life."

"Like what?" Kayla said defensively, uncomfortable with the confrontation.

"You're a sharp girl. I think you already know the answer."

Kayla was exasperated. "What? Sell my house?"

"Yes. Sell your house and buy something you can afford. Then pay off your credit card debt and maximize your 401K contributions."

"But it's my dream home…"

"You're young, Kayla. Buy your dream home later. For now, you should find a little home that you can fix up and sell for a profit. Do that a few times and then buy a dream home."

"You really think so?" Kayla asked, as the wisdom began to sink in.

Miranda smiled, happy to see that Kayla was looking her in the eye again. "Yes, I do. And when we meet next year, you will have no more credit card debt, you will be piling money up in your 401K, and you will be living in a home that you can afford. Really afford."

Kayla nodded.

Miranda spun around and opened the door of her credenza, pulling something from the stack. She spun back and placed it on her desk in front of Kayla. "And I want you to read this book."

Kayla picked up the little paperback. "*First Million*?"

"Yes, Kayla. I think it will help you," Miranda answered simply, and went back to Kayla's taxes. As Kayla flipped through the pages, Miranda checked her figures and marked receipts with her red pencil. She continued to ask Kayla patient questions as her tax return gradually took shape. Miranda finished her return within a few hours and handed the necessary forms to Kayla for her signature, along with her invoice.

"Thank you, Miranda," Kayla said, tucking the book and tax forms into her Prada bag. She stood to leave.

"My pleasure," Miranda stood and shook Kayla's hand. "I hope you enjoy the book."

Kayla nodded and patted her Prada bag. "I'll read it. Promise."

"Good. When you are finished with it, come see me and we can review your plans. I'm here to help."

"Are you holding me accountable?" Kayla asked, a little embarrassed.

"Maybe. But no charge for our next meeting. We'll just talk over coffee."

Kayla smiled. "Sounds like a good deal."

"And my God will meet all your needs according to his glorious riches in Christ Jesus."

—Philippians 4:19

8

STARTING FROM SCRATCH

Bam! Bam! Bam!

Kayla jolted awake. She was still adjusting to the sounds of the city; street sweepers and early morning bread trucks, police sirens and drunken shouts after last call, ships steaming out of the harbor and trains clattering just a few blocks away. It was a jumbled street symphony, with every new sound echoing down the valley of concrete and glass buildings. This was her new home.

Kayla had made several improvements to her downtown loft apartment. She added a thicker front door, with several deadbolt locks, and triple pane windows with sound-proofing inserts. She added a soothing slate wall fountain, and played music while she cooked, and listened to the white noise of the ocean on her smart speaker while she slept. Despite these measures, the hum of the city was always there, always exciting, always pulsing with life. Kayla was still adjusting to the pace, to the squeeze of the surrounding buildings, and to the ever-present sounds.

Bam! Bam! Bam!

But this was a different sound. And it was at her front door.

She removed her ear plugs and slipped out from her bed covers, negotiating her way through the throw pillows scattered across the hardwood floor of her loft bedroom. She carefully descended the spiral, wrought iron staircase to the center of her second floor living room and kitchen.

Bam! Bam! Bam!

She flipped on the light switch and illuminated the high brick walls, exposed steel beams, and floor-to-ceiling glass. At only five stories tall, her building was one of the smaller ones in the city, but her loft apartment was spacious, stretching through the top three floors, giving her three distinct levels and pocket view of the water. Beneath her apartment was a groovy, new art gallery that inhabited the first and second floors and had stirred her recovering neighborhood to life with bold colors and bolder artists that engendered a shabby-chic camaraderie. Her building was built in the early forties and had a gritty, bold personality as a fellow member of the Greatest Generation, who invaded France, defeated Hitler, and had been drinking hard ever since. The Santori Building was built as the Battle of Britain reduced the buildings of London to rubble and was currently fighting for status as a historical landmark.

Kayla dropped through her second floor, following a polished hardwood staircase that creaked with every step, echoing deep into her storage closet underneath, where she had packed the white elephants from her over-sized, former home. She reached her bottom floor, where she had her generous food pantry, storage closet, laundry room, and a home theatre that was currently under construction. The home theatre was filled with stacks of vintage posters and a cluster of reclaimed leather viewing chairs, with a vicious tangle of wires that snared and snaked across the floor.

Kayla had been chipping away at her home theatre project every weekend, watching internet videos to learn how to connect the expensive video equipment. It was the last piece in her three-floor puzzle. Kayla knew her new home was unorthodox, but it was also extremely cool. She had transformed a derelict hovel into a hip and expressive home, with the home theatre and storage on the bottom floor, the kitchen, dining, and living spaces in the middle, and her master bedroom and bathroom on the top, fifth floor.

She also had an exterior, metal staircase that scaled the final few feet of the building to her roof. Her roof deck occupied a quarter of the roof space with a teak deck, planter boxes, a genuine crumbling wall from the early forties, and a wild collection of old antennas, vents, and mysterious HVAC equipment. The most hideous of these features had been hidden behind trellises, covered by planted pots, and encased under the layers of her deck. It was an inspired space, with a 180-degree view of the surrounding city, the neon lights of a hundred restaurants, and the harbor beyond.

Bam! Bam! Bam!

"Who is it?" Kayla shouted through her thick front door and peered through the peep hole into the dark hallway. She reminded herself that she would need to install some better lighting outside her front door, so she could see through her peephole for its intended purpose. Maybe one of those old Quonset hut lamps from the 1930s that she saw at the reclaimed furniture warehouse down the street?

"Who do you think?" said a muffled and frustrated voice on the other side of the door.

"If I knew, I wouldn't shout through the door. Would I!" Kayla shouted back.

"It's Matteo! Your little brother. The one you love so much that you moved away and didn't tell him!" Matteo shouted back.

Kayla unlocked the series of deadbolts and opened her door. It was Matteo alright. He was drunk, disheveled, and disoriented. He staggered into the foyer, past Kayla, and then not recognizing the entry, spun around.

Kayla rubbed her eyes, totally exasperated. "I told you where I lived. I gave you a key. I invited you to my house-warming party. And I asked for your help with the move."

"But you never gave me the directions," Matteo slurred with his trademark smirk.

"You're so hopeless. You lost my address. Lost the key. Bailed on my party. And left me to move all by myself. And *now* you're here at.... What time is it?"

"Oh, it's early, Sis. Really early," Matteo proclaimed proudly.

"...at a crazy hour and you want to crash on my couch and eat my food..."

"You won't even know I'm here," Matteo swayed. "And you don't have to feed me."

"Why don't you stay at your place with Jessica?"

"I think you mean Cassi..." Matteo corrected.

"You broke up with Jessica? What happened? She's the best thing that ever happened to you!"

"Long story," Matteo whispered sincerely.

"And Cassi? What happened to Cassi?"

"Another long story. But that one's not really my fault."

"And neither one of these break-ups explains why you can't sleep in your own bed."

"That's more of a sad story. Lost my job. Then I lost my place."

"But you were doing so good, Matteo. What happened?"

"My boss didn't respect my free time. And my landlord didn't respect my late rent," Matteo replied, as he tried to focus on Kayla's face.

"Why didn't you tell me any of this?"

"I just did. Or weren't you listening?" Matteo laughed, then spun around as if he heard another voice. He turned back to face her, weaving slightly. "You never listen, Kayla."

"You could have called or texted me, instead of arriving at my front door like a lost cat."

"It all happened pretty fast..." Matteo began, and then shrugged.

"I would love to hear all about your latest sad story, but I have a massive meeting in the morning. I am presenting our new operating system to one of our board members. I need to sleep."

"You won't even know I'm here..." Matteo repeated and pointed up the stairs. "Is this where I am sleeping?"

Kayla sighed, thoroughly frustrated with her drunk younger brother. Yet she knew the fastest way back to sleep was to get him onto the couch. "Yeah. Follow the stairs to your favorite couch. It's one floor up."

Matteo started up the stairs, swaying slightly and using the metal handrail to steady himself. When he was halfway up, he turned and looked down at her. "Hey, Sis. I hate your new place. What were you thinking? I liked your big house… your big house in the gated community. I like that one better. That place was sweet."

"Then you should have helped me pay the mortgage," Kayla shot back.

"This place smells funny." Matteo ignored her. "Oh! And there's a bum sleeping on the sidewalk in front of your gate."

"And now there's a bum sleeping on my couch," Kayla retorted.

"Oh? Then where will I sleep?" Matteo slurred.

"I meant you, Loser!"

"Oh, that's funny!" Matteo laughed. "Sorry, I'm not as smart as you. I didn't get a scholarship to Who Are U and kiss a bunch of asses to get a fancy job."

Kayla rolled her eyes. At least Matteo was upfront about his jealousy of his big sister's success. Most siblings hide their feelings for decades and then let them pour out at Thanksgiving before the turkey is served.

Matteo continued up the stairs, slurring his words as he went. "And then you became some kind of a high-tech rock star and blew off your family and your friends. Because you would rather climb the ladder to Suc…cess!"

That hurt. This was new material for Matteo and it cut her deeply. But she knew there was no point in debating her brother in his current condition, especially since she was desperate to get a good night's sleep, which was in serious jeopardy.

"Whatever, Matteo. I'll bring you some blankets and a pillow."

As Matteo clomped unsteadily up the remaining wooden stairs, Kayla pulled blankets from the shelves in her laundry room.

"Got anything to eat?" Matteo shouted from her kitchen.

Matteo was snoring evenly as Kayla got up, showered, and slipped quietly down the creaky wooden steps through her front door. She stepped out on the sidewalk, relieved no one was sleeping in her path, and crossed the quiet street that was just beginning to come to life with the rhythm of a new day. She headed for her car parked in an underground lot two blocks away, stopping at her favorite corner coffee bar along the way. She greeted the happily caffeinated counter staff and ordered her daily scone and latte.

With the hot travel cup in hand, and a crisply heated scone calling to her from inside the carefully folded, brown paper bag, Kayla followed the parking ramp down a level to her new mini-SUV. She opened the door, slid into the soothing leather interior, and closed the door again with a satisfying thump.

Kayla sighed, savoring her favorite moment of the day. She took a slow, strong sip of coffee as Vivaldi gently stirred her senses to life. Her cell phone was tucked deeply into her Prada bag, her carefully selected clothes were crisp with the promise of a new day, and her hair was pulled back and safely tamed, just the way she liked it. A day of chaos stretched before her, but that was still several minutes and several miles away. For now, the peaceful, early morning was still hers, until she arrived at her cubicle.

Kayla sat down at her computer twenty minutes later, checked her phone, and received a savage tempest of tasks and issues. She was pulled immediately into a blurring vortex of emails, problems, and meetings, including her presentation to a very inquisitive member of the board. Kayla loved every minute of it and managed to remain joyful and radiant, while tackling every salvo that hit her cubicle. It was that same infectious attitude that had propelled her up the company ladder, with new raises coming in fast like the levels of a familiar video game.

It was dark outside when her day finally came to an end. She headed home, through a gentle evening commute, and parked her car in her assigned spot. As she emerged from the parking structure and crossed the street, she could smell the pungent spices from the Thai restaurant down the block. She closed her eyes and took in the savory scent, realizing how hungry she was. She reached her building, unlocked the front door, and immediately heard an R&B mix tumbling down the stairs from her living room, accompanied by the welcoming smell of grilled garlic and simmering tomato sauce. She was immediately grateful for her brother's talents in the kitchen, which unfortunately came in a complicated package of excuses, apologies, and broken promises.

While Matteo was adrift and searching for his place in the world, he was also a wonderful cook. He spent hours in the kitchen with their mom, Estella, where she taught him to cook and season his life with generous helpings of love and family. He was so close to her that his foundation shattered completely in the earthquake of her surprise death during their high school years. Matteo's confidence crumbled when the God his mom taught him to trust let her die of cancer. He had been a good student, comfortable in almost every subject. But the loss of his mom had completely derailed him. He barely graduated from high school and struggled for direction in the years that followed, often becoming angry and self-destructive. He was a disoriented soul, still looking for his mom.

Kayla was about to climb the stairs when she stopped abruptly. Her home theatre. What had he done? "Matteo!"

She stepped into the theatre, not understanding what she was seeing. "Matteo!"

A pot clanked in the kitchen, and she heard him clomp down the wooden stairs. He entered her home theatre, wearing her apron with a glass of red wine in his hand. His hair was carefully combed, his clothes neat, and his iconic smirk in place. "Hey, Kayla."

"What have you done?" Kayla demanded, her arms sweeping the contents of her home theatre.

"Oh, that?" Matteo asked. "I thought you were angry with me again."

"This is amazing. You did all of this today?"

"Yeah, well. I felt bad about what I said last night…"

"You mean this morning?" Kayla corrected him.

"Yeah, well, this morning. I felt bad. And I saw that you were never going to put this together. So, I rolled up my sleeves and got to work."

The home theatre was immaculate. Her new, big screen was mounted professionally, with the myriad of wires carefully concealed. Her vintage movie posters were framed and evenly spaced along the little theatre walls, with Chaplin, Bogart, Bergman, Hepburn, and Wayne smiling back at her. Matteo had added a bank of dimmer switches, that adjusted the light at the front, sides and back of the room, making the theatre at once elegant and exciting.

Kayla was stunned. She circled the room, weaving through the row of leather chairs. "This would have taken me months, Matteo. This is exactly what I envisioned. You saved me from a year of lost weekends."

"Now you can just enjoy your movies, Sis. By the way, I saw that you had a couple of streaming services, so I added a spare router and hard drive downstairs, so you can stream without interruption. I quickly learned that these old brick walls play havoc with your signal, so I built it close and compact." Matteo opened a little cabin at the back of the theatre to display the heart of the entertainment center.

"Wait. Matteo, this isn't my equipment. Where did you get this stuff?"

"I could ask you the same question, Sis. The equipment you bought was all top of the line. Really nice stuff. But it wasn't what you needed. I traded it in for the right equipment and, with the savings, I was able to add the local router and hard drive, and I added these," Matteo pointed up at the ceiling speakers mounted in the four corners of the theatre."

"What?" Kayla was shocked. "You added surround sound, too?"

"Yeah, it was the right thing to do. Those big speakers you selected were great for a different type of room, but these will give you the sound you want," Matteo added. Then he reached into his pocket and handed a roll of bills to Kayla. "This is what was left over. I used some cash to buy dinner. I hope you don't mind."

Kayla unfurled the bills, counting $350. "I get my home theatre and cash back, too?"

"I have a lot of contacts for this kind of thing. They were happy to trade. You still had most of the boxes and manuals, so it wasn't a problem."

Kayla threw her arms around Matteo in a grateful hug. "Thanks, Matteo."

"Oh, dinner!" Matteo broke their embrace. "I almost forgot."

Kayla followed after Matteo as he darted up the stairs. She reached the living room and could smell the pasta dinner coming together. Kayla set the table and tossed the salad, while Matteo pulled the final details of the meal together. When they finally sat down at the table, Kayla toasted her clever brother and her new home theatre.

They kept to small talk for a few minutes, catching each other up on mutual friends from high school. Then Matteo cleared his throat and began, "So, what's this all about, Sis?"

"What do you mean?"

"I mean this new place. I thought you were happy in your monster house in the gated community. Now you're living like an artist in a downtown loft. What's up?"

Kayla spun her fork in circles, rolling a bite of pasta into a tight ball. She took a thoughtful bite while Matteo waited. She finished and took a long sip of red wine. "You really are a good cook, Matteo. You should work in a restaurant as a chef."

"And you should stop pushing me to get a real job and answer my question. Why the new address?"

"It's more than a new address. It's a new lifestyle." Kayla explained.

"You didn't lose your job, did you?"

"Of course not! It's nothing like that. I met with my accountant a few months ago. She gave me a long lecture about my money choices. She also gave me a book and made me read it. It's a pretty simple book, but it made me see that my life was a mess. My mortgage was too much for me and I was swimming in debt."

Matteo stopped eating and looked up at Kayla. "What? My perfect little sister? The high achiever? I don't believe it."

"Believe it," Kayla said, working on her next bite.

"And that's why you moved here?" Matteo was warming to the conversation, eager to learn that he was not the only one in the family who was struggling. "Because of some book?"

First Million

"It's an investment. The mortgage is half of what I was paying at my other place. I used my little profit on the sale of my big house to pay off my credit card debt and I bought this dive, instead. I am fixing it up with plans to sell it in a couple of years from now. Or I might keep it as a rental property. Then I'll do the same thing again and work up to owning a big house. But the next time I live in a fancy, gated community I will actually be able to afford it."

Matteo nodded as he ate his meal. He was quiet for a while and thoughtful in a way that Kayla had not seen in a long time. He finally said, "Welcome back, Kayla."

"What do you mean?" Kayla said softly, already knowing what he was going to say.

"Just that you were hard to recognize before."

Kayla stared at the refrigerator as tears welled in her eyes. She was silent for a long time, with Matteo looking on, waiting for her inevitable rebuke. When her words finally came, they were gentle. "I just wanted to feel special. Like I was someone important. More important than the people around me. But I know that I hurt you and I caused pain for others. My big house lifestyle made my friends and family feel small… and I enjoyed it."

Matteo nodded again, grateful to hear her honesty.

"I also put all of my money into myself, and I had nothing left over for anyone else. I want to change that now. I want to have money left over to be charitable. I want a humble life that welcomes other people in."

Tears came to Matteo's eyes, too. "Like I said Kayla, welcome back. I missed you."

They enjoyed dinner and Matteo caught Kayla up on his roller-coaster love life and recounted how he lost his latest job and the ones before that. Every boss was to blame. They were all too rigid. They had no plans for growth. They had no respect for others. They had poor communication skills. And Matteo was always the victim. Kayla heard enough, she lifted her hand and got Matteo's full attention.

"I know you miss her very much, Matteo. I know your heart is broken. And I know that every girl you date is an attempt to recover some portion of Mom. Some piece of what we lost."

Matteo sat quietly, listening to her words.

"But she would want you to move on. She spent hours in the kitchen teaching you up, inspiring you, instructing you to be your own person. We don't have Mom anymore, but we do have her lessons. We have her example of a life well lived. And all of her words of wisdom."

Kayla was quiet for a moment and let the words sink in. Matteo was crying gently, nodding.

"There is so much of Mom in you, Matteo. And you have so many talents and gifts. You just transformed my mess into an awesome home theatre. In one day! And you still found time to cook this amazing meal?"

"Well, you were gone for a long time, Kayla. You really need to improve your work-life balance," Matteo joked as he got his tears under control.

"No, I'm serious. You have gifts, Matteo. You really should turn them into your own business. Then you'll finally have the boss you have always wanted."

"Who's that?"

"You, Loser!" Kayla laughed.

Kayla went to bed early, as Matteo listened to music and let her words sink in. He made up the couch for a second night and sunk into the blanket and pillows, waiting for sleep. His thoughts were rattling around in his mind, competing for attention. He was processing Kayla's words, remembering his Mom's wisdom, and recounting all of his broken relationships and lost jobs. He knew he had to change. It was time to move forward, to grow up, and to take responsibility for himself. It was true that he missed Mom deeply, and he had to turn his pain into purpose.

Restless and unable to sleep, he flipped on the light switch and sat up in his couch bed. It was then that he saw the little paperback book on the side table. It was the book that Kayla had read, and it had obviously reached something deep within her. The transformation in his sister was unbelievable. The princess was human again and making big changes in her life.

"*First Million*," Matteo said aloud, as he picked up the paperback and opened the cover. "I don't think I'm exactly millionaire material. No job. No income. No assets. I need a book called *First Thousand*."

He read the first page, and then the second. And before he knew it, the digital microwave clock flipped to midnight and he was still reading. When he finished the book, he felt different. He felt empowered and driven. He finally fell asleep with something new rattling around in his mind. He had a plan.

"And God is able to make all grace abound to you, so that always having all sufficiency in everything; you may have an abundance for every good deed."

—2 Corinthians 9:8

9

HUNDRED THOUSANDAIRE

"I have no idea what I am doing," Matteo confessed, as he took a chair across from Miranda's desk. His dark eyes were sincere, almost pleading. He fidgeted with a spiral notebook, with a pen tucked into the cover. His black hair was carefully combed, and he had shaved his trademark stubble. He looked younger, like a college student beginning his new fall courses.

"I hear that a lot," Miranda replied with a gentle smile.

"Wait. Really?" Matteo stammered, surprised by her answer. He felt uncomfortable sitting in a business office. Matteo was more accustomed to the counters, bars, and tables of his hourly jobs. He felt like he was back in his high school principal's office, with old Mrs. Cantwell pleading with him to work harder in school and show up for class. Mrs. Cantwell's efforts had failed, and so had Matteo's, unable to pull out of his emotional tailspin after the loss of his mom.

Matteo felt out of place. He wore a simple t-shirt and jeans, not really knowing how to dress. The effort of setting the appointment and then arriving on time was all that he could handle. He immediately felt his anxiety level rise as he entered the marble and glass lobby of the office building. His heart raced frantically as he rode the wood paneled elevator to the 8th floor. And his mouth went dry as he waited for Miranda in the leather couch of her waiting room, with the tech giants and finance wizards staring at him from the cover photos of *Forbes* and *Fortune*.

He was nearly speechless now. He had left his confidence back in Kayla's kitchen, where he could trust his hands to the simple discipline of utensils and ingredients. He was far from the places where he felt comfortable, with the people like him, who also struggled with the mysteries of an orderly life and clung to the bottom rungs of a heartless ladder. He was way out of his comfort zone but determined to see it through. He was determined for Kayla. He was determined for his mom. And, finally, determined for himself.

"Matteo, everyone who starts their own business has doubts. It's a scary proposition. I struggled with it, too. I left a high paying job with a top accounting firm to go out on my own. I remember the feelings, and I still have many of the same doubts. It's hard to know how to get started, how to pay the bills, and where to get your customers. But with a good business plan and some hard work, you can see it through to success."

"I don't know anything about those things," Matteo confessed. "I wouldn't know a business plan if it hit me in the face. I have no clue where my customers would come from. Or how much to charge. Or any of those things."

Miranda nodded. She understood completely. "Let's start with what brought you here."

Matteo shifted uncomfortably in his chair and surveyed her office. He was overwhelmed by the polished desk, big leather chair, framed degrees from prestigious universities, golfing awards, and pictures with local and national celebrities.

Miranda had seen it before, and she did her best to make him feel at ease, "Can I offer you a water, Matteo?"

"Uh, yeah. That would be cool." He stood and wiped his palms on the front of his jeans.

As she stepped out of her office and headed down the hallway to her little pantry, James followed her. "It's Kayla really. She said you could help me. And, uh, she's going to pay you for this meeting."

"That's nice of her. Kayla's a terrific person. I really like working with her," Miranda said as she opened the little refrigerator.

"Yeah, well she said that about you. Anyway, she said you were really good at this stuff, you know, went to business school in college and all that. And that you could help me, you know, start a business."

"And why do you want to start your own business, Matteo?" Miranda asked, handing him a cold bottle of water.

"Thanks," Matteo followed her back to her office. "Because I keep getting fired. Mostly for telling off my bosses. So, Kayla figured maybe I am not wired to, you know, work for someone else. Maybe I should be my own boss."

Miranda smiled and nodded her encouragement. "I hear that reason a lot."

"Wait. Really?"

"Yes, people may say it in a different way. They might try to hide the same answer with an articulate explanation for how they are ill

First Million

suited to take orders from someone else, or that the corporate world is stifling their creative spirit. But it's really the same thing. Not everyone is cut out to work for someone else. It's one of the top answers that I hear."

Matteo sighed deeply. "Oh, well that's good. I guess, I feel like I'm the only person alive who can't hold down a decent job."

"And why do you think Kayla sent you to me?"

"She, uh, thinks I have some special gifts. You know, handyman and stuff like that. Plus, I'm a pretty good cook. Kayla says I should think about, you know, a catering business."

Miranda nodded. "I have seen many people turn their gifts into very profitable businesses. When you are good at something, the money will follow. But whatever business you choose, you need to be all in. It must be something you can do for 10 or 12 hours a day and never doubt that you are doing the right thing. What would that be? Cooking?"

Matteo considered that for a moment, processing her words carefully. "Well, no. I don't think so. Cooking is sort of personal for me. You know, it's what I do to relax. It reminds me of my mom. And I just like cooking for the people that I love. So, I'm not sure that I want to turn it into a business. I don't want it to lose it's special place for me."

"I understand. That part of you is not for sale."

"Yeah. I like how you said it better," Matteo smiled.

"You have a very good sense of yourself, Matteo," Miranda replied. "That's really going to help you."

"Really? Uh... good."

"What about the handyman work that you mentioned. How do you feel about that?"

"I think that's what I can do for those long days that you mentioned. I like getting into a project and working with my hands and solving all of the little problems that pop up. I like to get lost for the day, you know. I think that's what I'm really good at."

"That's great, Matteo. And the handyman business is a solid choice. You could make a lot of money at it. You can scale it for growth or keep it simple and small. Either way, I have a feeling you will make more money with a handyman busines than at an hourly job."

"Yeah, that's what Kayla was saying. But I have no clue how to start. I also wanted to talk about this," Matteo said, sliding the paperback book to her across the desk.

"*First Million*?" Miranda picked up the paperback and smiled. She had given it to a few of her clients, but no one had reported back yet. "Did you read it?"

"Yeah, just the other day. I didn't really mean to, you know, but before I knew it, I finished it."

"It's a pretty simple book to read."

"Yeah, that's what I liked about it."

"So, are you interested in following the 5 steps and saving your first million?"

Matteo laughed nervously. Her direct question seemed so ridiculous. "Not really. I mean, a million dollars is a lot of money. I don't think that's for me."

"Why not? I think anyone can save a million dollars," Miranda stated evenly.

"But not people like me, though. Right?"

"I think that book was written exactly for people like you, Matteo. I think you can follow all of the steps within that book and save your first million, and a whole lot more."

"Really? Thanks. I don't know. I just don't see myself as a millionaire. That doesn't seem real or possible to me. It's just too much money. If I ever got close, I think I would lose it in a bad investment or blow it all on something stupid."

"I understand what you mean. It's hard to picture that level of success."

"Yeah. I just can't see it in my own life. Kayla's going to make it, though. I always knew she would make it. But I thought I would have, you know, a different goal."

"And what's that?"

"I thought I could just try to be a hundred thousandaire," Matteo said with a nervous laugh.

"Very clever. I think that's a really good idea," Miranda said with an encouraging smile. "So, you are proposing to save a hundred thousand dollars?"

"Yeah. You see, I have never really had anything in my life. I own some clothes and I have a car. But that's it. So, I think I should aim a little lower. So, it feels real."

"I think that sounds fine."

"Really? And you can help me?"

"Help you save a hundred thousand dollars? Absolutely."

Matteo sighed. "OK, good. Thank you. And Kayla will pay you for your time. Then I want to pay her back."

"Can you count on Kayla for some working capital to get your business started?"

"Yeah, she said she would help me. Maybe she could buy me some basic tools, get my name out there with some advertising. And maybe I could get a work truck."

"That sounds like a good plan, Matteo. I will help you with your business plan. We will include a budget for your initial working capital. And then we will create a personal budget for you to save one hundred thousand dollars."

"That would be great. Thank you!" Matteo was relieved. He had been so nervous to share his thoughts and dreams. They had seemed so silly as they rattled around in his head, but Miranda had them now, and she was going to shape them into a plan.

"You should thank, Kayla."

"Oh, I have. She has this new loft downtown that she's been fixing up. You know, after you told her to stop wasting money."

"She's a smart girl. I was pretty sure she would listen to my advice. She's really made a lot of changes. I am glad to see her saving her money. Plus, I think she made a great investment in her new place."

"Yeah, well, I am going to stay with her for a while and do all the handyman things she needs, plus do some cooking for her. And in exchange, she's going to help me get my business going."

"That's a great deal for both of you."

"Yeah, I know. I feel like I'm getting the better part of it," Matteo admitted.

"I don't. Kayla is getting the best deal, in my opinion."

Matteo nodded, but couldn't agree. He felt ashamed that his sister was bailing him out of his failed life.

Miranda sensed his feelings. They were familiar to her, and to so many of her clients. "Matteo, I think I know how you are feeling. What Kayla is doing for you is something that many people do for the people they love. It's very hard to get started on a new path. You need the help of others who are close to you. Whether it is encouragement, faith in your abilities, or some financial help. None of us really do it on our own. We all need help from someone."

"Thanks," Matteo replied uncertainly. "So, you are able to help me?"

"Yes, Matteo. I am very happy to help you. We can meet once a week as you get your business started. Then we can cut it back to once a month. And then we can meet a couple of times a year when I do your taxes. By then, you will be making the big bucks."

"I would like that. Thank you, Miranda. I think...."

"Under one condition." Miranda cut him off.

Matteo looked worried. "What's that?"

"After you save your first hundred thousand, and I know that you will, I want you to continue to save. Keep going until you make that next hundred thousand. And continue saving. I want you to promise not to quit."

Matteo considered it for a moment. "Alright. I'll keep going after the first hundred thousand. But let me get there first."

Miranda and Matteo worked on his business plan for the rest of the morning, developing an initial budget for his working capital. They discussed how to find his first customers, how to price his services, and how to build a referral program to grow his business. After a short lunch, they began tackling his monthly personal budget.

"I don't really know where to start. I don't even have any income, yet. Tell you the truth, owning my own business seems impossible. I just don't want to let Kayla down again."

"That's ok. This budget will start in 6 months, when you move out of Kayla's place. That's your deal, right?"

"Yeah. I got to be out of there in six months."

"No problem. We will use the income from your business plan, from month 6, to project what your income will be. I also want you to work a part time job, to help cover your expenses until your business is profitable. Sound ok?"

"Sure," Matteo agreed. "I guess I will apologize to my old boss."

"Actually, I have something else in mind. I think it really helps your business to work in a similar field. That way you are gaining your skills while you are growing your own business."

"Is that sort of what you did?"

"It is exactly what I did. While I worked at the big accounting firm, I started doing taxes for friends and family on nights and weekends. It really helped that I was doing the same type of work because I could use my knowledge for my new business. Once I had a good base of customers, I was able to leave my day job and start my own accounting firm. It gave me a much better chance at success."

"Sounds like a ton of work."

"It was. And it still is. But you will see, Matteo. When the work is for you, it's no problem putting the time in. There is something amazing about working for yourself."

"Alright," Matteo agreed awkwardly. "So, where would I work? I mean, what job are you suggesting?"

"One of my clients owns a few apartment buildings. He would like to meet with you about becoming his maintenance and repair guy." Miranda handed his business card to Matteo. "He is expecting your call, Matteo. I think you will like him."

"Wait. Really? You got me a job, Miranda?"

"No, I got you an interview. The job part is up to you."

"Alright. I get it. I'll call him after our meeting. Thank you," Matteo was stunned at her kindness.

"I am happy to help." Miranda continued, "So, you will have a part time job that will help you pay your bills, while you are growing your business. And we will keep your personal expenses really low, so you can begin saving."

"Whatever you say, Miranda."

They worked for the next hour on a humble budget, based on income from a part-time job and revenue coming in from his growing business. Miranda reminded Matteo that the focus was on freeing up money to begin saving. The resulting budget looked like this.

Matteo's Budget - Annual Household Income of $24,000.00

Monthly Income		
Salary Income (after taxes, social security, etc.):	$ 1,285.00	
Other Income: Business	$ 700.00	
Total Monthly Income:		**$ 1,985.00**
Monthly Fixed Expenses:		
Tithe & Charity	$ 200.00	
Rent	$ 400.00	
Groceries	$ 250.00	
Gas for Car	$ 200.00	
Car Payment	$ 124.00	
Minimum Credit Card Payments	$ 75.00	
Water Utility	$ 25.00	
Cable	$ 00.00	
Cell Phone	$ 75.00	
Electricity & Gas	$ 25.00	
Car Insurance	$ 55.00	
Health Insurance	$ 200.00	
Renters Insurance	$ 20.00	
Total Fixed Monthly Expenses:		**$ 1,649.00**
Remaining Balance:		**$ 336.00**
Additional Expenses - Cash:		
Savings	$ 200.00	
Meals & Entertainment	$ 50.00	
Miscellaneous	$ 25.00	
Christmas & Gift Fund	$ 25.00	
Personal / Clothes Fund	$ 30.00	
Total Additional Expenses:		**$ 330.00**
Remaining Balance:		**$ 6.00**

Matteo looked over the budget that Miranda helped him to create. He had never seen his income and expenses detailed before. He had always just spent the money he made and usually ran out well before the end of the month. He wasn't credit worthy, so his single credit card had a limit that kept his spending in check. As a result, his credit card debt was under $2,000, so his minimum monthly payment was only $75.00.

"Looks good, I guess," Matteo said after surveying the numbers. "What's this tithe at the top?"

"It's really important to give, Matteo. You will see. When you are generous with your money, amazing things happen. I believe God blesses us when we tithe, giving 10% to his church and other charities."

"I've never done that before," Matteo said defensively. "I don't feel like I can afford it."

"It's a step of faith, for sure. But it will pay major dividends. You will see. You will be really happy when you are giving regularly. And you are opening yourself up to God's blessings. You can't out give God. Be a faithful giver and He will always take care of you."

"I'll trust you on this, Miranda," Matteo agreed. "But it seems crazy to me."

"Don't trust me, Matteo. Trust God."

"I'll try," Matteo agreed. "But how do I rent a place to live for only $400?"

"That's your budget for a spare room in someone's home. It's a humble start, but this is what you need to do at first."

"Yeah, I'm ok with that. I just need a place to crash. Nothing fancy."

"As you increase your income, you can improve your living situation. But the most important line item on this budget is saving $200. You need to set that money aside every month. The first thing you should do is write yourself a check or take the cash to the bank. Better yet, invest it automatically. Make it so you can't touch it."

"But it's only $200. How can it make much of a difference?"

"Check this out, Matteo," Miranda replied and began building a table that showed Matteo how the money would grow overtime with compound interest.

40 Years of Savings – With Compound Interest:

Years:	Monthly Savings:	Annual Savings:	Interest Rate:	Savings:
5	$200	$2,400	10%	$15,434
10	$200	$2,400	10%	$40,291
15	$200	$2,400	10%	$80,324
20	$200	$2,400	10%	$144,797
25	$200	$2,400	10%	$248,632
30	$200	$2,400	10%	$415,858
35	$200	$2,400	10%	$685,178
40	$200	$2,400	10%	$1,118,920

"Wait. Really?" Matteo was stunned as he looked at the numbers. "You're saying I can save this much money by socking away $200?"

"It's the miracle of compound interest," Miranda explained.

"So, I would be a hundred thousandaire in 20 years?"

"Yes, if you just save $200 a month. And you will be a millionaire in 40 years," Miranda pointed to the final column.

"There you go again. You're trying to make me into a millionaire." Matteo shook his head in exasperation, with a faint smirk.

"I think anyone can be a millionaire, if you start early enough and save every month."

"That's pretty amazing," Matteo admitted, as he looked at the numbers. "I don't get why it starts off so slow. In the first 5 years I only save like $15,000. Doesn't seem like much."

"Yes, I think a lot of people see their savings growing slowly in the early years and they quit or spend the money on something they think they need. So, they miss out on the benefits of saving over the long term."

"Yeah, but just 15 more years and that $15,000 becomes over $100,000. Why would I save so much more money in the last 15 years than I did in the first 5 years?"

"It's a good question, Matteo," Miranda agreed. "It's because you have more accumulated savings to generate the new income. You are still putting $200 into savings each month, but the 10% interest on your savings of $15,000, $60,000 and then $80,000 is putting in even more. Remember that 10% income from $80,000 is $8,000 each year. So, your money grows faster. That's the powerful part of compound interest."

"Really powerful," Matteo said, looking over the numbers again. Something clicked in him in that moment. He began to see the money listed in the table as his own, as if he had already saved it. He knew that, if he stuck with Miranda's plan, he could do it. But he still had doubts.

"But now I have to invest the money somewhere, right?"

"Yes, that's the next step," Miranda agreed. "There are many solid options for you. Stocks, bonds, annuities, real estate…"

"But I have no idea where to put it. I don't know anything about stocks or bonds or anything like that."

"You don't need to," Miranda explained. "There are hundreds of great companies that will do that for you."

"You mean stockbrokers? I don't trust those guys. Don't they charge really high fees?"

"Yes, but I think the fees can be worth it. Financial planners and stockbrokers can really help you with your long-term financial goals."

"But I have to pay them?" Matteo asked.

"Yes, you would. But several of my clients do their investing on their own. I am not sure that I would recommend that for you. But it is an option."

"So, I can skip those fees, if I do it myself?"

"Yes, there is definitely a way to handle your investments on your own, without any fees."

"How do I do that?" Miranda had Matteo's attention.

"To get you started, I can recommend a few companies that allow you to purchase stocks in ETFs, or exchange traded funds, without any fees. You just select the ETF that matches up with your goals and place your money there. Then diversify by purchasing multiple ETFs over time, so you don't have all of your money in one place."

"Wait. What? You just lost me there. I have no idea what you are talking about. ET whats?" Matteo was frustrated, feeling like the big money went to the people on the inside of the game, while the little people on the outside got crushed.

"And I don't know anything about connecting the wires on a home theatre system," Miranda replied, "But you do. We both have knowledge that the other one doesn't have. But you are here to gain some of my knowledge, so let me show you how easy this is."

Miranda showed Matteo several investment sites that offered Exchange Traded Funds (ETFs) for zero costs or commissions. "See, these exchange traded funds are groups of stocks or bonds that are designed to grow, protect your money, or pay you a dividend."

Matteo stopped her, "That's what I mean. Dividend?"

"Oh, dividend is just a fancy word for income from your investments."

"Go it. Thanks."

Miranda continued. "So, you just select the ETF or stock fund that best fits your needs. And they have a team of experts who actually buy the stocks that make up the funds. If a stock is struggling or its future doesn't look very good, the experts will sell it and buy something that looks to perform better. You don't have to do anything."

"But there are so many of them," Matteo said, looking down the list on Miranda's computer screen.

"And there are tons of equipment choices if I want to create a home theatre, right? Once you do it a few times, you get comfortable with it. Take a look at this one. This ETF is made from a bunch of growth stocks from the DOW Industrial Average, and this one is from the Stocks in the S&P 500."

"What's the difference?" Matteo was frustrated again.

"The DOW has 30 big stocks, while the S&P has 500 stocks."

"Why would I buy 30 stocks when I could have 500?" Matteo asked.

"Good point, Matteo! And that might be the best reason for you to select their S&P 500 Growth ETF. They will then select the best companies from the S&P 500 stocks and drop the ones that they do not think will grow. But the 500 stocks may not grow as fast as the 30, in most cases. Because more stocks are involved."

"How much will they grow. I need to make 10%, right?"

"Yes, and this chart here shows you what the fund has done over the last several years. That percentage there shows you the rate of growth each year."

"But that says over 20%," Matteo wondered.

"Yes, that's because the fund is professionally managed, and these people really know what they are doing. Instead of growing your money by 10% a year, it looks like within this S&P 500 fund, they can grow it at over 20%. But look here, some of the years they actually show losses. Losses come with gains, but overtime, this fund is returning over 20% per year without any fees."

"That's a lot more that 10%" Matteo was impressed.

"But you can't bank on 20%. That is pretty rare. So, I plan for 10% in these funds when I do my projections, but then if the returns are higher, you will save even more."

"I get it. You're being careful just in case there are some bad years in there."

"Exactly. I want to make sure that the money you expect is there for you in 20 or 30 years. If it turns out to be more money, I figure you won't complain."

"But you're saying that I might be able to save more than $100,000 in 20 years and more than a million in 40 years?"

"I think you should. But let's keep to the 10%, just in case."

"And these companies won't charge me anything?"

"No. Just keep buying their ETFs every month with the $200 you are saving. And then roll in the dividends, the income that the funds make, back into more purchases. It will start off slow, but after about 10 years, your money will really grow."

"That book you gave Kayla explained all this, but it really helps to see it for myself, you know, with my own money."

"Good. That's the idea. Once you do a plan for yourself, the money becomes real. And you can see what it will mean to your future."

Matteo sat back in his chair and looked around Miranda's office. He was not used to her world of college degrees and ETFs. But once he stepped off the elevator to her office some of the mysteries of life were explained to him. He imagined stepping off the elevator on the other floors of the building and solving other mysteries.

Then a negative thought entered his head, the old doubts that seemed to wait in ambush.

"What if I can't make the $24,000 a year?"

"It's a good question. If you fall short, you will need a plan. You must save the $200 per month. What would you do?"

"I guess if I fall short, I could move in again with Kayla, or a friend, until I can get my income back to where it needs to be."

"I think that's a good plan. Is it worth sleeping on a couch for $100,000?"

"Totally. I'm not proud."

"But so many people are. And they miss out on so much because of that pride."

"I can see that. But I'll do whatever. You know, to get there."

"That's the spirit, Matteo. But I think your business will earn a lot more than $700 per month. And I think your part time job will earn more than your budget, too. Your income will grow and then you can move to a nice apartment and spend more money on insurance and clothes and entertainment. But as you do all of these things, you must continue to save the $200 per month. And, as you continue to succeed, see if you can increase it so you are saving $400 per month, then $500."

"And continue to grow my savings while my life gets better," Matteo continued.

"Exactly," Miranda smiled.

"You really are determined to make me a millionaire," Matteo laughed, but he appreciated her confidence in him.

"I think you are already on your way."

"**Every good and perfect gift
is from above, coming down
from the Father of the heavenly lights...**"

—James 1:17

10

FIRST MILLION

Several years later, Matteo strolled down the sidewalk with his travel mug in hand, enjoying a rare day off. The cul-de-sac was crowded with families and cars double-parked along both sides of the street. Music was playing from a giant speaker set-up in the back of a vintage pick-up truck, with folding tables and blankets filling every driveway.

Milton Lusbee, the owner of the mid-century modern on the corner, was cooking free sausages from the edge of his driveway, while Jenny Grevance served up free pastries, coffee, and orange juice from the porch of her Cape Code Classic across the street. Both were accepting donations for the food, as the customers felt inspired to give.

It felt like the neighborhood was hosting a carnival, but it was a community garage sale. Each of the neighbors in the cul-de-sac had agreed to participate to raise money for cancer research. They were honoring the memory of a dear neighbor who had just passed away after a long battle with lymphoma. The event had been well-advertised, with an impressive article appearing in the community newspaper. Serious bargain hunters started arriving an hour early, while the homeowners were still setting up their garage-based thrift shops.

Matteo had been up for hours and needed a break after working so hard to get everything ready. He toured his neighborhood, while his wife and sons covered the shoebox cash register in front of their own garage. He greeted neighbors, surveyed the crowd of customers, and gauged the prices for the different items; from old couches to used water skis, from a set of steel drums to a vintage Snoopy Snow Cone Maker, and thousands of valuable and worthless odds and ends from decades of attic storage.

Matteo was following the sidewalk through the cul-de-sac, making his way through the gathering of value shoppers and fellow neighbors, when a collection of paperback books caught his eye. The little bookshop was set up at the end of Tag Harrison's flag lot, with little paperbacks and oversized coffee table booked lined up in neat rows on bookshelves pulled from several homes. The collection stretched from the Harrison's driveway across the front lawn of the Sexton's Spanish-style stucco. Several people were browsing through the titles and Matteo joined them, curious about the prices. He was surprised to see that most of the books were offered for under a dollar.

He saw a familiar title and paused to pick it up.

"*First Million*?" John Bosch said from over his shoulder. John lived in a ranch-style three doors down from Matteo. He was a friendly attorney who specialized in insurance law. His kids had gone off to college, so John and his wife, Samantha, were traveling the world and bringing back souvenirs and exciting stories. "You seem to be well on your way already, Matteo."

"Hey, John," Matteo looked up from the little book. "How are sales at your house?"

"Great. I got rid of my old rowing machine. What a relief! The guilt of walking past that dusty thing was driving me crazy."

"What did you sell it for?"

"An even hundred," John declared victoriously. "It was in pretty good shape. Unlike me."

"You look good to me, John," Matteo encouraged him.

"Bless you, Matteo," John put a hand on his shoulder. "How about your house?"

"We're mostly selling the kid's old toys. I'm looking forward to having the extra space. And the kids are having a blast selling their old things for charity."

"It amazes me how much we spend on junk, just to sell it a few years later at a garage sale," John said thoughtfully. "Makes you think about how much money we waste on unimportant stuff."

"That's what this book is all about," Matteo said, holding up *First Million*.

"Do you recommend it?" Charlie Brixton joined Matteo and John from a folding table filled with Tupperware and used kitchen appliances on the carefully manicured lawn of Mel Bailey's Country French. He was holding a bread-maker with a $10 price tag on it.

"Morning, Charlie!" John said warmly.

"Hey, Charlie!" Matteo shook his hand and welcomed Charlie into their conversation. Charlie had moved to the neighborhood about a year ago. He was the youngest resident in the cul-de-sac. His wife, Christine, was pregnant with their first. He was an engineer and had moved from the Bay Area to be part of a start-up. Charlie lived next door to Matteo, and they had a few conversations about what it took to start a business.

Charlie was grateful to see some familiar faces in the crowd. "I had to get away from our garage for a while. It's been crazy. We sold almost everything that we had."

"You got rid of most of your old furniture, right?"

"Yeah, Christine was eager to clean house, ever since we moved here. She has her eye on some expensive new furniture. I think she's trying to keep up with Matteo Rios and his family," Charlie said in a conspiratorial whisper.

"Don't fall into that trap," Matteo warned. "We're neighbors. We don't need to compete with each other."

"Easy for you to say," Charlie replied. "By the looks of your home, you've already made it."

"That's because I don't waste my money," Matteo replied. "It's a throwback from my days of poverty. I was sleeping on other people's couches when I started my business. I've been careful with money ever since. Because I had to be. I learned it from this book right here. And a few good friends."

"Really?" Charlie was suddenly interested. "*First Million*?"

"Actually, I give a copy of this book to every new employee that I hire. I make them read it and then spend a few hours with them talking about the importance of saving."

"You have that handyman business, right?" Charlie asked. "With the commercials showing the guys in the clean uniforms."

"Yeah, that's us," Matteo admitted.

"So, all of the people we see in your ads have read this book?" Charlie said, taking the paperback from Matteo's hand.

"Yeah. It's part of our training program when we bring people on board."

"And it works? The training, I mean," Charlie flipped the book over and studied the back.

"For some," Matteo explained. "It's exciting to see some of my employees embrace the training and improve their lives. But others just aren't ready to make those changes."

"Their loss," John added. "Sounds like they are missing out on some life-changing wisdom."

"Hey, this used copy is only 15 cents," Charlie marveled. "What a bargain."

"Let me borrow your pen," Matteo indicated the ever-present pen in John's shirt pocket. He handed it over with a shrug.

"May I?" Matteo asked Charlie for the book. Charlie handed it over, wondering what Matteo was up to. With a careful pen, Matteo altered the price tag from 15 cents to $150. "That's more like it."

"$150?" Charlie asked. "I was going to buy it for 15 cents."

"You get what you pay for," John laughed.

"He's right. Buy it for $150 and you will naturally get more out of it," Matteo explained. "For only 15 cents, you might not take the time to read it."

Charlie contemplated the higher price tag and was skeptical.

"Look, Charlie," John stepped in. "You are just getting started. You're building your life. I've known Matteo for a long time. I have never met anyone with a better work ethic in my life. You should have seen the distressed home he bought out of foreclosure about 8 years ago…"

"It's been twelve years," Matteo corrected.

"Right, the last housing crisis. His place was a wreck. Totally falling apart. Matteo moved in and rescued it. He remodeled it patiently over time, as he had the extra money to do it. He built his business with the same careful, frugal approach. You won't find a wiser man when it comes to money matters. If Matteo says this book is worth $150, I'm not going to question him. In fact, I think I'll buy it. My son needs to…."

"Sorry, John," Charlie interrupted. "Let me buy it. When I'm done, I'll give it back to you so your son can read it."

"You're going to pay $150?" John asked.

"Hey, it's for charity," Charlie replied. "Plus, I can't pass up a bargain like this."

"Command those who are rich in this present world not to be arrogant nor to put their hope in wealth, which is so uncertain, but to put their hope in God, who richly provides us with everything for our enjoyment."

—1 Timothy 6:17

11

YOUR TURN

You have met Betsy Grant, a single mom who transformed her debts into a life of success with a simple budget.

You were introduced to her son, James Grant, who used the same wisdom to pay his way through college, start his own business, and buy a home. All without taking on any debt.

You got to know Caden McBride and his family, as they simplified their extravagant lifestyle to pursue their dreams.

You witnessed the legacy of Ernesto Sanchez, a multi-millionaire entrepreneur, who used the important principle of hard work to escape prison and build an enduring organization.

Miranda Flores shared the same principles with each of her clients and encouraged them on their path to financial independence. Kayla Rios changed her life's priorities so she could free up resources to help others, while becoming true to herself. And Matteo Rios, who was heading for a life of disappointment, lifted himself off the couch and changed the course of his life with a simple plan of action.

You have the tools you need to save your First Million. You know everything you need to know to become financially independent. And the characters of this book encourage you to start today. Their lives may be works of fiction, but they are based on real-life people who are out there right now, making it happen for themselves.

It's your turn now. And you are just 5 steps away.

"A good person leaves an inheritance to their children."

—Proverbs 13:22

THE 5 STEPS TO
FINANCIAL INDEPENDENCE

Step 1: Budget First

- Include all of your expenses as you create your budget.

- Reduce expenses until you are saving at least 10% to 20%.

- If you can't save 10% to 20% with your current income and expenses, it's time to make some larger adjustments. If you have car payments, sell your current car and buy a used car with low miles. Sell your home and find something more affordable with solid potential for appreciation. Or rent a less expensive, new place. Join the revolution of cord-cutters and eliminate your cable bill. Drop your gym membership and find no cost ways to exercise. Cook at home. Make your own coffee.

- To increase your income, take advantage of the gig economy. Drive others on nights and weekends, deliver meals, take on a fun part-time job, or start a side business. Save this extra money.

- Tithe. If you honor God, He will bless you. You can't out give God. If you tithe or give to a charity faithfully, you will be amazed at how the money you give comes right back to you, often multiplied many times over.

Step 2: Debt Free

- Create a list of your debts. Order them with the ones with the highest rate of interest at the top.

- Include your credit card, car loan, mortgage, student debt, and money you owe to friends.

- Pay off the debts with the highest interest rates first. These are probably your credit cards.

- Once you pay off your first debt, use that monthly minimum payment you were making to pay off the next one. Each time you eliminate a debt, use that former payment to tackle the rest of your debts. This cascading effect of increased monthly money will allow you to pay off your debts very quickly.

- Use the 10% to 20% of monthly savings from **Step 1: Budget First** to pay off your debts first, until they are all gone. Then begin saving.

Step 3: Live Simply

- Live beneath your means. Make sure you have plenty of money left over each month for saving.

- Stop trying to compete with or impress others.

- Reject luxury and status items and buy quality necessities.

- Take advantage of the free features of your community: parks, beaches, libraries, hiking trails, and special events.

- Focus on living very comfortably on 80% to 90% of your current after-tax income.

- Enjoy the amazing benefits or a life where you no longer worry about money.

Step 4: Save and Reinvest

- Save 10% to 20% of your income each month.

- Begin building a stock, bond, or real estate portfolio.

- Use the services of a financial planner or investment counselor to help achieve your savings and investment goals.

- Do not spend the growth, equity, or dividend income from your investment accounts. Roll the dividends back into your investments and continue to diversify your portfolio. Over time, the compound interest will allow you to save your first million.

The Miracle of Compounded Interest

Compounded Interest - Example 1: Saving $200 per month for 40 years at a 10% rate of growth will allow you to save over $1,000,000.

Compounded Interest - Example 2: Saving $500 per month for 30 years at a 10% rate of growth will allow you to save $1,000,000.

Compounded Interest - Example 3: Saving $1,000 per month for 30 years at a 10% rate of growth will allow you to save $2,100,000.

Compounded Interest - Example 4: Saving $2,000 per month for 30 years at a 10% rate of growth will allow you to save $4,3000,000.

Step 5: Work Hard

Hard work creates unlimited opportunities for greater wealth and purpose. Promotions, raises, new jobs, more customers, second jobs, and side businesses give you a big head start on saving your first million. Hard work will also provide more money-making opportunities and allow you to create an income portfolio, so you no longer rely on a single income source to build your first million. And, finally, hard work builds a feeling of satisfaction, pride, and confidence deep within your soul.

BOOK TWO

WIPEOUT!

5 DARING SCHEMES TO OVERCOME COLLEGE DEBT

By Oliver Powers

For My Sons

"...to them he gave the name sons of thunder."

—Mark 3:17

1

"Was I on drugs? Owe UT $93K!"

Kelsey was shocked to receive such an honest text. She wished she had the courage to go public, too. Her parents never talked about money, so she never did. She was ashamed of her student loan debt and determined to hide the truth. Yet, here was Max, one of her old high school buddies, laying it all on the line.

A moment later he added, **"Job pays $48K. Rent eats half. Taxes insane. Kill me now!"**

Kelsey found herself in similar straights. She depleted her 529 in the second semester of her sophomore year and took out loans for the rest of her undergraduate degree and MBA. Her parents had offered to help, but she waived them off. They needed to save for their retirement, and she knew the stronger they were financially, the better off she would be in the future.

Kelsey, like so many of her college friends, had high expectations after graduation. The reality was devastating. No one seemed impressed by her degrees, and few job offers waited for her after graduation. She was facing the abyss.

After she completed her MBA, Kelsey retreated to her hometown to be close to family and friends. If she was going to be broke, she would do it in a place where people loved her.

She found a cheap apartment, not far from her parent's home, and paid the rent with part-time jobs and tax prep work, while she searched for her first career job. It took her nearly a year, and her salary left a lot to be desired, but she was now the assistant manager of accounts payable at a regional trucking company. It was a humble start.

She was facing 20 years of debt, and a monthly loan payment of over $600. By the time she paid it off, the final balance would be almost double what she had borrowed for her education. Kelsey felt like her university had somehow taken advantage of her. She had believed their claims about her amazing career opportunities and thought the addition of an MBA gave her the extra edge she needed to land her dream job. She started to believe that MBAs were a dime a dozen, and work experience was what every employer really wanted.

Kelsey now had a job, and she worked hard to convince herself that she was climbing the ladder of success. But late at night, she would lay in bed as the darkness pulled her into despair. The truth was undeniable. She had worked hard in college and grad school for 5 years and invested a fortune into her education. Now she was under-employed, at a company she hated, and carrying a lifetime of debt. She felt completely trapped.

Her despair resurfaced as the texts from Max hit her phone, but it also felt good to know she wasn't alone. Plenty of her friends and classmates had been led down the same tree-lined walkways, seduced by the lovely brick buildings, and hooked by the allure of a framed diploma.

"Same dealer? Georgetown soaked me for 200 large. Still owe $128K. #Suicide Squad."

Kelsey laughed as Clayton chimed in with a text reply. He was one of those rare kids who never studied and excelled in everything he did. His parents had both played college basketball and Clayton was a top varsity athlete in every sport he tried, but his real gift was academics. One of the few black students at Kelsey's high school,

Clayton was thoroughly brilliant and managed to pull straight As through all four years, regardless of the number of advance placement classes he added to his schedule. Clayton was recruited by several top schools, and selected Georgetown and their generous scholarship offer. However, his scholarship was pulled in his second year at Georgetown when he began to skip classes, changed majors, and let his grades fall below the required B average threshold. So, with his easy, always-on-vacation smile, Clayton stayed at Georgetown, went deeper into debt, and eventually graduated in five years with a double major.

Kelsey put her phone down, took a cold sip of coffee, and went back to her computer screen. Thoughts of her student loans frog-marched her into another accounting project. Her phone chimed again, and she couldn't resist.

"**Vast conspiracy! Gotta fight back.**" Max replied.

"**No way, Man. Crush us like bugs.**" Clayton fired back.

"**Can't pay enough. Can't earn enough. Already crushed.**" Max retorted defiantly.

"**Does crushing beer cans count?**" Clayton asked, and Kelsey could imagine his smile.

"**Does at UT!**" Max immediately shot back.

"**What were we thinking? Academic appetites larger than our savings.**" This text came from a new number.

Kelsey gasped when Nicole Chen jumped in. She hadn't seen Nicole since the summer after her junior year. She was always the grounded one. The girl with a plan. She oozed confidence. Not Nicole, too?

Nicole followed up with a second text. **"Drinks Thursday Night. McGinty's. Bring your evil schemes for getting out of debt. We shall overcome!"**

"Good!" Clayton replied.

"I'm in! 6ish?" Max texted back.

"I'll be there." Joe Frisco had joined the rebellion. Kelsey's heart skipped a beat. He was in this text group, too? Now, she was definitely in. But she played it cool.

"K." She typed simply, then tucked her phone into her top desk drawer and got back to her spreadsheet.

Bring your evil scheme? Kelsey smiled. She had one. It was a product crafted by several months of musing. It was a plan devised over hundreds of early morning yoga sessions. It was a fantasy born of necessity. Was it time to take action and implement it?

The walls of McGinty's were covered with license plates, autographed dollar bills, local celebrity photos, and neon beer signs. A vintage juke box played country, while the bar tenders pulled their taps to the beat. The wait staff raced by in patriotic t-shirts, serving up drinks and wise cracks. The customers shouted over the din, munching happily on peanuts from metal buckets, and tossing the shells on the floor.

Kelsey found Max and Clayton in a corner horseshoe booth, under a mounted jack-a-lope. The antlered rabbit was wearing a quizzical expression and a light blue tie. Her old high school friends slid out of their booth and wrapped Kelsey in big, warm hugs.

"Hey, Princess!" Max shouted over the music. He had come straight from work, with rolled up sleeves and loosened tie. He had his same eager, boyish face, dark hair cut short, and stocky build. Kelsey thought he looked like a kid playing dress up. She noticed a backpack in the booth with him. She was tempted to ask if he had to hit the library for some extra studying after dinner.

Clayton just smiled. His looked very fit and was taller than she remembered. Clayton looked like he had stepped out of an Abercrombie catalog, with a casual plaid button-down, over a "this old thing" t-shirt, and jeans torn at the knees.

"It's so great to see you guys," Kelsey shouted back.

"Totally. We gotta do this more often," Max agreed, following Clayton back into the booth. Kelsey slid in on the other side.

"You look amazing," Max continued enthusiastically. And she did. Kelsey had left work early to shower and dress for the evening. She wore black, polished cowboy boots and a red dress under a denim jacket, her blonde hair loose to her shoulders.

"Thanks, Max. You look pretty dashing yourself!"

Max shrugged and took a sip of his beer. "You still working at the same place? Trucking and such?"

"Still there," Kelsey admitted, clearly disappointed. "Not my dream job, but it could be a lot worse."

"Yeah," Max agreed, leaning forward over his beer. "You could be washing cars at Rider Rental Car and pretending to be in a prestigious management training program."

"Hey, I hear that's a pretty solid program," Kelsey replied, also leaning forward to hear a little better.

"Oh, it's fine," Max shrugged again. "Glad to have a job. Just not what I thought I would be doing after 4 years of grinding in the UT business school. Funny. All through business school we did these case studies about what to do when you are running a multi-billion-dollar conglomerate. And not one of them mentioned washing cars!"

"Oh, yes! And I know how to *audit* those same multi-billion-dollar companies. But now I'm doing payables for a trucking company," Kelsey marveled.

"It's just the first step..." Clayton began, with his reassuring smile.

"Can I bring you something?" Their waiter interrupted, smiling sweetly at Kelsey. He was wearing a black cowboy hat with a silver band, and a t-shirt with "Proud to Be" emblazoned boldly across an American flag.

"Sure. Red wine?" Kelsey asked.

"Merlot ok?" He asked, as he scribbled on his order pad.

"Sure. Surprise me."

"You got it." He scanned the table with open hands. "You fellas want a refill?"

"Another," Max replied holding up his mug. Clayton nodded.

"Back in a minute." The waiter crunched his way over the peanut shells and disappeared into the crowd.

"Sorry, Clayton. You were..."

"Just a first step," he shouted again over the music.

"I hope you're right about that," Kelsey shouted back.

"You are so smart, Kelsey. You got this. Just put in your time and the doors will swing wide open for you," Clayton said with his easy smile.

"Thank you. You're too kind, Clayton. And where are you working now?"

"Had to leave the brokerage. They just had me cold calling for new clients." He took a long sip of his draft beer. "Really? Georgetown degree and I dial for dollars. Unbelievable!"

"So, what are you doing now?" Kelsey asked, trying not to shout, while keeping her voice over the music.

"Couple things. I am consulting for a party rental company, helping them expand multi-state and leveraging their existing assets to expand their product line. I am also building modeling software for tracking crypto-currency value gaps. China is moving very quickly into crypto and I think there will be a Wild West component in the exchange worth exploiting."

Max and Kelsey exchanged glances, amazed at his casual brilliance. Same old Clayton.

"Wait? Weren't you a philosophy major?" Max asked.

"Double-major. Philosophy and political science," Clayton sighed. "And I'm going to law school in the fall. I didn't really have the grades, but I guess I crushed the LSAT."

"Really! Back to Georgetown?"

"Yeah, I figured I'd consolidate my debt," Clayton laughed.

Max whistled, but the country song drowned it out. "Dude, you will owe them a packet by the time you finish."

A waitress with red hair and faded jeans arrived with a tray full of drinks and announced each one as she placed them on the table. Her "I Love Our Troops" t-shirt quickly vanished into the crowd.

Clayton took a sip of his beer. "I know. Over the top. But I figure law school will have a decent ROI."

"You sure about that?" Kelsey asked, taking a sip of her merlot. She did a doubletake, surprised by the quality of brand served at McGinty's. "I've calculated ROI for law school and it's pretty bleak. When you consider..." She stopped mid-sentence.

"Don't let me interrupt you," Joe Frisco stood at the edge of the table. His eyes were fixed on Kelsey, as if she were the only person at the table. He wore a tie and blue sport coat over black jeans. He was more handsome than she remembered, and his eyes were a shade bluer, even under the dim lights at McGinty's.

Kelsey was frozen, unable to scramble up a reply. Max and Clayton quickly jumped to her rescue.

"Joe!" They shouted in unison, sliding out of the booth to exchange hugs and fist bumps. They commented on everyone's appearance and agreed they needed to get together more often. Finally, they sat down, and Joe slid into the booth, next to Kelsey. "Nicole called. She had a work thing. She'll be here later."

"What?" Max exclaimed. "But she set this whole thing up."

"She's always working," Clayton replied. "Girl's determined to climb that corporate ladder."

"She still coding?" Max asked Clayton.

"No. More like scaled platform support," Clayton corrected. "She's in enterprise cloud solutions for a division of Interloper. She's BIG TIME."

"We're all big time," Kelsey tried, finally entering the conversation. She raised her glass and they each toasted their official status.

"Yeah, big time debt," Max groaned.

"That's why we got together, right?" Joe asked.

"That's why I'm here," Max stated boldly.

"Yup," Clayton agreed. "Call me the poster boy for crushing student debt. And I'm just getting warmed up."

"Same, Kelsey?" Joe asked, finding her eyes again.

She nodded. "Yeah. I don't really like to talk about it…"

"I remember that about you," Joe smiled.

"You do?"

"Yeah. You keep your cards pretty close to your vest."

"Sorry," Kelsey apologized.

"No. I think it's cool," Joe said. "But you're here now. So, you must need to be here."

"Yeah," she admitted. "I need to be here."

"And you did your homework?" Max asked.

"Homework?" Clayton asked, studying Max with a quizzical expression.

"Yeah, like Nicole said. Did you bring your evil scheme?"

"Oh, I carry that with me always," Clayton replied.

"Wait? Seriously?" Joe asked.

"Of course," Clayton replied. "Always ready to roll. Just working up the nerve."

"Can't wait to hear it," Joe said, as the black-hatted cowboy waiter arrived for his order. Joe pointed to the beers and the waiter nodded and made his way to the bar. "Do you have an evil plan, Kelsey?"

"I do," she declared, as a second plan began to form.

"Excellent. Have you been scheming for a while?" Joe asked.

"I have," Kelsey smiled mysteriously and took another sip of wine, letting her heart slow.

"I guess I need to come up with something," Joe said a little defensively.

"I'll go first," Max stated. "That will give you some time to come up with yours."

"Shouldn't we wait for Nicole?" Kelsey asked.

Joe looked at his phone. "She just texted. Another 45 minutes."

"We better order dinner," Kelsey suggested. They all grabbed menus and placed their orders, including Nicole's order which Joe received by text.

"Looks like you're up, Maxie," Clayton announced. "Let's hear your plan."

2

VANISH

Max Hiatt: Marketing Major, University of Texas.

Remaining Student Debt: $93,715.78

Current Position: Account Coordinator, Management Training, Rider Rental Car Company

Annual Salary: $48,500 + Bonuses and Overtime.

Max grabbed his backpack and climbed out of the front seat of his rideshare, thanking the driver. "Thanks again, Paul. Have a great time in the Bahamas."

Paul beeped and drove off, leaving Max on the sidewalk in a rough and tumble part of town, in front of a Chinese restaurant with a painted window advertising fresh Peking duck. Max opened the glass front door and the bell rang, announcing his arrival. No one seemed to care. He walked through a collection of empty tables and stopped at the counter. A plastic golden cat, with a single paw raised in the air, stared at him suspiciously.

"You want my money, little friend?" Max asked, a little nervously.

"What's that?" A voice startled him. Max looked over to see an older woman with stern eyes and graying hair. She was wearing baggy jeans and a yellow Hawaiian shirt, with a red crayon over one ear.

"Where'd you come from?" Max tried to meet her stare but dropped his eyes back to the friendlier cat.

"What did you say?" She asked again.

"Oh, sorry. It's, uh, nothing..." Max stammered.

"What do you want?" She continued, tersely.

Max cleared his throat and chose his words carefully. "I was told to order the Cantonese Fireball Soup. Single Bowl."

Her expression remained wooden, but her eyes seemed to challenge his order. "Who told you about the Fireball Soup?"

"Tony. He told me what to order. Uh, here, at this restaurant," Max explained, trying hard not to upset her.

"Which Tony?" She probed further.

"You mean there's more than one?"

"Lots of Tony!" She insisted. "Which Tony?"

"Uh, Tony Lombardi?" Max tried.

Her eyes narrowed. "You mean Tony Chains?"

"Uh, yeah. I guess that's..."

"Four fifty!" She interrupted.

"You mean four *hundred* and fifty, right?" Max confirmed.

"Four fifty!" She nodded. "Cash only!"

Sid, the old guy who rented the apartment above Max, had introduced him to Tony Lombardi just a few days ago. Max had only talked to Tony for a couple of minutes, but it was enough to give him the address to the Chinese restaurant and directions for what to order. He was surprised by the angry Chinese woman, but ready for the price. He pulled a roll of bills out of his jeans pocket and handed it to her.

She counted the money quickly. "Through the kitchen! Upstairs!"

"Uh, the kitchen?"

"Upstairs!" She repeated.

Max watched her slip the roll of bills into the pocket of her Hawaiian shirt, as he went awkwardly behind the counter. "Uh, alright. Through here?"

She turned away and started working on a racing form with her red crayon. Max headed into the kitchen. The staff of three were busy prepping food in a jungle of stainless steel, steam, and exotic smells. They didn't look up. Max took the stairs and headed to the top, where he found three doors, with no indication for which was the right one. He tried the first and found a dusty storage closet filled with brooms, rolls of pink toilet paper, and large bags of rice. The second door opened to a tiny bathroom, which he was relieved he didn't need to use. The third door was locked.

Max tried the handle and it refused to turn. He then heard a loud, automatic "Click" and the door popped open. He stepped into a foyer with highly polished, hardwood floors. Water cascaded gently down the slate facia of an ornate wall fountain. The walls of the foyer were white stone veneer, with cut-outs that displayed intricate jade sculptures. The door closed behind him and he stood, marveling at the transition from hole-in-the-wall Chinese restaurant to luxurious secret office. The foyer was round, with two closed doors and an open door. He stepped through the open door onto plush, white carpet and stood in front of an imposing desk, surrounded by chic, modern art.

He was alone. Max let his eyes roam across the artwork and elaborate furnishings, completely surprised by the elegance. He finally took a seat in one of two carved, teak chairs and waited for his host.

A few minutes passed. Then a tall, wiry man in his early thirties entered the office from the foyer. "So, you're friends with Tony Chains!"

Max stood and shook the man's extended hand. He was surprised at the strength of his grip. He had a perfect, white smile and wore expensive ripped jeans, red Converse All Stars, and a Coke t-shirt. He had grey piercing eyes and jet-black hair. The gold watch on his wrist looked like a Rolex, although Max had not seen enough of them to be sure.

"Friends? You mean with Tony?" Max hesitated. He was expecting to meet a seedy gangster, not a young, fit guy who could join him at the park for a game of pick-up hoops. "Not sure I know him well enough to call him a friend."

"But you're here on his referral. Right?" His host was still smiling, but his eyes were studying Max carefully.

"Yeah. He's friends with my neighbor, Sid. Said I should come and talk to you."

"Ah, a friend of a friend. I get a lot of those." His host took a seat behind the enormous desk, his grey eyes never leaving Max.

"I'm sorry! I didn't catch your name," Max asked.

"That's because I didn't give you my name. I find it works better that way... for both of us."

"Suits me," Max shrugged, and sat back down. "What should I call you?"

"Well, if you must, you can call me Max."

"But that's my name." Max protested.

"Exactly."

"Wait! How do you know my name?" Max was stunned.

"I know everything about the people who come to see me. I have to be very careful in my line of work."

"So, I'm guessing Tony told you?" Max began to feel uneasy, like he had opened a door that should have stayed shut.

"You can guess, but that's not why you're here," his host continued studying Max's eyes.

"And you know why I am here?" Max asked carefully.

"You want a new identity. So, you can disappear," his host replied smoothly, as if this were the case with everyone he met.

"Yeah, that's right. I need to get out of my massive college debt," Max sighed. "I need to start over."

"Tell me about it," his host exclaimed. "I went to Oregon under-grad. That out-of-state tuition is ridiculous. No idea what I was thinking. Then I got my MBA at USC. I was so deep in debt I thought those collections agents would never leave me alone. Until I started this business."

"So, you disappeared, too?" Max asked, relieved he wasn't the only one to dodge his student debt this way.

"It's possible," his host shrugged. He lifted an iPad from his desk and handed it to Max. "Fill out this questionnaire. Don't worry, it's fully encrypted. I need to know what you want your future to look like, where you plan to live, religious preferences, that kind of thing. You fill that out and I will send you an encrypted text with my banking instructions. You will wire my fee to the account I provide to you. I will then have a locker key left on your desk at work, with the address to find the locker."

"Wait, you know where I work?" Max shuddered.

His host ignored his question and continued. "Inside the locker, you will find everything you need. New identity. Driver's license. Passport. Credit cards. Resume'. College diploma. Brief story of your new family. And an airline ticket. The rest is up to you."

Max nodded, uncertain of what to say. Then thought of something. "The resume'...."

His host nodded, "Every company name listed on your new resume' will verify you worked there, at the dates listed. It will all be arranged. Your references, too."

"That's pretty slick. You really do a thorough job."

His host smiled at the compliment. "For a little bit more, I can have a car registered in your name waiting at the airport, and an apartment leased and furnished for you. I can even have a job lined up for you."

"I think that's out of my budget," Max replied, regretfully. The deluxe package sounded like the way to go, but he needed to conserve his money. "I'll stick with the standard package."

His host nodded. "Any questions?"

Max hesitated, "What about the real me?"

"You mean Max Hiatt?"

Max shuddered again. It was creepy that this underworld character knew so much about him. "Yeah, I guess. Do I check the local paper one morning and see my obituary staring back at me?"

His host nodded again. "I can do that for you. Some people like the closure. I even have clients who attend their own funerals. In disguise, of course."

"Like Tom Sawyer?" Max laughed. "That's pretty cool."

"Yeah, I guess so. But I don't recommend it. It's better just to vanish."

Max was disappointed for some reason. He wanted closure on his present life. However, this guy was an expert and he was probably right. A death could lead to questions and inquiries. It was better to disappear.

"A word of caution," his host warned. "You don't want to unwind this new identity of yours. Once you wire my fee, you are committed. You need to vanish and stick with the plan. So, you must be absolutely certain that this is what you want."

"Oh, I have no doubts," Max declared, eager to convince his host.

"And don't come back to me. Under any circumstances," his host cautioned him. "You won't find me anyway. I move my office every couple of months."

"Wait. Really?" Max was amazed. "But your office is so elegant…"

"What about your family?" His host interrupted.

It was a good question.

"My dad died when I was in high school," Max began, reluctant to continue. But he remembered that his host probably knew all about his sad, little life. "My mom couldn't handle it and turned to drugs. It was bad. Then she remarried a total jerk. He and I were like oil and water. So, I moved in with my friend's family until I graduated high school. I saw my mom every so often, but she had a new family and it was super weird. They moved to Europe while I was in college, and I haven't been in touch. No siblings. So, pretty simple."

"You paid your way through college?" His host asked, but it felt like he already knew the answer.

"More like I borrowed my way through college," Max mused.

His host nodded with what appeared to be compassion.

"My dad's life insurance gave me enough to get started," Max continued. "I borrowed the rest."

"What about your friends?"

"I'll make new friends," Max said evenly. "I'm a friendly guy. It's easy for me."

"Sounds like you've thought this through." His host nodded with an approving smile. "Be sure to quit your job and provide your employer with plenty of notice. Tell them you have a new job out of state. You don't want anyone filing a missing person's report."

"Got it! And I took a cash advance on my credit card to pay your fee," Max explained.

"Yeah, that's the spirit. Max out all of your credit card with cash advances. You will need as much cash as you can carry. Use it as your nest egg when you disappear."

Max nodded. He had been considering this move for a while. He had a new backpack, tucked under his bed, with a single change of new clothes, and a trash bag he was filling steadily with cash.

"And you know to change your look, right? New hair color, different style. New clothes. A beard is always a good idea. And don't come back here. No college reunions. No old girl friends. You need to truly disappear."

"Yup! I'm ready," Max insisted.

His host nodded again and stood to leave. "I'll let you finish the questionnaire. Just leave the iPad on my desk. I'll send you the encrypted text tomorrow with the bank account details for the wire. Once the funds hit the account, I will get to work. It will take about a month. One day, the key will appear on your desk with the instructions you'll need, leading you to a locker with all of the documents I prepared for you."

Max hesitated again.

"Yes?" His host asked, a little impatiently.

"It's just that I work at a rental car company, and there are keys all over the place, especially on my desk," Max explained.

His host held up a hand. "I know all about Rider Rental Car. Don't worry. You'll recognize my package when it arrives."

Max stood to shake his hand, but his host had already left the room.

Eight weeks later, Scott Turley (formerly Max Hiatt) walked through the Cheyenne Regional Airport terminal carrying his new backpack. It was filled with his new passport, a new Wyoming driver's license, a diploma from Boise State University, a new birth certificate, and family history notes for his new persona. Scattered and hidden throughout his personal belongings was over $25,000 in cash to start his new life. He felt like he was walking across campus on his first day of college, eager to start his classes and make new friends.

"Scott" followed the signs to the ride sharing area and hopped into his waiting car. The driver took him into Cheyenne and dropped him at a diner. Scott paid cash for his meal and walked the half mile to his motel room. He paid cash again for a single night and slept for twelve hours straight. It was the best night of sleep he had in years.

The next morning, he showered, dropped his room key in the lobby slot, and ate a big breakfast at a different diner across the street. Well rested and full, Scott slung his backpack over his shoulder and walked a mile to a car dealership on Westland Road. He paid all cash for a used Ford F150 and drove it to Jackson, Wyoming.

It was late spring, and his plan was to grow a beard and sign on with a river rafting company. He would also try to find work as a fly-fishing guide and supplement his income working nights as a bartender. In the winter, he would trade his paddle and flyrod for a snowboard. He would give snowboarding lessons, work the lifts, and continue to tend bar. He thought he might even cut firewood to earn some extra money.

While he worked, Scott (Max) planned to study for his real estate license. He wanted to start selling homes the next spring. He would meet a local girl, switch his college football allegiance from the Texas Longhorns to the Boise State Broncos, and begin saving to open his own real estate company. He was finally free. And he planned to stay that way.

3

THE STING

Kelsey Sizemore: Accounting Major and MBA,
University of Arizona

Remaining Student Debt: $104,812.61

Current Position: Assistant Accounts Payable Manager,
Leebrick & Singleton Trucking

Annual Salary: $31,300

Kelsey Sizemore was an overachiever. She was famous for late night study sessions, impressive grades, and her carefully drawn roadmap for success. She had earned her accounting degree with honors and went straight into the MBA program, graduating with both degrees in just 5 years. She had expected plenty of job offers upon graduation, but Tucson, Arizona was a small city, and the offers were scarce and located in cities where she preferred not to live.

With some encouragement from her parents, Kelsey moved back to her hometown and continued her job search in earnest, with little improvement in her situation. It turned out that she was one in a large herd of overachieving accounting majors with an MBA, and the competition for open jobs was fierce. So, she settled. After several months of searching, Kelsey finally accepted a position at Leebrick & Singleton Trucking, a non-glamorous company with low wages and little room for advancement. But it was a job.

Her trouble was not just her dead-end job, but the crushing debt she had accumulated to get that job. She owed over $100,000 in student loans and would be paying them for the next twenty years.

Kelsey knew she had the vision and the skills to turn Leebrick & Singleton Trucking into a very profitable company. She could see the potential. Leebrick & Singleton had cultivated an enviable market share in the southern states, with competitive prices and strong customer relationships. If they could just get a better handle on their cash flow and receivables, they would be able to purchase additional trucks and expand into new areas. With an expanded sales team and updated corporate brand, she was confident that Leebrick & Singleton Trucking could be transformed into something special.

No one else seemed to share her vision. In fact, when she accepted her position at Leebrick & Singleton, she felt like she had traveled back in time. The wood paneled walls, brown shag carpet and clunky computer monitors were just the first indications that Leebrick & Singleton Trucking was still operating in the late seventies. The other indicators were more sinister, centered on a misogynistic owner who had a particularly insulting way with words, and ruled the field of cubicles with an iron fist. For all his bluster, Mr. Singleton was blind to the potential of his family company, especially the potential to steal from it.

Kelsey was not a natural thief. She considered herself an honest person who worked hard to guard her integrity. However, as her humiliation increased, she felt her resolve to be honest disintegrating. She knew she was clever and believed she could run circles around the rest of the staff at Leebrick & Singleton Trucking, but no one valued her talents. With each passing day, Kelsey contemplated a righteous corruption designed to prove her ingenuity, while paying off her hideous student loans. She convinced herself that no one would be hurt, and no one would ever know.

Thinking through the angles of her scheme helped her push the despair away and made her feel like she had some control over her life, even if her plan stepped across the legal line. Kelsey was careful to craft a plan that did not include any "stealing", technically, but it did involve a great deal of diverting. She would just let the funds pass through her fingers, until they could be returned to their original purpose, like a salmon caught downstream and returned to the water a few miles upriver, never the wiser.

She resisted the temptation, at first. But her resolve faded with every pathetic paycheck she received. Her determination to do what was right was diminished by every monster student loan payment she made. And her will to rise her above her circumstances vanished with every abuse she endured from Mr. Singleton, and every demeaning comment she received from her immediate supervisor, Mrs. Sledge. As the humiliations piled up, Kelsey set aside her prudish restraint and advanced her plan to harness the power of her employer's payables.

The concept was a simple one. Kelsey noticed that Leebrick & Singleton Trucking did millions of dollars of business each year subcontracting deliveries with a handful of smaller trucking companies. If Leebrick & Singleton could not fulfill an order, they would tap one of these other trucking companies to transport the load for them. This allowed them to keep their customers happy, while increasing their revenues. The subcontracted work amounted to over $15 million dollars in revenue each year. This was an impressive sum by most standards, but just a small portion of Leebrick & Singleton Trucking's annual revenue.

So, Kelsey decided to play the gap.

During her lunch hours, she contacted her counterparts in the accounts receivable department in each of the 20 plus subcontractor companies that Leebrick & Singleton Trucking used. Kelsey used her business savvy to negotiate a 2% discount if she paid their invoices within 10 days, instead of the standard 30 days. Almost all of the subcontractors agreed, as cash flow is a critical component in running a successful moving company, and they were eager to secure payment as soon as possible.

In order to earn the 2%, Kelsey would just need to pay each company invoice in 10 days, while Leebrick & Singleton Trucking released the payments in 30 days. For the scheme to work, Kelsey would need a few million dollars in working capital to have the funds necessary to cover the 20 day float between payments of 10 days and the checks cut in 30 days, without the funds going missing.

To secure the working capital, Kelsey did some creative editing to a few million dollars of supplier invoices. When the invoices arrived at Leebrick & Singleton Trucking, Kelsey slid them into her briefcase and took them home each night. She then re-typed each invoice using a simple Word template, using logos copied from her supplier's websites, and matching the fonts and invoice designs. It was surprisingly easy to do.

She then altered the invoice date and the due date for each payment. If the real invoice was dated March 15th and the due date was April 15th, Kelsey would change the invoice date on her fake invoice to February 15th and move the due date to March 15th. She then took the fake invoices back to the office and paid them immediately. The volume of orders at Leebrick & Singleton was too high for anyone to notice the invoices had been paid 30-days early, and Kelsey had sole control over this part of the accounting department, with no one looking over her shoulder or checking the little details of her work. Her job was to pay bills, and they let her do it.

After several weeks of paying fake invoices 30 days early, Kelsey had secured a few million dollars in funds, which allowed her to pay each subsequent invoice early, in 10 days rather than in 30.

However, she could not simply send the checks from Leebrick & Singleton Trucking directly to the subcontractors 10 days early. If she did that, Leebrick & Singleton and not Kelsey Sizemore, would receive the 2% discount.

So, Kelsey formed a corporation, with a series of DBAs ("doing business as" subsidiary companies) to receive the checks she wrote from Leebrick & Singleton Trucking, and a single corporation that took the place of Leebrick & Singleton to distribute the funds to each subcontractor. The key to her plan was to create company names that were similar to each subcontractor, so she could write checks from Leebrick & Singleton Trucking and receive the funds into her fleet of dba companies, while also creating a company with a name similar to Leebrick & Singleton Trucking for the checks to be sent back out to the subcontractors. She kept a list of the dba companies that she created and the subcontractors they mirrored.

Actual Subcontractor Company Name	Kelsey's Created Company
American Trucking Company	American Logistics Company
Desert State Trucking	Desert State Group
Lehigh Logistics	Lehigh Trucking Company
Southland Trucking Company	Southland Group
Central West Trucking	Central West Logistics Group
Wilson & Watkins	Wilson and Watkins Trucking
And so on...	And so forth...

The mock companies Kelsey created allowed her to deposit the checks from Leebrick & Singleton into her own business accounts. Rather than mail the checks from Leebrick & Singleton Trucking, she just pretended to mail them and then took them home and deposited them electronically into her dba company accounts.

She also created a mock company called Leebrick & Singleton Logistics Group and paid each of the subcontractors from that account. The name and address were similar enough to Leebrick & Singleton Trucking that each subcontractor quickly deposited the checks. And if any of them ever called her with a question, Kelsey would take the call and explain the name change was part of their new, 10-day payment plan.

From her created Leebrick & Singleton Logistics Group account, using the few million dollars she had secured by early paying her altered invoices, she wrote the checks to the real trucking companies and paid each within 10 business days, securing the 2% discount. So, each month she early-paid the supplier companies from her own business account, then paid her business account back at the higher amount in 30 days.

For example, if Leebrick & Singleton Trucking owed Wilson & Watkins $13,780 for a long-haul order, Kelsey would copy the invoice and take it home. She would then pay Wilson & Watkins from her personal Leebrick & Singleton Logistics Group account at a 2% discount, or $13,504.40. This would allow Kelsey to personally keep the 2% discount of $275.60.

So, for every invoice she paid, Kelsey was pocketing 2%. Leebrick & Singleton spent over $15 million per year on subcontractor trucking companies. By working her scheme for just over a year, Kelsey was able to net almost $300,000 on the gap, by keeping the 2% fee for herself. It technically wasn't stealing, as every supplier invoice was paid and no money was actually taken from Leebrick & Singleton Trucking. And she was the one who did the work and used her ingenuity to secure the 2% discount from her early payment negotiations.

After 12 months of this, Kelsey had paid all of the float money back to Leebrick & Singleton and she had paid off her $104,000 student loan debt. She was also able to place another $180,000 into an investment account. She then closed each of the dba companies she had used to orchestrate the float.

Now it was time to pay the money back to her employer. Kelsey arranged a meeting with her supervisor, Mrs. Sledge, and the company owner, Mr. Singleton. They were both reluctant to take the meeting and more than a little rude when it began.

"What is this meeting about, Chelsea?" Mr. Singleton demanded. They were sitting in his office, and the afternoon sun was streaming through the windows, making it hot and stuffy. With the combined glare of the sun and the company owner, Kelsey began to perspire.

"It's, uh, Kelsey," she corrected.

"Sorry!" Mr. Singleton waived his hand across his desk. "All you pretty girls have the same name. I can't keep track of them."

"Excuse me, Mr. Singleton?" Kelsey replied, stunned.

Singleton scoffed at her discomfort, "You know what I mean! And you're new here. It takes me a while to learn everyone's name."

"But I've worked here over a year..."

Mr. Singleton cut her off. "And you're welcome. Now, what is this about?"

"Please, Kelsey," Mrs. Sledge insisted crossly. "Mr. Singleton is a Very.... Busy.... Man."

Kelsey pressed on and tried to ignore their condescending tones. "I'll get right to it, then. I wanted to let you know that I have negotiated an early payment discount with almost every one of our subcontractor trucking suppliers. If we pay them within 10 business days, rather than the usual 30 days, we will receive a 2% discount."

"2%!" Mr. Singleton blustered. "That's a rip off! You're a fool to cut that deal."

"Excuse me…" Kelsey said again, floored by his rudeness.

Singleton quickly interrupted. "You don't understand the value of cash flow, Chelsea! I'd rather keep their money for the whole 30 days! We can use it to power our operations, make our payroll, and leverage our float."

"But, Mr. Singleton, the savings would equal $300,000 a year," Kelsey insisted.

"Pocket change! As I tried to explain to you, I want to keep the cash for the entire 30 days. In fact, I think we should change our payment terms to 45 days."

"But…"

Singleton cut her off, again. "Before you come to me with an idea like this, and waste my precious time, not to mention the precious time of our trucking subcontractors, I suggest you bring it up with Mrs. Sledge, first."

"Yes, Kelsey. There are protocols for this type of a meeting here at Leebrick & Singleton Trucking," Mrs. Sledge agreed. Mr. Singleton stood, and Mrs. Sledge followed his lead.

"This meeting is over!" Mr. Singleton declared.

Kelsey remained seated, shocked at their treatment of both her and her idea. She could clearly see her future at Leebrick & Singleton, and she did not like what she saw. Mr. Singleton placed his hands on his hips and tried to stare her out of his office, while Mrs. Sledge cleared her throat emphatically.

"Thank you for stating your position in such clear terms," Kelsey began.

Singleton interrupted her again. "Now, look here, Missy. This meeting has gone on long enough..."

This time it was Kelsey who interrupted. "For the last time, Mr. Singleton, my name is Kelsey! I can spell it for you if that will help. And I happen to have an MBA and an accounting degree from the University of Arizona. I am a well-educated and talented accounting professional. Furthermore, I have just provided you with a terrific business advantage that will allow you to expand your company, so you can become even more profitable. Not to mention, this $300,000 in annual savings would allow you to pay me, and some other people around here, a decent wage. I have come to you with a solid idea and it should have been received with respectful consideration. But please don't trouble yourself with my initial plan, because I now have a better one."

Singleton's eyes narrowed and he rasped, "And what is that?"

"I am putting in my 2-week notice. I will be leaving Leebrick & Singleton Trucking and taking my ideas with me." With that, Kelsey Sizemore stood up and left his office.

A few weeks later, she completed her notice period and walked into the sunshine. She had paid off her $104,000 student loan debt and now had $180,000 of working capital to start her own accounting company.

4

PLAYING BANKER

Clayton Moss: Philosophy & Political Science Major,
Georgetown University

Remaining Student Debt: $128,893.03

Current Position: Entrepreneur and
Part-Time Assistant Manager, Fiesta Party Rentals

Annual Salary: $12,450

"Banker!" The dealer declared, tapping the King of Clubs and 9
of Diamonds with his long, delicate fingers. He deftly slid the chips
across the felt to each gambler who played Banker, clicking and
stacking the chips with professional flourish. In the same motion, he
swept the chips away from the gamblers who had played Player
and Tie.

Clayton Moss held back a smile, as the chips in front of him
doubled. He was all business and careful to conceal his racing heart
behind a practiced, blank expression. He knew people were watching him. There were hidden cameras feeding video to the control
room, where people trained in the art of deception studied his
every move. The busy waitresses watched, too, gliding across the
floor in their low-slung dresses, serving drinks and gauging players. The subtle eyes of his dealer confessed that he did more for the
casino than flip cards, as he followed Clayton's every twitch, like
the dancing needle from a lie detector test. The pit boss was ever

present, roaming the back tables like a caged tiger, watching nothing and seeing everything.

Clayton was sure they saw him. They would always see a six-foot-tall black man in his early twenties wearing a crisp, white tuxedo and sipping patiently on a rum and Coke, while steadily playing Banker at $500 a hand. The ice in his glass had melted over an hour ago, and the waitresses bounced into view every few minutes to offer a fresh drink. Clayton smiled and waved each of them off, only sipping occasionally, as he treaded water in a calculated assault on the casino's Baccarat table. He was up $1,500, which was not the point. He would have preferred to have a small loss posted. He did not want them - the collective them of cameras, waitresses, dealers, and pit bosses - to suspect that he knew what he was doing. But, of course, he did. He knew exactly what he was doing.

Clayton could see patterns.

He had the rare ability to discern probabilities, recognize trends, calculate likelihoods, and sense the pulse of what was coming next. His intelligence was startling, and he would have been an academic superstar at Georgetown, but he placed a low priority on his grades. Rather, he fed his insatiable thirst to learn new things, which compelled him to skip many of his classes and lectures at Georgetown University.

Clayton's brilliance and natural athletic abilities had always allowed him to coast through elementary school and high school. However, at a university like Georgetown, everyone was brilliant, and his absence in class and the library held him back. This was a calculated risk. Without the burden of studying and attending regular classes, Clayton was free to pursue a wider range of academic interests.

Clayton had aced the LSAT, and would be attending Georgetown Law in the fall, even though his university grades were below average. If he had attended his classes, he would most likely have secured a position on the stage at graduation, or at least a Magna Cum Laude sash. Rather than securing a perfect grade point average, Clayton sat in on lectures across the campus on a myriad of subjects, debated professors during their office hours, and even attended an archaeological dig in Egypt in his junior year, with a completely different university. Clayton was fascinated by life, whether it was science, politics, mathematics, computer science, religion, philosophy, foreign language, architecture, or engineering. It all interested him, and he quickly mastered the foundation for many of these subjects. It was all so exciting for him, that he refused to be pinned down to a traditional set of four courses for an entire semester, which provided a rather strong gravitational pull on his GPA.

As his grades fell, Clayton eventually lost his scholarship and borrowed his way through the balance of his undergraduate degrees in philosophy and political science, which required an extra year to graduate and racked up debts of over $128,000. Clayton knew he would never have the discipline or focus to pay his debt off over time. He would need to pay it off quickly, in one fell swoop.

He was quite aware that there were several ways to raise capital to eliminate his debt. He toyed with using his crypto-currency model, which would one day make him millions, but he lacked the ready cash to invest in such a volatile enterprise. He also felt confident that he could hack Georgetown's mainframe and simply erase his debts, but stealing was beneath his abilities. So, Clayton turned his mind to gambling.

He was eager to put his innate abilities of mathematics and pattern discernment to work against the highly trained gambling establishments in Las Vegas. He had studied the various games of chance and calculated his winning percentages against a variety of game scenarios. Clayton was quick to decide that sports betting was too unreliable, poker held too many variables, and horse racing lacked the empirical science needed to cultivate a significant advantage. He finally settled on Punto Banco, better known as Baccarat.

Baccarat is considered a game for the wealthy, with minimum bets of $500 and a reputation for attracting moguls and secret agents bent on breaking casinos with their daring bets. However, it is also an ideal game for a bold and brilliant college student who is interested is wiping out his student loan debts.

Baccarat is simple to play and, therefore, easy to master. It also offers a relatively small advantage for the casino, while also allowing for extremely large bets. To win at Baccarat, you just need to get 9, or closer to 9, than the other hands. All 10s and face cards are counted as 0, while the other numbered cards are counted at face value. If a pair is dealt, like two eights, you add them together and subtract 10, so your total is 6.

Clayton also knew that Baccarat was a game of trends, streaks, and patterns. In fact, Baccarat, more than any other game, is similar to the toss of a coin. While the odds of a coin toss are even, you instinctively know that a coin will not land with certain accuracy on a pattern of heads, tails, heads, tails. Clayton knew that streaks developed where a coin would land heads, heads, heads, tails, heads, heads, heads until the streak of heads went dry.

Baccarat is all about discipline, nerves, and patience. It was a matter of waiting for a streak to develop and then capitalizing on it boldly, almost ruthlessly, until the streak was over. And Clayton planned to leverage his gift to see these developing streaks to his advantage.

Clayton did not need to worry about whether to play Banker, Player or Tie, the only three outcomes in Baccarat. He was all about the probabilities. Tie was a fool's bet, with an advantage to the casino of 14.36%, while Player offered a much leaner casino advantage of 1.24%. Banker was king, with a casino advantage of only 1.06%. An advantage so low that you are required to pay the casino a commission of 5% each time you win. Clayton was happy to pay the commission and eager to play the best odds Las Vegas had to offer.

Clayton could also count cards. Most Baccarat tables use a standard shoe of 8 decks of cards, so his ability to count would be largely minimized. However, he would be able to spot patterns, for example, if a face card did not appear after five straight cards, Clayton could quickly gauge the probability of the next one appearing.

He had devised a stratagem for winning enough money to pay off his student loan debt in a single weekend. He just had to wait for the streak to arrive. He would then begin to place increasingly larger bets, doubling and tripling them, until he had won the money he needed. If he didn't lose his nerve, Clayton knew he would emerge a winner. He just needed to follow his instincts and not blink. And he needed a tremendous amount of cash to see his plan through.

To get the cash, Clayton went no further than his mailbox. He gathered up the twenty or so special credit card offers that targeted young consumers and had arrived in his mailbox over the past few weeks. He applied for all of them. Once approved, Clayton took his collection of credit cards to a series of banks and received the largest cash advances allowed. By the end of his session, Clayton had over

$48,000 in borrowed cash. He tried not to think about the 19% interest rate on each.

He then bought a one-way ticket to Las Vegas, uncertain of how long he would need to stay to play out his scheme. He also rented three tuxedos, one white and two black, with different jacket styles. He took a week off from his part-time party rental job and flew to Las Vegas on a hot Thursday in late September.

Clayton had carefully researched the various casinos and knew where he would play. He was careful not to stay where he was playing, choosing a non-gaming resort close to the strip. He planned to alternate between a few casinos each night, until he spotted the streak he wanted.

With his dark features and tall, muscular body, Clayton Moss looked like a black James Bond as he walked across the floor of the casino and took his seat at the Baccarat table. He ordered a single drink and began to implement his consistent, unemotional plan.

After an hour of steady play, no patterns had materialized. Clayton treaded water and waited for the streak to develop, his mind racing ahead of the game to discern the next outcome. The cards were vague and the patterns blurred, so he pushed for another hour and called it a night. He paid the dealer a 5% commission on $2,500 of winnings and left a generous tip.

The next night found Clayton at a different casino, a larger and richer casino famous for its Baccarat tables. It was Saturday night, so Clayton arrived early to select his chair, wearing a black tuxedo and sipping on a gin and tonic. He sat at the table of 14 chairs, slightly right of center and watched the cards flip as he played Banker and his mind raced ahead with the probabilities. His plan was to make a big play on this Saturday night, at this specific casino, when the tables were crowded with weekenders from LA and the Bay Area. He would be one of hundreds of young people of interest and it would allow for a smoother play. He knew it was possible that he would need to stay in Las Vegas for several more days, but he was hoping for a Saturday night streak that he could ride to black. And, to his delight, this one came well before midnight.

The Baccarat dealer was a veteran with silver hair, sleepy eyes, and incredibly efficient hands. His teeth were perfectly white and built a confident smile that dazzled the table over a name badge that announced he was "George from New Jersey". In another life, this dealer could have played a successful CEO, or a model for a compassionate Medicare ad. Clayton wasn't fooled. This elegant, older man was the grim reaper, visiting death on half the gamblers at the table with every deal.

George, the dealer, reset the game and flipped the new cards in rapid succession. Clayton sat behind another $500 bet.

"Banker!" The dealer declared smoothly, stacking and snatching chips in quick succession. He doubled Clayton's $500 into $1,000. This was the third straight Banker, after a long series of predominantly Player wins.

It was time to test the streak. Clayton pushed another $1,000 out to match the chips in front of him. He took a brief sip of his gin and tonic, watching George from New Jersey flip a Queen Eight for Player, and a Ten Seven for Banker. The dealer quickly pulled Clayton's $2,000 in chips away with an apologetic smile.

Clayton didn't flinch. Instead, he pushed $5,000 forward onto Banker again, his largest bet of the weekend. Prior to this bet, Clayton had tread water at $500 bets, and the occasional $1,000. But he was implementing his scheme now and was ready to ride it to bust. He could see the streak developing in his head and knew the timing was perfect. His mind was clear, floating high above the table in a world driven by advanced mathematics, while his heart raced at the excitement of what he knew would come next.

The cards flipped quickly, and the dealer shouted "Banker!" He pushed $5,000 in chips at Clayton, making it an even $10,000. George paid each banker at the table, while he pulled the chips away from the losers. If he had noticed Clayton's first big win, the dealer didn't let it register on his face. The table was full now, with other gamblers from destinations all over the world. While Clayton was dashing in his rented tuxedo, he was just another face in the crowd of desperate and confident gamblers. That was about to change.

With $5,000 in winnings, Clayton didn't hesitate. He quickly slid another $10,000 in chips onto the Banker square, making a bold $20,000 bet. George's sleepy eyes were suddenly awake, and he looked up to study Clayton with a new appreciation.

George dealt again and Banker caught a pair of Eights, while Player turned a Three Six. The $20,000 was quickly pulled from Clayton's mark and George gave a slight shrug, while the players around Clayton gawked at his massive loss.

But Clayton was expecting the loss and knew the time was right. He pushed a full $40,000 onto the Banker's square, all of the money he had remaining. Lose and he would be in debt $176,000. Win and he still had some cards to play. But he knew he would win.

"Bets, please," the dealer requested. He gave Clayton an extra second to consider his bet. Clayton did not touch his chips, leaving $40,000 on the table, sitting Banker again. The other gamblers noticed Clayton for the first time and bet accordingly.

The cards flipped quickly, too quickly for Clayton's taste. He wanted the moment to last a little longer. And, so it would.

"Tie!" George declared. The dealer from New Jersey tapped the Player square, tapped the Banker square, and paid the Tie.

Clayton let the $40,000 ride into the next deal, while the other gamblers scrambled to make their bets. He took a quick sip of his gin and tonic, as the new cards flipped into place.

"Banker!" the dealer called, flipping a King Nine to beat Player's Jack Seven. A collective gasp escaped the other players around the table and people from other tables began to gather.

"That fella just won $40,000," a husky middle-aged man in a white cowboy hat, black button-down, and crisp new jeans whispered to his wife. He was watching the game from behind Clayton's back and, for the first time, Clayton sensed a crowd pressing in on his table.

The old cowboy's wife put a motherly hand on his shoulder. "Honey, you should take it and run."

Clayton sat still and ignored her wise advice. George stacked the $40,000 in winnings in front of Clayton, making it a cool $80,000. His heart was racing, but Clayton's mind remained crystal clear. He knew he had it. He nodded to the dealer that his bet would stay at $80,000.

George from New Jersey glanced up as he pulled cards and chips back towards him. He made a slight gesture that no one else noticed. The pit boss came over and saw Clayton's bet. He tipped his head slightly to the right and passed on, pretending not to watch.

"Bets, please!" The dealer called coolly. Every other player, and the crowd behind them, had their eyes on Clayton's $80,000 bet. They studied his calm, surveyed his command of the situation, noticed his spotless tux, considered the gin and tonic he had barely touched, and envied the massive pile of chips that sat in front of him. And they all bet Banker, too. Many of them doubled their bets. All 14 gamblers were sitting on Banker, ready to live or die with Clayton Moss and his bold $80,000 bet.

Clayton smiled for the first time all night. He raised his glass to his fellow Bankers and they raised their glasses back. But no one spoke. Even George was surprised by this moment at his table, and he had been dealing in Las Vegas for over a decade. He pulled the cards slowly from the shoe, flipping an Eight of Spades for Player. Everyone sighed. Then he tossed a King of Hearts for Banker, and everyone cheered. Then George turned a Ten of Diamonds for Player and everyone gasped, afraid to speak. They were staring down an Eight, and only a Nine could win for them now. Finally, the dealer flipped the Nine of Hearts and the table erupted in cheers. The crowd pressed in, patting Clayton on the back and high fiving the other players. A few other gamblers tossed chips at Clayton, to thank him for his luck.

George searched Clayton's eyes, his knowing look was warm and kind. "Care to bet, sir?"

Clayton shook his head and pulled $160,000 in chips off the Banker square. "I'll sit out this hand."

George nodded and the rest of the players placed their bets. The dealer turned cards across the table, while Clayton did quick math in his head. He calculated his $128,000 in student debt, added in the $48,000 in credit card advances, and factored in the 5% commission for his winnings, plus a nice tip for the dealer.

"Player!" The dealer called, and Clayton smiled again, knowing what would happen next. After the dealer clicked the wins onto each square and pulled the loser's chips off the table, Clayton pushed $25,000 into the Banker square. He was now playing with house money.

Once again, every one of the other thirteen players pushed their chips onto Banker, joining Clayton on another bold bet. The people standing behind Clayton crowded in tighter.

"You should just keep your winnings!" The cowboy shouted from behind him, as more people gathered around. The stack of chips in front of Clayton was staggering and it drew both crowds and admiration for the young black man in the tuxedo.

"Last hand," Clayton said. The dealer nodded, allowing a slight grin to form. He was pulling for Clayton, just as everyone else was.

The dealer deftly flipped the cards, and everyone gasped. A pair of Nines fell for Banker, beating the Player with a sitting Queen Six.

The table erupted for a second time. Clayton was jostled again with high fives, hand- shakes, back slaps and tips slid onto his square. Everyone was genuinely happy for him, and largely in his debt. Clayton took a deep breath for the first time all weekend.

George from New Jersey smiled and paid Clayton first, out of order, but no one cared. He made another imperceptible signal. The pit boss came over to congratulate Clayton as his betting chips were matched to total $50,000.

Clayton pulled the new chips off the square to join the $135,000 of his previous winnings, giving him a total of $185,000. Clayton slid the $6,850 in commissions to the dealer, who was instantly impressed that he knew the exact commission amount. Clayton also slid a $1,000 chip over to him and whispered a quiet, "Thank you."

The dealer nodded and the other gamblers cheered as Clayton stood up to his full six feet. The crowd behind him stepped back to give him and his chips some room.

His final winnings left him with enough to pay off the $48,000 in credit card advances, his Student loans of $128,000, and his expenses for hotel, airfare, food, and tux rentals.

Clayton sighed, "Time to go home. Can I borrow a chip carrier, please?"

"Certainly, sir!" George waved his hand and a clerk from the cashier's window appeared. She quickly stacked Clayton's chips into the carrier and led him through the crowd to the cashier's window.

As Clayton began to follow her, the man in the cowboy hat stopped him, as the crowd listened in. "That was one hell of a play. I have the feeling you knew what you was doing."

Clayton just smiled.

"Are you a professional, or something?"

Clayton didn't know if he meant gambler or athlete, but replied. "I just graduated from college with $128,000 in student loan debt and $48,000 in credit card debt. Tonight was about paying it all off."

The cowboy immediately took off his white hat and gave it to Clayton, as his wife beamed warmly. Clayton handled the man's hat carefully, respectfully, and placed it on his head at a slight angle, smiling back at his new friend with genuine gratitude. The crowd cheered again and started another round of high-fives and back slapping, as Clayton made his way through the crowd to the cashier's window to collect his check.

He flew out the next morning, exhausted and debt free.

5

CHAPTER 7

Joe Frisco: Film & History Major, UCLA

Remaining Student Debt: $54,822.17

Current Position: Part-Time Teacher and Stunt Double, Working on a Documentary Film

Annual Salary: $27,750

Joe Frisco prided himself on his creativity. He double majored at UCLA in film and history, with big plans to earn his PhD in history so he could be a professor at the college level, while developing cutting-edge films on a wide range of historical topics. He had a long list of student film awards to his credit and several impressive internships at Hollywood production companies.

Several times, Joe had been assigned a project on a Friday afternoon, written the script, recruited actors, filmed at various sites, edited the film down to compelling quality, and submitted his work before the weekend was over. His creative talents had captured many prizes and awards. During those pressure-cooker assignments, Joe's creativity had propelled him to success. But today, as he looked up at his mountain of $55,000 in college debt, Joe could not think of a single creative idea for eliminating it.

He had planned his future career out very carefully, down to the sequence of historic battle films he would produce for his growing YouTube channel. Each film of the series would be designed to make

those ancient struggles impactful and exciting for the next generation of students, while generating a solid income for Joe and his
future family. But he had failed to come up with a single suitable plan
to earn the funds he needed to get his masters degree, or his PhD,
without going deeper into debt.

Joe had also bravely laid his body on the line for extra pocket
money, playing stunt doubles for several lesser films and actors. He
had jumped off buildings into giant inflatables, rode his motorcycle
through barriers, and taken many real and imaginary punches. Yet
Joe lacked the cold-hearted bravery to ask his wealthy family for help
with his debt, even though they were in the comfortably enviable
position to make it all go away. He wanted to pay for college on
his own.

As the months slipped away, Joe Frisco drove to substitute teaching gigs by day, while editing his current movie by night. He watched
helplessly as his dreams of higher education drifted further and further away, dreading the thought of asking his family for help.

Then one morning, as Joe taught his yawning students about the
industrial age of Vanderbilt, Rockefeller, Carnegie, and Morgan and
discussed the inevitable bankruptcy that awaited their competitors,
a simple idea struck him. He would take on more debt, as much as he
would be allowed to borrow. He would go back to school to complete
his masters, and then his PhD, all on debt. He would load up his
credit cards to purchase all of the things he wanted. He would transform his life overnight with debt.

Then at the pinnacle of his debt, he would file Chapter 7 bankruptcy. He would slip into the protective arms of the government,
who would shield him from his creditors. They would be forced to

stand down and leave him alone. By that point, Joe would have his masters and his PhD, and have many fine things purchased on credit.

"I max my credit cards. Buy cool stuff for my home. New editing equipment, a TV for every room, couches, paintings, clothes..."

Joe smiled at the thought and took a sip of his beer. "I declare bankruptcy and wipe out my student debts – all of them. Then, since I can't borrow money from anyone for a few years, I sell the stuff I bought, turn it into cash, and invest that money for the future. I don't need to steal from my employer or run away from home. In 7 years, I have the bankruptcy off my record, take the cash I invested, and use it to make my films. A bright future with a clean start. That's my plan," Joe announced simply.

"Sorry, Joe," Nicole Chen said flatly. "Your plan won't work."

"No?" Joe looked up. "So, Max's plan is ok? Kelsey's plan is ok? I already know Clayton has a fighting chance to pull off his plan. I'm not going to bet against him."

Nicole had arrived at McGinty's just as Max had changed his identity to Scott Turley and was strolling through the Cheyenne Airport on his way to a new life. She had laughed along with her old friends as they took turns sharing their daring schemes for eliminating their debts. She was awed by their bravado, shocked at their cunning, inspired by their creativity, and disappointed in their morals. She had listened patiently, enjoying dinner and her friend's clever devices for dodging their debt, while she sipped the delicious merlot recommended by Kelsey.

But when Joe mentioned filing Chapter 7 bankruptcy, she had to interrupt.

"I am sorry, Joe. I have thought about Chapter 7, too. But student debt is not eligible for bankruptcy, except in very extreme circumstances."

"Those bastards!" Max shouted. He was on his fourth beer and enjoying their conspiratorial meeting immensely.

"The system is so rigged against us," Kelsey sighed. "There's no way to get out of student loan debt, unless you slave away for twenty years making those crazy high payments."

"True that," Clayton agreed. "I'm not going down that way. I need to take my debt out with one sudden coup."

Nicole sighed. The others had been drinking longer than she had, and they were fairly committed to their schemes. But she knew there was only one option. She tried a new tact. "You guys are braver than I am. And crazier. But I see this as a good thing."

"Come on, Nicole," Max protested.

"No, hear me out," Nicole insisted. "I think our student debt is going to make us stronger, more resourceful, and more creative people. I think our debts today are exactly what will make us super successful tomorrow."

"What do you mean?" Max interrupted. "How can our debt make us stronger, better people, when we are just broke and beaten people?"

"I just don't see it, Nicole," Joe agreed.

"Look no further than the Greatest Generation, Professor Frisco," Nicole reasoned. "Think about it. That generation grew up in the depression, most of them didn't have anything. They grew up on rural farms, inner cities, and small towns with absolutely nothing. Many of them didn't even have a pair of shoes. We all have ten pairs of shoes! And most of them never went to college. They went to war, instead. But they overcame their hardships. They shipped out to Europe and Asia and they won the toughest war our world had ever seen. And, today, they are rightly called the Greatest Generation. We can be like them."

Joe nodded thoughtfully. "You're saying we can fight against our student debt, the collective student debt held by our generation, and be like the Greatest Generation. We just have a different enemy. We can learn how to overcome debt, become amazing savers, and develop profitable enterprises to advance our culture."

"Exactly," Nicole agreed. They were all listening now. They all knew about the Greatest Generation. It was made up of their grand-parents and great grandparents, and they had always admired them. Everyone did.

"So, is this your plan, Nicole?" Kelsey asked.

"Yes," Nicole replied. "My plan is to overcome."

6

POWERS TO OVERCOME

Nicole Chen: Computer Science and Software Engineering, San Jose State University

Remaining Student Debt: $39,412.89

Current Position: Project Manager, Enterprise Cloud Solutions, Interloper, Inc.

Annual Salary: $125,000

In high school, Nicole Chen was always known as the girl with a plan. She proudly excelled in STEM (science, technology, engineering and math) courses and knew early on that she would have a career in high tech. She was accepted to many prestigious universities across the country, and selected San Jose State University. The cost for San Jose State was relatively low, it was ranked as one of the top schools in the country for software engineering, and Nicole was able to have a series of high-profile internships at high tech companies in Silicon Valley.

Nicole secured an internship at Interloper Technologies in her senior year, and they hired her in immediately upon graduation, allowing her to work in her choice of cities. She planned to go back to school in a few years, on Interloper's dime, to complete her masters. As a result, Nicole did not have as much student loan debt as her contemporaries, and her career was well on its way. Unfortunately, Nicole did have a love of brand names and the affluent lifestyle that went with them. She financed her expensive tastes with a series of credit cards, until they began to challenge her student loan debt for dominance.

Even though Nicole had a high salary, she was deeply in debt and eager to eliminate it as quickly as possible. She was on the fast track, and her student loan and credit card debt were holding her back. She felt like she was driving in the fast lane with the emergency brake on. Nicole was eager to create a plan to get out of debt in just a few short years.

"This guy, Oliver Powers, just wrote a book called *First Million*," Nicole explained, as they finished their plates.

"What's it about?" Kelsey asked, leaning in over her empty plate.

Nicole continued. "It's all about how to save $1 million by following 5 steps. I just finished reading it. It's a pretty cool book, and I think we could use the same steps to pay off our student loans pretty quickly."

"Seriously? You want us all to read a book?" Max shook his head. "I think I'd rather disappear."

"But you already told us your plan, Max! We all know that you're going to change your identity and disappear in Wyoming. So now it won't work," Clayton laughed.

Max hadn't considered that. He was stunned, as if his only means of escape had been permanently blocked.

"Here's a copy, Max," Nicole said, taking the book out of her purse and handing it to him. "It's super easy to read. Anyway, the author, Oliver Powers, is speaking at my church next Thursday night at 7:00 pm. I think we should all go and see what we can learn."

"What can it hurt?" Kelsey agreed. "I'm so desperate to get out of debt, I'm willing to try anything."

"Including embezzlement?" Clayton laughed.

"No judgement," Joe insisted, stepping in for Kelsey. "We were all stupid enough to get ourselves into this mess. It's not cool to bag on anyone's plans. And I think Kelsey had the best of all the plans."

"Thank you, Joe!" Kelsey raised her glass. "Glad someone has my back."

Clayton rolled his eyes.

"So, you guys are in?" Nicole asked. "It's totally free."

Everyone nodded and saved the date into their phones, as an old song from Will Keys began playing.

"Dude, I haven't heard this song in years," Joe said, as he set his phone down next to Kelsey's. "Total one hit wonder."

"Didn't Dave Roscoe discover this guy?" Clayton added.

"Yeah, before he launched the Deranged Prophets," Joe agreed.

Max rolled his eyes. "You guys and your obscure music trivia…"

"How are the Deranged Prophets obscure?" Clayton shot back.

"We can do this!" Nicole announced, getting them back on topic. "If we stick together and encourage each other, I bet we can get out of debt in three years or less."

Joe looked up. "Then I'm in."

"Me, too," Max agreed.

Clayton was quiet, surveying the empty glasses and dinner plates on the table. "I guess it's time to…."

"Hey, Max," An attractive woman in her early forties walked up to the table. She was wearing a McGinty's polo shirt, jeans, and a pair of polished cowboy boots.

"Holly!" Max climbed out of the booth and gave her a hug. "Hey, everyone, Holly is the owner of my favorite fly shop."

"Thank you, Max. It's my favorite fly shop, too," Holly replied and greeted everyone.

"I didn't know you worked here," Max exclaimed.

"Yup, I've worked here for years. I manage this place," Holly explained.

"And you run the fly shop, too?" Max was surprised.

"And I am the single mother of two perfect kids, and lead Bible studies at my church. You know me, Max. I've got too much energy to just sit around. Plus, I need to save money for my kid's college funds. I'm not going to let them take on a bunch of student debt."

They all laughed and toasted with their empty glasses. Max caught her up on the reason for their dinner. "Well then, let me buy you one last drink," Holly offered.

Another round of drinks was served, as they settled-up their tab. Holly pulled a barstool up to their horseshoe shaped table, with a Coke in hand. "Whew. Busy night."

"You guys were packed," Joe agreed. "Tired?"

"Oh, I'm used to it. I love working here. Always a fun crowd. Everyone's so friendly. The fly shop is great, but it gets a little quiet in the middle of the week," Holly took a long sip of her Coke.

"When's the last time you went fly fishing?" Max asked, enjoying his free beer.

"I'm actually going right now," Holly confided.

Max was intrigued. "Really? Where can you fish at 10:00 at night?"

Holly smiled. "You mean 11:00?" They all look at their watches, shocked at the time.

She had Max's undivided attention. "You don't mean Cherrocks?"

Holly smiled conspiratorially. "Of course, I do."

"But that place is just a legend," Max insisted.

"You mean legendary," Holly corrected him. "And it's a warm night with a full moon. The fishing will be epic. You should all come along."

Max didn't hesitate. "Seriously? We are in!"

"No, we're not!" Kelsey stated emphatically. "It's almost midnight and we have to work tomorrow."

Clayton agreed. "It's pretty late…"

Max cut him off. "What Clayton? You worried about sleeping through your party rentals job?"

"He's got a point there," Joe chuckled.

"Sorry. We can't just go fishing at midnight," Nicole insisted.

Max pleaded earnestly. "You don't understand. Holly is offering to take us to Valhalla. This is a once in a lifetime opportunity."

"He's right about that," Holly agreed. "This place is pretty secret. Private water. I have friends in remote places. I don't usually take people up there with me."

"What about fishing gear?" Joe asked, he was quickly warming to the idea.

Holly laughed. "I've got enough gear to outfit all of you. At least 10 fly rods in my suburban, all rigged for night fishing."

Kelsey looked at the cute outfit that she had put together with so much care. Her new dress, polished cowboy boots and denim jacket. "There's no way I'm going fishing in these clothes."

"I have 6 or 7 pairs of waiters in my truck. I'll set you up. I might have a shirt you can wear, too. Don't worry. I got you covered," Holly said kindly.

"And for Nicole?" Max asked.

"No problem," Holly smiled at Nicole.

"Alright, then. Tomorrow's Friday and I got a bunch of conference calls. I was going to work from home anyway," Nicole finished her drink and looked expectantly at Kelsey.

"But I don't fly fish," Kelsey protested.

"I'll teach you," Joe offered.

"OK. I'm in," Kelsey said a little too quickly.

Clayton laughed and exchanged glances with Max. "How were you planning to get home, anyway?"

"Drive," Kelsey shrugged.

"You mean you brought your car?" Max asked.

"Yeah, didn't you?"

"I took a rideshare here and I will take one home."

"Wait, seriously? You drove here? Didn't you learn anything at college?" Clayton teased.

"Yeah. What exactly did they teach you?" Max piled on.

"Accounting," Kelsey declared defiantly.

"Worthless!" Clayton decided.

"I am beginning to believe that," Kelsey agreed.

"You never drive at night," Max insisted. "You rideshare at night."

"So, I spent $200,000 for a college education and I never learned to do this?" Kelsey shook her head.

"You got ripped off!" Max proclaimed.

"We all did," Joe agreed.

"But especially, Kelsey," Clayton laughed.

They piled into Holly's suburban and took the highway east toward the foothills. Holly, Joe and Max spoke about fly fishing, as the others listened, trying to learn what they could. They left the lights of the suburbs behind and slipped into the quiet night of the country, lit by a full moon.

"Did you have student loan debt, Holly?" Kelsey asked, eager to talk about something other than fishing.

"Sure, I did," Holly replied over her shoulder, while she kept her eyes fixed on the road. "I come from a big family, with four brothers and sisters. My parents gave each of us a fixed budget for college. Anything above that budget was our responsibility. College was a lot less expensive back then, but I still needed to make about $10,000 a year to cover my part of the tuition and such. I was determined to graduate without any debt, so that meant working my way through college."

"That's cool," Joe commented. "I did the same thing. But I still graduated with a bunch of debt."

Holly nodded. "It's so much more expensive now. I remember working at a movie theatre near my college campus on the weekends. I was making peanuts and just knew I wouldn't be able to keep up with my college costs. So, I started my own business. I began promoting the movie theatre and a few other little businesses in the area on my college campus, creating special events, college student discount nights, coupon books, posters, that kind of thing. I charged these little businesses a flat monthly fee to post their flyers on campus and spread the word about their special college kid discounts. It was fun. And I made enough to cover the extra money I needed."

"Great idea," Kelsey was impressed. "And you graduated without any debt?"

"I remember at the end of each month my clients would pay me my fee and I would turn it into cash and walk it straight to the financial aid office. The people there knew me by name. They would take my cash right there in that little office and show me on the computer how they would apply it against my loan. I did that every month that I was in college. Sometimes it was a little cash. Sometimes it was a lot of cash. But I kept visiting that little office until I paid it all off. I was able to graduate without any debt. And all of those kind people in the financial aid office came and watched me graduate. It was really sweet."

"Wait? Really?" Clayton said from the front seat next to her. "That sounds like Mayberry. I don't think they do it like that anymore."

"Clayton, I don't think they did it like that then. They must have made an exception for me. I think they thought it was cute that I was carrying my cash payments in every month. I was being so careful to take control of my debt, they had pity on me. They probably had to jump through a bunch of hoops to make it work. You know, convert my cash to a check and work out the other details with the big money university lenders. But they did it and I learned a lot from that experience. I haven't been in debt since. I pay cash for everything."

Holly took a remote offramp with a large billboard sign declaring a new housing development would soon be built by Bannister-Sanchez Construction. She took an obscure right at the end of a horse fence and turned onto a dirt road, passing a colorful collection of mailboxes. The road narrowed as she drove further east and became bumpy and riddled with potholes. She began weaving between road ruts and fallen tree branches, following an old road that snaked through oak trees and along ravines. She spoke passionately of fly fishing while she drove and enjoyed entertaining her eager audience.

Holly stopped mid-sentence and jumped out of the suburban. She opened a metal chain-link fence that blocked the road and opened the combination lock. She drove past it, and Joe hopped out to close the gate and lock it behind them. They drove up to two more gates just like the first one, Holly unlocked each one, and continued following a twisting road deeper into the foothills.

As the clocks on their cell phones hit 11:55 pm, Holly pulled into a dusty turn-out and parked the suburban. They climbed out of the car to a chorus of summer crickets and the deep-throated greetings of frogs. Holly lined them all up on the dusty road, their voices excited with the adventure, and set them each up with waiters, fly rods and vests. The vests were filled with fly boxes, leaders, line, pliers, flashlights, and scissors - everything they needed to be dangerous.

"Alright, Friends," Holly said cheerfully. "You are all rigged up. Follow me. The path is a little tricky, so watch your step. And please keep your voices down to a whisper, so we don't spook the fish."

They followed Holly over the edge of the dirt road and down a steep trail that entered a stand of oak trees. The full moon lit their path, until they reached the trees and were quickly swallowed into dark shadow. They flipped on their flashlights and continued down the trail toward the bottom of the canyon, stepping over fallen branches and granite rocks. When their descent cleared the thick line of trees, they were almost blinded by the bright reflection of the moon in the Cherrocks pool.

It was a wide, oval body of water, completely still, expect for the ripples of fish as they rose to feed just below the surface. They reached the edge of the Cherrocks pool and Holly whispered instructions for which way they should head and how to cast.

"The most important thing is to make the smallest possible splash and be real quiet," she whispered. Then she sent them around the south perimeter of the pool, telling them to spread out to cast. Holly headed along the bank in the other direction, to a proven spot that only she knew.

As Nicole, Kelsey, Clayton, Joe and Max stumbled along the path in the moonlight, they were filled with a new boldness they had not experienced in a long time. They all felt a euphoric joy, a youthful newness in the embrace of their midnight adventure, like the late morning sun streaming through the windows on the first day of summer. They felt like kids again and something clicked in all five of them. It was a belief that they could do anything.

"Y'all can do this," Max promised, slipping into the country boy persona he reserved for fishing trips and eating BBQ ribs.

"What? Catch a fish?" Someone replied in the darkness.

"Not with the noise you're making," Joe whispered.

"No. Y'all can get out of debt," Max continued.

"How?" Kelsey asked, as she grasped Joe's hand in the darkness.

"I just have this feeling, like we're almost free," Max explained.

"I feel it, too," Nicole agreed. "This is amazing. We can totally do this."

"You guys are just drunk on beer and moonlight," Clayton drawled.

"No, it's more than that," Nicole agreed, a little breathless from the hike.

"Can we do it together?" Kelsey asked.

"Totally. We can help each other," Nicole continued.

"And we don't have to embezzle?" Clayton laughed.

"It's not embezzling if I don't actually take any money," Kelsey whispered harshly, then started giggling.

"And we don't need to vanish into thin air," Nicole started giggling, too.

"Or gamble away our future?" Kelsey fired back.

"Or declare bankruptcy," Joe replied.

"Shhhh!" Mas was adamant. "Have some respect for Valhalla."

They all went quiet and continued to follow the little path around the pool, winding through trees and scrub brush. They reached a rock outcropping and scrambled up the boulders, white with moonlight. They stood on the rocks and looked out over the Cherrocks pool, sparkling in the silver moonlight. They watched as the pool rippled with the pulse of feeding rainbow trout.

"OK, now what do I do?" Nicole whispered, holding her flyrod awkwardly over the water from the height of the rock.

"Wait. Where did Joe and Kelsey go?" Max whispered back.

"I think they took another turn," Clayton laughed. "Probably found a good spot."

"For fishing?"

"For something," Clayton jumped to another boulder a few yards away and then climbed down to some other rocks at the water's edge. He checked the brush behind him and saw he had the clearance he needed. He did a few false casts and shot his line out over the water. Clayton may not have been an experienced fly fisherman, but he was a gifted athlete and picked it up quickly.

"OK, Nicole," Max whispered, pointing out over the water. "Cast right there, out to the reflection of the moon. I just saw a fish rise there."

Nicole back cast her rod clumsily, but the line fed out smoothly enough and the fly skipped across the water with minimal splash.

A fish hit her line almost instantly. "Oh! Wow!"

"Shhh!" Max tried, but then started laughing.

"Whoop!" Clayton shouted at the same time. "I think I caught ol Nessy."

"Shhh!" Max tried again.

The water was alive with thrashing trout. Nicole's line was taut, and she held the reel steady against the pulsing fish as he fought the invisible tension. Max helped her steady her rod and showed her how to play the trout in gently. He whispered, "Nicole caught a lunker, too."

Max helped Nicole bring her fish to the shore. He was silver spotted, nearly two feet in length, and quivering just under the surface. Max showed her how to steady the fish in the water with wet fingers. Nicole reached into the cold pool and felt the slick weight of trembling fish as he rested in her hands.

Max slipped in close and, using pliers, quickly released the fly from the trout's mouth with a flick of the wrist. Nicole gently massaged the fish under water as Max gave instructions, until his tail began moving. Then, in an instant, the trout shot through Nicole's fingers and back into the depths of the pool, free from the tiny hook.

"Wow! That was awesome," Nicole whispered, beaming with a wide smile and drunk on the experience. "Now I see why you like fly fishing so much."

"Congratulations. That was a great fish."

"I can't believe I caught him."

"This place really is Valhalla." Max helped Nicole reset her rod and pointed her where to cast again. "You got this, girl."

Max stepped back and watched her cast again. Then climbed onto another boulder and deftly cast his own line out over the water, feeding more line out over the pool. His fly landed gently, presenting a perfect midnight snack. A large trout zipped up from the murky depths, breached the smooth surface of the moonlit pool, and snapped up the fly. Max's rod bent with the deep weight of the fish, as he raced for the bottom with the invisible line.

"Bang!" Max whispered and began to carefully play his trout. "I'm telling you, we can do this thing."

7

FREE ADVICE

The church was full of members and guests, interested in learning the principles for attaining financial independence. The building was large and contemporary, like a music hall, with comfortable chairs in neat rows that completed a semi-circle. The stage was a curved half-circle, with a single podium and a large screen displaying the slides for Oliver Powers' presentation.

Powers was in his early-thirties and wore a dark suit jacket over jeans and a light blue dress shirt, with highly polished, black dress shoes. His hair was wavy, light brown, and he had a habit of sweeping it out of his eyes with his hand to reveal blue eyes and a warm smile. He looked like the older brother that you could trust with an important secret.

Powers was soft spoken and matter of fact. He wasn't touting a get-rich-quick scheme, but a disciplined lifestyle that allowed everyone to save the money needed to become financially independent. His short book, *First Million*, shared the concept of financial independence as the amount of money a person needed to save in order not to draw an income from a salary, pension, or Social Security.

"So, as you can see, the concepts are pretty simple. It is about taking on a radical new lifestyle that paves the way to real financial security," Powers concluded. "Are there any questions?"

Several hands shot up, but Nicole stood up in the center of the church and boldly asked, "What about student debt? My friends and

I are not candidates to save a million dollars right now. We need to get out of our massive debt first."

Powers smiled and nodded. "Thank you for your question. I agree with you. You must get out of debt first, before you can begin saving your first million..."

"It's not that easy," Max interrupted, standing up beside Nicole. "We owe serious money. Almost a million dollars between the five of us. Clipping coupons just won't cut it."

The crowd erupted in laughter and Max turned to acknowledge them. Kelsey, Joe, and Clayton sunk down in their seats a little, pretending they weren't with Max.

Powers was laughing, too. "No, I get it. College debt is robbing the future from your generation. It is probably the number one impediment to your success. But you can also use it as a catalyst for great accomplishments."

"You mean, if we can get out of our debt, we can do anything?" Nicole asked.

"That's exactly what I am saying," Powers agreed. "If you can stay after the presentation for a few minutes, we can talk some more."

Max and Nicole thanked him and sat down with their friends, who were still sunk low in their chairs.

"Yes," Powers pointed to a balding man in the third row.

"So, I'm a little confused. Are you saying that I should fully fund my 401K, or invest independently?"

"Both, actually. You see..."

Powers concluded his presentation and thanked his audience again. He came down from the stage and joined Nicole and her friends in their chairs, sitting sideways as they stood or remained as they were. He listened carefully as they each discussed their stories of debt and their impossible predicaments. They also shared their daring schemes for getting out of debt. Powers was understanding, but not very sympathetic. They had each made the decisions that led to their current situations.

"I don't mean to sound harsh," Powers began. "But you all must acknowledge that your universities didn't hold a gun to your heads. They clearly stated the cost of their tuition, housing and meals and you all readily signed up for it. You should not be surprised. Your level of debt was completely predictable and 100% your responsibility. You all had many options to go to less expensive universities. You could have lived at home for the first two years while you knocked out your general education courses at community college. That simple move would have cut your debt in half. But the allure of a four-year college is very real. College is fun. Football games are fun. Those campuses are beautiful. But all of it comes with a high price tag."

They listened intently, not arguing, knowing that he was right.

"The college experience is this generation's rite of passage. There are no glorious wars to fight, or religious campaigns to sign up for, and the Peace Corp seems to have lost its luster for most young people. So, now you conquer a four-year college. And it isn't easy. You all worked hard to get into the very best college that would accept you, regardless of the price. And you can join the chorus of people who boast about their prestigious degrees and cheer for their football teams. This has become part of our culture. And the massive student debt that comes with it is part of the package, part of your rite of passage."

Wipeout!

"Alright, alright. You got us," Max said. "We all feel a little stupid right now. We drank the Kool-Aid and we are in serious trouble. So, what do we do? Will I be working at Rider Rental Car for the rest of my life to pay off my debt?"

"You can overcome it, just as previous generations overcame their challenges," Powers answered simply. "Don't lose hope. There is a way to eliminate your debt and put your lives back in the fast lane."

"That's why we're here," Kelsey sighed, eager to learn the way out. She was sitting next to Joe and he had his arm over her shoulder. They had seen each other every night since McGinty's and the midnight fly fishing adventure. Suddenly, Kelsey's life seemed 100% better and her job at Leebrick & Singleton Trucking a lot less awful. Joe was also more inspired and worked late into the night on his documentary, while taking every substitute teaching job he could find. He even started researching where to get his masters in history.

"Would you be willing to meet with us individually? Maybe you could help us create a plan to get out of debt as fast as possible?" Nicole asked. This had been her plan all along. She knew that a one-on-one coaching session with a mentor like Oliver Powers would be just the advantage they needed to stay focused and overcome their student loan debts.

Powers dropped his chin to his chest and studied his dress shoes, letting a lock of hair fall across his eyes. His mind was turning, and they all watched patiently. When they began to wonder if he had fallen asleep, Clayton spoke up. "It's cool, Man. We don't want to bother you."

Powers looked up and met Clayton's eyes. "No, it's not that. I am happy to help. I just wanted to think through a few things with my schedule. I have a proposal for each of you actually."

"It's got to be better than the proposals we came up with," Joe joked.

"I hope so. Although, I have to say that I am genuinely impressed with the ideas you each came up with to eliminate your debts. They were complex, well-reasoned, and worked to eliminate your debt. It is actually those ideas that tell me that you have the focus and determination to get out of debt in a more traditional way. Your creative approaches have given me an idea that could help all of us."

"What do you have in mind?" Nicole asked.

"I just published *First Million*. I want to start working on my next book. I am thinking that I could work with each one of you to develop a plan to get out of debt. I could meet with each of you and help you get on your way. Then, with your permission of course, I will tell your individual stories in a new book about how to eliminate student loan debt."

"You would feature us? And use our real circumstances?" Kelsey asked.

"That's what I have in mind. I think it could be helpful for others to read how you worked through your college debt. Each situation is unique. My readers would benefit from seeing the practical approach you each use."

"Would you use our real names?" Nicole asked.

"Only if you want me to. I think it might be better to create names for each of you. This will allow me to write about your real debts, salaries and budgets, without bringing any exposure or embarrassment."

"That works for me," Max said quickly.

"Max, why are you in such a hurry to change your identity? Clayton teased.

"We love you just the way you are," Joe piled on.

"So, you will coach us one-on-one and help us develop a plan to get out of debt? And, in exchange, you want to publish our stories in your next book? Is that right?" Nicole asked.

"Yes, with one addition. I think accountability groups are powerful. I want you to meet with each other once a month to go over your budgets, discuss your expenses, and help each other through the temptations of life. I think it will help you stay on track," Oliver explained. "The accountability group, brain trust, or personal board of directors is a popular concept for achieving your goals. It would be one of the steps I would want you to follow as you work through your debts collectively."

"You want us to meet once a month at McGinty's? And share our dirty laundry with each other?" Max asked. "Sounds awesome."

"Let's find a cheaper happy hour," Kelsey said. "I get the feeling we're going to be living on a tight budget for a while."

Powers nodded. "The power of an accountability group cannot be understated. Whether you are trying to beat an addiction, or start a business…"

"Or get out of massive student loan debt," Kelsey chipped in.

"Exactly. You will all behave differently in the context of the group. You will prioritize your lives to make sure that you are keeping up your side of the bargain. This approach will help you each get out of debt very quickly."

"How quickly?" Joe asked.

"We'll have to see," Powers replied. "Your current debt path is set for ten or twenty years. But I want to see you eliminate your debts in more like two or three years."

"Really!" Kelsey was over-joyed. "That would be a dream."

"Sign me up," Joe agreed.

"When can we start?" Max joined in.

"Does everyone have their calendars?" Oliver Powers asked, pulling his phone out of his suit pocket.

8

FIVE STEPS TO ELIMINATE
YOUR COLLEGE DEBT

Prior to his next meeting with each of his new friends, Oliver Powers worked on a list of the steps he believed were needed for paying off college debt, which was similar to the 5 steps he shared in his book *First Million*. The steps were meant to be easy to follow and easy to remember, while yielding the results that would get each of them out of debt in just a few years.

After careful thought and research, this is what Oliver came up with:

Five Steps to Eliminate Your College Debt

1. **Form an Accountability Group**

2. **Set Your Goals**

3. **Face Your Debt**

4. **Lower Your Overhead**

5. **Create a Budget with Money Left Over to Quickly Eliminate Debt**

He then enumerated the concepts of each step:

Step 1: Form an Accountability Group:

- Create a group of people who are approximately your age and share your set of challenges.

- Develop a culture of honesty where everyone tells it like it is. This means that you share your amount of debt, your income, your expenses, and your personal struggles with each other.

- Meet frequently. Once a month is recommended, so you can review each other's monthly expenses, offer suggestions to save money, encourage each other to stay on your plan, and discourage each other from spending on items that are not in your budget.

- Invite an older, more experienced person to attend the group and act as a coach, mentor, or counselor. Have them work with each person individually to refine their plans to pay their debt off faster.

Step 2: Face Your Debt

- Create your list of debts. Order them with the highest rates of interest at the top.

- Include your student loans, credit cards, car loan, mortgage, and money owed to friends.

- Pay off the debts with the highest interest rates first. These are probably your credit cards.

- Once you pay off your first debt, add the monthly payment from that debt to pay off the next one. Each time you eliminate a debt, use that former payment to tackle the rest of your debts. This cascading effect of increased monthly money will allow you to pay your debts off faster. Then focus on eliminating your long-term student loan debt.

Step 3: Set Your Goals

- Within the context of the group, develop your goals for your life and for eliminating your student loan debt. Write them down and commit them to memory. Refer to them daily.

- Review your goals with your accountability group. Then share your results. Continue to refine your goals to fast track your debt repayment and accomplish your life dreams.

- Work hard on your goals. Hard work creates unlimited opportunities for greater income and ways to save money.

Step 4: Lower Your Overhead

- Live beneath your means. Make sure you have plenty of money left over each month for tackling your student loan debt.

- Stop trying to compete with or impress others.

- Reject luxury and status items and buy only quality necessities.

- Refrain from spending money unnecessarily.

- Alter your entertainment expenses and look for free or inexpensive ways to spend your time. Take advantage of the free features of your community: parks, beaches, libraries, hiking trails, and special events.

- Focus on living very comfortably on 80% to 90% of your current after-tax income.

- Enjoy the amazing benefits or a life where you no longer worry about money.

Step 5: Create a Budget with Money Left Over to Quickly Eliminate Debt

- Include all expenses as you create your budget.

- Reduce expenses until you are saving at least 10% to 20% each month.

- Use the 10% to 20% of monthly savings to pay off your debts. Then begin saving.

- If you are unable to save 10% to 20% with your current income and expenses, it's time to make some larger adjustments. If you have car payments, consider selling your current car and buying an inexpensive used car. Consider selling your home and finding something more affordable with solid potential for appreciation. Or consider renting a less expensive home.

- Join the revolution of cord-cutters and eliminate your cable bill. Drop your gym membership and find no cost ways to exercise. Cook at home. Make your own coffee.

- To increase your income, take advantage of the gig economy. Wait tables, drive for a ride share service on nights and weekends, deliver meals, take on a fun part-time job, or start a side business. Save this extra money and apply it to your debt.

- Pay cash for everything that you can. This will not work for your rent or your mortgage, but almost everything else can be purchased with cash. Cash is harder to spend than using a debit or a credit card. You are more likely to want to hold onto that $20 bill. Create cash envelopes for different expense categories like Groceries, Entertainment, Hair Care, Clothing, and Miscellaneous. Then set a budget, withdraw the cash at the beginning of each month, and place it in the envelopes in a secure lock box at home. Once you spend the money in an envelope and it is gone, do not replace it with more cash or begin using credit cards for these categories. Once the money is gone, you are done spending on that category until next month. For higher ticket items, save the cash in your envelopes for a few months until you have enough to buy what you want. Cash envelopes are incredibly effective and will help you stay on budget. You can spend the cash on these categories guilt free, knowing that this is part of your plan.

- Consider Tithing. If you honor God, He will bless you. You cannot out give God. If you tithe or give to a charity faithfully, you will be amazed at how the money you give comes right back to you, often multiplied many times over.

Oliver typed up the 5 steps and made copies for each person in the group. He was ready for his first coaching session.

9

MAX HIATT

<u>Max Hiatt:</u> Marketing Major, University of Texas.

Remaining Student Debt: $93,715.78

Current Position: Account Coordinator, Management Training, Rider Rental Car Company

Annual Salary: $48,500 + Bonuses and Overtime.

"It sounds like a good first job," Oliver commented, as Max described his management training program at Rider Rental Car, including his base salary, and the overtime bonus structure. Oliver was wearing sneakers, faded jeans, and a polo shirt. Max matched the casual dress code with jeans and a hoodie sweatshirt.

They were sitting in a conference room that Max had borrowed from one of his friends from church. They were on the fourth floor of a building that looked out over the freeway and the foothill neighborhoods beyond it. The room was spacious and well-decorated, with modern art, a glass conference table, and comfortable chairs. Oliver had brought a stack of grid paper, pens, and his laptop. They were both sipping ice-cold Diet Cokes from the minifridge tucked inside one of the credenzas that curved along the wall, opposite the floor-to-ceiling glass. It was the sort of office building Max was hoping to work in for his next job, rather than racing back and forth across a dusty parking lot to his car rental office.

"I guess so," Max replied as he watched Oliver fire up his laptop. "I just thought I would be doing something bigger. You know, more impressive."

"I know the feeling," Oliver commiserated and handed Max a pad of grid paper, along with the 5 steps he created to eliminate college debt. "My career started a lot like yours. I was just a low-level employee at a search engine optimization company. I put a few years in there and noticed that my skillset was super valuable to companies who needed help with their online marketing. That led to my next job in hotel marketing. And it was through that job I was introduced to the 5 Steps and wrote *First Million*. So, now I am doing this. Just be patient and work hard. The opportunities will find you. They always do."

"Thanks. I need to hear that. Because right now my self-esteem needs a major boost. I have so much debt and so little salary."

"I get it," Oliver said with understanding. He spent a few minutes going over the 5 steps with Max, including the notes he had typed up as a guideline. "I would like you to work with the others as an accountability group. If you work as a team and follow these guidelines, I am confident that you will get out of debt quickly."

Max studied the 5 steps and the accompanying notes. After a few minutes he looked up at Oliver. "This all seems reasonable to me. It's really common sense when you think about it."

"I am glad to hear you say that. Accepting the mission to get out of debt is the biggest step."

"Slam dunk. So, what do we do next?" Max was eager to get started.

"It's time to follow the 5 Steps. But before we dive in, can you share your plan with me again?"

"My plan? You mean the spoofs we put together for Nicole? Our daring schemes for getting out of debt?" Max asked, as he skimmed over the 5 Steps.

"That's exactly what I mean."

"But why? They were mostly illegal and pretty unrealistic," Max asked, as he wrote some notes at the top of the pad of grid paper.

"Because your scheme tells me a lot about you; how you think, what your goals are, and what you are willing to do to get out of debt," Oliver explained, taking a quick sip of his Diet Coke.

"Oh, I see, Professor Powers. It's like a *Rorschach* test," Max laughed.

"Exactly," Oliver said. "But I'm not a professor, Max."

"You are to me," Max laughed and recounted his scheme to pay someone in the underworld to create his new identity. He would become Scott Turley, vanish from his current life, walk away from his debts, and move to Wyoming. To support himself, Max planned to work as a fly-fishing guide, a river rafting guide, and a bar-tender while pursuing his real estate license. "So, what does that tell you about me?"

"A few things," Oliver replied, after hearing Max's plan again. "It tells me that you have a creative imagination. You are willing to work nights and weekends to make ends meet. You enjoy the outdoors and crave a more relaxed lifestyle. And it sounds like you have a long-term goal of owning your own business."

"Yeah, you nailed it," Max shook his head. "I didn't realize I was so easy to read."

"As you put your new plan together, it is important to understand who you are and what you are prepared to do to reach your goals."

"That makes sense," Max took a sip of his Diet Coke and leaned back in his chair. It was an early Saturday morning, and his friend had said they could use the conference room all day, while he worked in his office down the hall to catch up on a project.

"Let's get started on your new plan and we will follow the 5 Steps as you put it together." Oliver repeated the 5 Steps to provide the structure for Max's new plan.

Step 1: Form an Accountability Group

Step 2: Face Your Debt

Step 3: Set Your Goals

Step 4: Lower Your Overhead

Step 5: Create a Budget with Money Left Over
to Quickly Eliminate Debt

"Got it," Max said after reviewing the list. "OK, step one form an accountability group. I can check that box. Clayton, Joe, Kelsey, and Nicole. We have already started meeting."

"You're off to a good start. And step two? Facing your debt?"

"I haven't gone there, yet," Max declared. "It's not pretty."

"I understand. But you need to know what you are fighting against. Use the grid paper and make a list of your debts," Oliver replied smoothly, using their momentum to encourage Max to take the next step.

Max sighed and wrote his debts out on his pad. To get the most accurate numbers, he had to make some calls and visit the necessary websites to check his balances for his credit cards, car loan, and each student loan debt, while Oliver waited patiently. It was an important exercise and Oliver reassured him along the way. It took nearly an hour, but Max was able to gather the latest details for his list.

"That was painful," Max sighed, totally discouraged. "Pretty grizzly stuff, Professor Powers."

"Have you ever listed them out like this before?"

"Never. I have always been too afraid."

"I understand. But a key step to this process is facing your debt. As you look at your debts, what are you thinking?"

Max considered that for a while. "I guess it is better to see them all on one page. I knew about my debts, but I never really put them all together before. I guess you're right. It is better to meet your enemy face-to-face."

The final list of Max's debts looked like this:

List of Max's Debts	
Credit Cards	$ 3,978.00
Department Store Credit Cards	$ 873.00
Car Loan	$ 17,455.00
Student Loan #1	$ 3,500.00
Student Loan #2	$ 84,675.00
Student Loan #3	$ 5,450.00
Total Debt:	**$ 115,931.00**

Oliver read over the list again. "Now you just need to create your goals for paying them off."

"Seems totally impossible," Max insisted.

"One step at a time. Every great journey begins with a single step. And that is how you will pay off your debts. One step at a time."

Oliver ordered sandwiches to be delivered and they continued working through lunch.

"Now I need to create my goals for step three," Max spoke while he chewed his sandwich. "Let's see…"

Max wrote for a few minutes, erasing and rewriting a few times until he created the following list of goals:

1. **Get Out of Debt as Fast as Possible.**
2. **Do This on My Own.**
   Do Not Ask Anyone for Financial Help.
3. **Find a New Job that I Really Like.**
4. **Never Get in Debt Again.**
5. **Save Up and Take a Trip to Europe to Celebrate.**

"How do you feel about your goals?"

"I like them," Max said admiring his list. "It seems totally impossible, but if I could accomplish everything on this list…"

"What?" Oliver pressed.

"It would be amazing," Max proclaimed.

"Good. And you will do it. All of it," Oliver encouraged him.

Max was suddenly energized. "What's next? Step four is lower my overhead. I don't know. I feel like I am already living a pretty Spartan life."

"There are thousands of ways to adjust your lifestyle to make it more affordable. This will become evident as we work through your budget. I sent you a text, asking you to put a detailed budget together for your current expenses. Were you able to get that done for today?"

"It's right here, Professor Powers," Max replied and presented his budget to Oliver.

This is what his first draft looked like:

Annual Income of $48,500.00

Monthly Income		
Salary Income (before taxes, social security, etc.):	$ 4,042.00	
401K Contribution	$ 00.00	
Subtract Estimated Taxes Withheld Each Month	$ 800.00	
Total Monthly Take Home Income:		**$ 3,242.00**
Monthly Fixed Expenses:		
Rent	$ 1,600.00	
Car Payment	$ 315.00	
Minimum Credit Card Payment	$ 50.00	
Gym Membership	$ 25.00	
Student Loan #1: Non-Consolidated ($3,500 @ 2% / 5 years)	$ 61.00	
Student Loan #2: Consolidated ($84,765@ 5.75% / 20 years)	$ 595.00	
Student Loan #3: Perkins Loan ($5,450 @ 4.5% / 10 years)	$ 56.00	
Cell Phone	$ 89.00	
Home Phone / Cable / Internet	$ 214.00	
Water / Electricity & Gas	$ 119.00	
Car Insurance	$ 84.00	
Total Fixed Monthly Expenses:		**$ 3,208**
Remaining Balance:		**$ 34.00**
Additional Expenses – Cash or Credit Card:		
Savings	$ 00.00	
Groceries	$ 300.00	
Meals & Entertainment	$ 50.00	
Gas for Car	$ 250.00	
Personal / Clothes Fund	$ 50.00	
Total Additional Expenses:		**$ 650.00**
Remaining Balance:	Negative	-$ 616.00

Oliver looked over Max's budget line by line and jotted some notes. "This is a great start. I see a few changes that should really help you. And I have one key word for you, Max."

"What's that?"

"Overtime."

"Really? You think if I volunteer for more overtime it will make a big difference?"

"It will be life changing." Oliver smiled, jotting some more notes. "I have a few more questions before we start to rework your budget."

"Sure…" Max took a final bite of his sandwich.

"It looks like you are negative each month for about $600. Is that right?"

"Yeah, but it's worse than that. In reality, I use my credit card a lot to go out and such."

"Your short fall, and your social life, explains your credit card debt?"

"Pretty much…"

"And you are renting?"

"Yes, I've had the same place for a while. It's a one bedroom."

"So, no roommates?"

"No, after college, I needed a break from roommates. You think I need to change that?"

"Or move home with your parents."

"That can't happen. My dad died and my mom lives in Europe with her new family."

"That must have been very difficult for you. I'm sorry."

"Thanks. It's been an adjustment," Max admitted candidly.

"I can't begin to imagine. So, yes, you need to change your living situation and take on a few roommates. And look for a better deal. Your goal should be to lower your rent by about $1,000 per month."

Max sighed deeply. "I thought you might say that. It sounds like I will be moving inland, away from the beach."

"Yes, if you are serious about eliminating your debt quickly, this is a lifestyle change you need to make. Unless you can find an inexpensive room to rent closer to the coast. But I would suggest that you look for a place closer to your job. That will cut down on your monthly gas expenses."

"Right..." Max said, with little enthusiasm.

"Is there anything missing, Max?" Oliver looked up from the budget.

"Well, yeah," Max said, a little reluctantly. "I'm pretty active in my church. They really helped me through my tough times. I want to make God a priority in my life. I want to tithe, but I just don't see how I can right now."

"I understand. Tithing is important. Giving to charity is important. And it has been my experience that the more you give, the more the blessings come back to you. It's an amazing dynamic and I want to encourage you to begin giving as soon as you can."

"But not right now?" Max asked.

"I think you should get out of debt first," Oliver said sympathetically. "But there are other ways that you can give. You can volunteer your time, donate clothing and canned food, help as a greeter or an usher, set up their mission trips, or feed the homeless. You can tithe your time, until you can afford to give money."

Max brightened. "That sounds cool. I can do those things."

"Well, let's see what we can do with the help of a few roommates and some overtime," Oliver replied. "And a different car."

"A new car?"

"It will be new to you. You need to get rid of your current car."

"But I think I'm upside down on it," Max replied.

"Yes, it's too bad you don't work in the auto industry and have access to some nice used cars..."

"So, you're saying I should try to work a deal through my employer, Rider Rental Car?"

"That's exactly what I am saying. See if your manager can help you unwind your current car loan, and help you find a cheaper used car."

"He's not that kind of a guy. He's all business. If you know what I mean..."

"You might be surprised, Max. Plus, you are about to offer to cover every extra shift he can give you legally. With the overtime you are going to be working, you are about to become his favorite employee."

"Oh, I get it. You want me to cut a deal," Max nodded. "He helps me make more money and nail down a better car deal, and I become his indentured servant."

"Something like that," Oliver laughed. "But at the end of your servitude, you will be debt free and have a ton of great work experience. This is the perfect job to get out of debt, Max."

"I'm not convinced," Max replied skeptically, "But let's see what you have in mind."

Oliver got to work on a new budget. This is what he came up with.

Annual Income of $62,500.00

Monthly Income		
Salary Income (before taxes, social security, etc.):	$ 4,042.00	
Overtime & Bonuses	$ 1,166.00	
Second Job	$ 800.00	
401K Contribution – Max it out, after debts are paid	$ 00.00	
Estimated Taxes Withheld Each Month	$ 1,200.00	
Total Monthly Take Home Income:		**$ 4,808.00**
Monthly Fixed Expenses:		
Tithe (10% once debt free)	$ 00.00	
Rent	$ 515.00	
Car Payment	$ 00.00	
Minimum Credit Card Payment	$ 50.00	
Gym Membership	$ 00.00	
Student Loan #1: Non-Consolidated ($3,500 @ 2% / 5 years)	$ 61.00	
Student Loan #2: Consolidated ($84,765@ 5.75% / 20 years)	$ 595.00	
Student Loan #3: Perkins Loan ($5,450 @ 4.5% / 10 years)	$ 56.00	
Cell Phone	$ 89.00	
Home Phone / Cable / Internet	$ 72.00	
Water / Electricity & Gas	$ 43.00	
Car Insurance	$ 58.00	
Renters Insurance	$ 35.00	
Total Fixed Monthly Expenses:		**$1,574.00**
Remaining Balance:		**$3,234.00**
Additional Expenses - Cash:		
Savings	$ 00.00	
Groceries	$ 300.00	
Meals & Entertainment	$ 25.00	
Gas for Car	$ 150.00	

Personal / Clothes Fund	$ 25.00	
Total Additional Expenses:		$ 500.00
Remaining Balance:		$2,734.00

"A second job?"

"Yes. But make it a fun job. Drive for a rideshare company, deliver meals for restaurants, tend bar or wait tables on the weekends. Mow lawns or wash cars. Start a little moving company. Anything that will help you earn another $200 per week, or $800 more for the month."

"You mean like work in a fly-fishing shop?"

"Why not?"

"I got it," Max said, unfazed by the extra work. "So, I have an extra $2,700 per month?"

"$2,734," Oliver corrected.

"Right," Max shrugged. "So, what do I do with it?"

"First, you buy a used car and get rid of your expensive car loan. Then you tackle your largest, scariest, highest interest rate debt. And keep paying it down until it's gone."

"What's my budget for the new car?"

"Try to keep it to two or three months of this extra money. $5,000 or $6,000, ideally."

"Alright. I will see what I can do. Then, which debt do I pay off first?"

"It's tempting to pay off your largest student loan first, but I want you to eliminate your credit card. It has a much higher interest rate. And you can pay it off in 2 months."

"And then I tackle the big monster student loan debt?"

"Exactly. And then the smaller ones. So, your debt payment structure will look like this," Oliver said and made the following table:

List of Max's Debts		
Purchase Used Car	$ 5,400.00	Month 1 & 2
Credit Cards	$ 3,978.00	Month 3 & 4
Department Store Credit Cards	$ 873.00	Month 4
Car Loan	$ 00.00	
Student Loan #1	$ 3,500.00	Month 36 & 37
Student Loan #2	$ 84,675.00	Month 4 – 35
Student Loan #3	$ 5,450.00	Month 35 & 36
Total Debt:	**$ 103,876.00**	**Paid: 3 years, 2 months**

"Wait! Really?" Max felt tears in his eyes. "You're saying that if I work lots of overtime, take on some roommates, get rid of my cool car and buy a junker, find a cheaper place to live, quit my gym and take up jogging, and work a crazy fun job every Saturday, I will be out of debt in just over three years."

"Yes, that's the plan."

"And I don't need to change my identity and vanish?"

"No, you just need to work your ass off, Max," Oliver explained. "And live humbly for a few years. And this plan does not include raises, or a new job with a higher salary, which you will earn if you work this hard. So, I think you will be out of debt even faster. Then you can start tithing, contribute the maximum amount to your 401K, save up to pay cash for a new car, and start to raise your standard of living."

"Wow! Professor Powers, you have made me a believer," Max was overjoyed with relief and close to tears.

"I'm glad I can help. You have a plan that works. Just to stick with it and don't quit. Even when it gets hard, don't quit," Oliver insisted. "And it will get hard."

"Nothing is as hard as facing my mountain of debt. I'd run through brick walls, if it would help. I'm all in, Professor."

10

KELSEY SIZEMORE

Kelsey Sizemore: Accounting Major and MBA, University of Arizona

Remaining Student Debt: $104,812.61

Current Position: Assistant Accounts Payable Manager, Leebrick & Singleton Trucking Company

Annual Salary: $31,300

"Max told me you helped him create a plan to eliminate all of his debt in about three years," Kelsey said as she settled into her chair. They were sitting on the patio of a local coffee shop. It was an early Saturday morning and there were few other people up. Kelsey was bundled in a thick, zip-up hoodie sweatshirt and jeans, and held her steaming latte in both hands to warm them.

"Is it too cold out here for you?" Oliver asked.

"No, I love it. I am stuck inside a creepy, dark office all week. I try to stay outside all weekend, no matter how cold it is," Kelsey explained. "Is this ok for you?"

Oliver was wearing a sweater under his jacket and looked warm. "I'm fine, thanks. I'd rather be outside, too."

"So, Max..."

"Yes, that's right. He had about $116,000 in total debt, as you know from your accountability group. With the plan he created, he will pay it all off in about three years."

"That's amazing," Kelsey said enthusiastically, slurping her hot coffee.

"I think so, too," Oliver smiled and watched the sun begin to clear the trees on the ridge to the east.

"But you do this all the time, right? So, it must be kind of old hat for you," Kelsey wondered.

"I saw it in my own life and became a believer. But it always amazes me how quickly debt can be eliminated when you really put your heart into it. It's powerful," Oliver said.

"Max is totally stoked. He called all of us to say how excited he was. He really thought he was sunk. He's already moved to a new apartment with some friends from his church and traded his car payment in for a used car that Rider Rental Car helped him find at auction."

"Yeah, he texted me a picture. It looks like a good car for $5,400."

"Is that all that he paid?"

"Yeah, there are plenty of cheap cars out there, if you take the time to look for them."

"Well, I already have a car. My parents helped me buy it in high school. So, I am lucky. I don't have a car payment."

"And you can drive it for the next few years?"

"Definitely. It's nothing fancy, but I am happy with it. I like owning it and not having a car payment."

"I know exactly what you mean," Oliver nodded and took a sip of his coffee. "Did you bring your assignment?"

"Yes, I have a list of my debts, my goals and my budget," Kelsey said as she pulled a small spiral notepad out of her purse. She handed them to Oliver and he began leafing through them. "I also read the notes you emailed us, with the 5 steps to eliminate our college debt. Those were really helpful."

"Good. I am glad they helped. You already have step one in action, since you have your accountability group," Oliver said, looking up from her notes.

"Yeah, it's really weird for me to share my salary and debts with other people. My family taught me that money should never be discussed with other people."

"Is it helpful?"

"I was surprised. Once I shared it with my friends, and they shared their situations with me, I quickly saw how helpful it is to talk through my money troubles. Everyone had good ideas."

She handed her notes to Oliver and he began to look them over. As he wrote in the margins, Kelsey spoke a little nervously. "So, Max told me how you took his budget and made a bunch of adjustments to it to set aside a few thousand dollars to tackle the debt. So, the budget you have in front of you is what I am doing now. I also put together a second budget, you will see a few pages in. That is the budget I want to get to, with your help."

Oliver turned the pages and began reading through the second budget. "This is really good," He said. "You're an accountant, right?"

"Yes, for Leebrick & Singleton Trucking," Kelsey reported, taking a nervous sip of her coffee.

"But in this second budget, you have a completely different salary," Oliver commented. "Tell me about that."

"I have decided that I need to find a new job. I have been at Leebrick & Singleton Trucking for almost a year. I hate my job and I need to leave. I want to find a new job that pays better and has more potential."

"That's a great idea. You have some solid work experience now. I am sure you will find something soon. There is something about looking for a job when you already have one that is really powerful."

"Like you're a hot property, or something?"

"Yes, when you don't have a job, employers sense a level of desperation. That desperation is replaced by confidence, options, and opportunities when you already have a job."

"Yeah, I think that's true," Kelsey agreed. "A few of the sub-contractors that we work with have asked if I would be willing to come to work for them. I'm not interested in moving to another city right now, so I have said no."

"But it's nice to have the interest, isn't it?"

"It's great. And it made me realize that I am not the same person I was a year ago. I have more value and more confidence. I think my next job search will be a lot more successful."

"And tell me about your daring scheme," Oliver said, looking up from the second budget.

"Oh, that!" Kelsey laughed. "Max warned me you would want to talk through it."

"Are you ok with it?"

"Yeah, but it was kind of a joke really. I meant to share it only with my friends. I would never really do it."

"Do what?"

"Embezzle from my employer..." Kelsey admitted reluctantly.

"Really? Sounds interesting."

Kelsey went through her scheme, sharing the nuances of her office and the people she worked with. She explained the early payment discount concept, and how she could set up a series of companies to float the money.

"So, it's not really stealing…" Oliver said, as she wrapped up the details of her scheme.

"Technically, no."

"You don't look like a thief."

"Thank you." Kelsey smiled. "And I'm really not. But Nicole mentioned a daring scheme to get out of debt and I had been watching the situation for a while. There is a fortune in savings available for my company and it frustrates me that they don't take advantage of it."

"Did you really negotiate those savings with the subcontractors?"

"I did, and Mr. Singleton shot me down. He wasn't at all interested. Said I was wasting my time."

"But then you got some job offers from those same subcontractors, because they saw how you were taking the initiative to make your company more profitable," Oliver said carefully.

"That's right," Kelsey replied, surprised that he had connected the dots so quickly.

"So, just because Leebrick & Singleton Trucking does not appreciate your talents, it doesn't mean that another company won't."

"Exactly. That's what has encouraged me to start looking for a new job."

"Then your plan worked," Oliver commended her. "You have a talent for ringing profit from a company's operational budget. That is a gift that many companies will be interested in."

"Thank you," Kelsey was encouraged. "I like the way you said that."

"And how about your list of debts?" Oliver asked, taking another sip of coffee.

"Max warned me about that, too. It should be on the third page." Kelsey also took a sip of coffee, letting the heat run deep into her chest.

List of Kelsey's Debts	
Credit Cards	00.00
Car Loan	00.00
Other Debts	00.00
Student Loan	$104,812.00
Total Debt:	**$104,812.00**

"So, just the student loan debt?"

"Yeah, I figure that's enough..."

"I agree. You've done a great job in managing your finances. You've kept it simple."

"Well, I am an accountant."

"An accountant with goals?" Oliver asked, hopefully.

"Oh yeah, I've got lots of goals," Kelsey replied with a smile. "But I just put the major financial goals on page two."

Oliver flipped back to page two and read over her goals. He was impressed.

1. **Find a New Job that Pays at least $50,000 per year**

2. **Eliminate All of My Debts**

3. **Save $90,000 for a Down Payment for a House**

4. **Start My Own Business**

"These are great goals," Oliver replied after reading through them.

"Thanks," Kelsey replied. "I have more, but they are kind of personal."

"No, this is fine," Oliver tapped the list and flipped back to the first pages in her notepad. "And you are ready to take step three?"

"Lower my overhead? Yeah, right away. Whatever it takes."

"Super. Now let's take a look at your first budget. This is what you are doing now?"

"Yes, but not for much longer. I am inspired to make some changes pretty quickly."

Annual Income of $31,300

Monthly Income		
Salary Income (before taxes, social security, etc.):	$ 2,608.00	
Estimated Taxes Withheld Each Month	$ 521.00	
Total Monthly Take Home Income:		**$ 2,087.00**
Monthly Fixed Expenses:		
Student Loan- Consolidated ($104,812.61@ 4.5% / 20 years)	$ 663.00	
Rent	$ 600.00	
Home Phone / Cable / Internet	$ 123.00	
Car Insurance	$ 74.00	
Cell Phone	$ 69.00	
Water / Electricity & Gas	$ 62.00	
Gym Membership	$ 45.00	
Total Fixed Monthly Expenses:		**$1,636.00**
Remaining Balance:		**$ 451.00**
Additional Expenses - Cash:		
Groceries	$ 250.00	
Gas for Car	$ 100.00	
Dinner Out & Entertainment	$ 50.00	
Personal / Clothes Fund	$ 50.00	
Total Additional Expenses:		**$ 450.00**
Remaining Balance:		**$ 1.00**

"You did a great job on this budget, considering..."

"Considering I don't make very much money?" Kelsey replied, a little ashamed.

"Well, yeah. It's really difficult to live on $2,000 per month."

"You're telling me!"

"So, you rent an apartment. Do you have a roommate?"

"Yeah, Stephanie and I went to college together. We share a little place near the train tracks. It's very glamorous."

"I can imagine," Oliver smiled. "And I can see by your second budget that you are planning to move home?"

"Yes, I don't see any other way to take out my debt. It's not something I want to do…"

"Loss of independence?"

"No, my parents are super cool. I guess it's just a pride thing. I mean, I have my MBA and top grades from a good university. It's humbling to live at home after what I have accomplished."

"But the debt is more humbling?"

"Miles more…. It keeps me awake at night."

"You will save a fortune living at home," Oliver said, taking another sip of his coffee.

"My parents are really happy about it. They offered to take care of my student loan debt, but I don't want them to do that. They need to save for retirement. I want them to be financially secure as they get older. It will make my future life easier, too."

"You won't have to worry about them. That's smart. But they can help you a great deal by allowing you to live at home."

"Exactly…"

"So, let's look at your new budget. The one you are so excited about."

"It is exciting. I save so much money by moving home. I can basically devote my whole salary to my debt."

"Plus, you list the higher salary for a new job?"

"Yes, this whole budget will go into effect in three months. I needed to give my roommate notice and I will need time to find a new job."

Annual Income of $50,000

Monthly Income		
Salary Income (before taxes, social security, etc.):	$ 4,166.00	
Estimated Taxes Withheld Each Month	$ 850.00	
Total Monthly Take Home Income:		**$ 3,316.00**
Monthly Fixed Expenses:		
Student Loan- Consolidated ($104,812.61@ 4.5% / 20 years)	$ 663.00	
Rent	$ 00.00	
Home Phone / Cable / Internet	$ 00.00	
Car Insurance	$ 74.00	
Cell Phone	$ 69.00	
Water / Electricity & Gas	$ 00.00	
Gym Membership	$ 45.00	
Total Fixed Monthly Expenses:		**$ 851.00**
Remaining Balance:		**$ 2,465.00**
Additional Expenses - Cash:		
Groceries	$ 00.00	
Gas for Car	$ 100.00	
Dinner Out & Entertainment	$ 50.00	
Personal / Clothes Fund	$ 50.00	
Total Additional Expenses:		**$ 200.00**
Remaining Balance:		**$2,265.00**

Oliver finished his review of Kelsey's new budget. "Very impressive. This is really going to help you get out of debt quickly."

"Yeah, I'm exciting about it."

"So, it looks like your debt repayment will look something like this…"

List of Kelsey's Debts		
Credit Cards	00.00	
Car Loan	00.00	
Other Debts	00.00	
Student Loan	$104,812.00	Month 3 - 48
Total Debt:	**$104,812.00**	

Kelsey sighed. "Yeah, four more years of living at home. I wanted to get it done a lot faster than that."

"And you will, Kelsey. We're not finished yet."

"Really?"

"Yeah, we haven't talked about your weekends, yet."

"My weekend? What do you mean?"

"You're an accountant. You can help people with their taxes."

"On the weekends? You think I should?"

"Absolutely! You can earn big bucks, especially during the tax season working on your own, or for one of the larger tax preparation chains."

"Yeah, I used to do that. I guess, I am so tired after the work week that I never considered working weekends, too."

"It's up to you, Kelsey. But it will get you out of debt a lot faster if we can add tax prep to your income. Plus, this could be the beginning of owning your own business."

"Let's do it," Kelsey grabbed her calculator and ran the numbers, based on what she thought she could charge and how many hours she thought she could bill. She was able to add an additional annual income of $18,000. The resulting budget looked like this.

Annual Income of $68,000

Monthly Income		
Salary Income (before taxes, social security, etc.):	$ 5,666.00	
Estimated Taxes Withheld Each Month	$ 1,140.00	
Total Monthly Take Home Income:		**$ 4,526.00**
Monthly Fixed Expenses:		
Student Loan- Consolidated ($104,812.61@ 4.5% / 20 years)	$ 663.00	
Rent	$ 00.00	
Home Phone / Cable / Internet	$ 00.00	
Car Insurance	$ 74.00	
Cell Phone	$ 69.00	
Water / Electricity & Gas	$ 00.00	
Gym Membership	$ 45.00	
Total Fixed Monthly Expenses:		**$ 851.00**
Remaining Balance:		**$ 3,675.00**
Additional Expenses - Cash:		
Groceries	$ 00.00	
Gas for Car	$ 150.00	
Dinner Out & Entertainment	$ 50.00	
Personal / Clothes Fund	$ 50.00	
Total Additional Expenses:		**$ 250.00**
Remaining Balance:		**$3,425.00**

"Now I feel like I am earning MBA money," Kelsey announced, excited at the added income.

"Exactly. Our earning potential should not be defined only by our main jobs. It is always best to create a scenario where your income comes from multiple sources, especially when you are so deep in debt," Oliver explained.

"So, what does my debt repayment schedule look like?"

"I think you will really like the change…"

"Enough to work weekends?"

"Only part-time. You can have a flexible schedule and work nights and weekends as you wish. You'll see. It will be a lot like college when you went to classes and lectures all day…."

"And studied all night?"

"Exactly…"

List of Kelsey's Debts		
Credit Cards	00.00	
Car Loan	00.00	
Other Debts	00.00	
Student Loan	$104,812.00	Month 3 - 34
Total Debt:	**$104,812.00**	

"Now, I will be out of debt in just under three years!"

"The time will fly. And this does not include raises, or new jobs opportunities that you will surely earn."

"Thank you, Oliver," Kelsey said, standing up to give him a hug. "I feel like I just got my life back."

11

CLAYTON MOSS

Clayton Moss: Philosophy & Political Science Major, Georgetown University

Remaining Student Debt: $128,893.03

Current Position: Entrepreneur and Part-Time Assistant Manager, Fiesta Party Rentals

Annual Salary: $12,450

"Have you always been a risk taker?" Oliver Powers asked. He was fresh from a radio interview and was wearing a jacket and tie. While no one could see him through the radio, Oliver wisely dressed up for the inevitable social media photos. Oliver reasoned that it helped to look professional when trying to convince people that you have the wisdom to help them save a million dollars.

They were sitting in a large warehouse owned by Fiesta Party Rentals. Folding chairs were stacked all around them, with columns of neatly stacked tables, large cases of linens and artificial trees and bushes. Twinkle lights were wound on reels that filled the shelves, along with candles in a hundred styles.

"Pretty much," Clayton confided. He was wearing a black Fiesta Party Rentals polo shirt and tan slacks. He was reclined in a plastic chair, with his feet propped up on a crate of tiki torches. "I have played sports since I was a little guy. I learned quickly that when you take a risk, whether it's taking a shot down the field, or driving inside to the hoop, that's where scoring happens. So, I guess I developed a high tolerance for risk."

"That matches up with your story," Oliver agreed.

"Oh, you mean my daring little scheme?" Clayton laughed.

"Have you played much Baccarat?"

"Enough to know how to win," Clayton replied confidently.

"So, what's your next play?"

"Law school at Georgetown. Not much risky about that," Clayton sighed. "Except for the additional debt I'm going to have to take on."

"But you don't seem too worried about it," Oliver mused.

"Not really. I have a lot of ideas for the future and they don't involve being in debt for long. I think I will be making a lot of money in the future, so I'll just add to my debt and take care of it after law school."

"What will your debt total be by then?"

"Let's see, with housing and tuition, I will owe another $210,000. Add in my $128,000 and I should get it up to $338,000."

Oliver whistled. "And you are ok with this?"

"Well, not really. But I plan to work summers and I should be able to get some well-paying internships in DC. So, I don't think it will really get that high."

"Fair enough," Oliver agreed. "Did you happen to put together your goals or your budget for this meeting?"

"Not really. I threw a budget together just before you arrived." Clayton handed Oliver a print-out of his spreadsheet. It was surprisingly organized and well considered. "I've got so many goals a single piece of paper wouldn't hold them."

Oliver nodded, hiding his disappointment that Clayton wasn't as committed to the process as his friends. He shrugged it off and focused on the work Clayton had done.

"This looks like you put a lot of time into it," Oliver commented, looking through the numbers.

"Not really. I know my numbers. It's just that they are about to change again."

"That's ok, this will get you through August and you should be able to take a nice bite out of your debt, before you go back to Georgetown."

"That's what I was thinking," Clayton agreed, dropping his feet off the crate and leaning forward to look at the same spreadsheet.

Annual Income of $12,450

Monthly Income		
Salary Income (before taxes, social security, etc.):	$ 1,050.00	
Total Monthly Take Home Income:		**$ 1,050.00**
Monthly Fixed Expenses:		
Minimum Credit Card Payment	$ 100.00	
Gym Membership	$ 45.00	
Student Loan - Consolidated ($128,893 @ 5.25% / 20 years)	$ 869.00	
Cell Phone	$ 59.00	
Car Insurance	$ 83.00	
Total Fixed Monthly Expenses:		**$ 1,156.00**
Remaining Balance:	Negative	-$ 106.00
Additional Expenses - Cash:		
Meals & Entertainment	$ 50.00	

Gas for Car	$ 200.00	
Personal / Clothes Fund	$ 50.00	
Total Additional Expenses:		**$ 300.00**
Remaining Balance:	**Negative**	**-$ 406.00**

"You're going negative every month?" Oliver asked, as he looked at the bottom line.

"Pretty much. I use my credit card as I need to," Clayton explained. "But my parents have a sweet little guest house, so I live there rent free and help out with repairs and such. I'm pretty fortunate."

"That's great," Oliver agreed. "Do you have a list of your debts?"

"No, but I know basically what they are," Clayton flipped the spreadsheet over and listed his debts quickly.

List of Clayton's Debts	
Credit Cards	$ 12,800.00
Department Store Credit Cards	$ 4,500.00
Student Loan	$128,893.00
Total Debt:	**$146,193.00**

"Pretty impressive," Clayton said with a smile.

"I've seen a lot worse," Oliver admitted. "If that helps."

"Oh, I'm sure you have. I'm only 24. Just imagine the debt I can pile up by the time I'm thirty."

"Good point. So, your focus is to pay down your debt over the summer?" Oliver persisted.

"That's what it says on paper," Clayton dodged.

"Do you have another plan?"

"Not one that I'm willing to share," Clayton was elusive.

"I'll let it go at that."

Clayton's phone buzzed. "Sorry, Oliver, I just have a few more minutes. I have a conference call at 2:00."

"No problem," Oliver looked up from the spreadsheet. "Anything else I should know?"

"Yeah, Nicole pulled some strings and helped me land an internship at Interloper in their analytics department, building forecasting models and what not."

"Sounds impressive..."

"Yeah, I guess so. It pays something like $25.00 an hour. So, I'll keep this job and work there some, too. Should help with the debts."

"OK." Oliver used a pen to mark-up Clayton's budget. "So, would your summer budget look more like this?"

Clayton looked at the mark-up and said. "No, actually, I'm going to give Interloper 40 hours a week. They said I can work nights and such. So, I'll keep this job, plus the 40 hours at Interloper."

"Nice...," Oliver was impressed. "Then your budget for the three months of the summer will look like this?"

"Yeah, that's about right."

Annual Income of $12,450

Monthly Income		
Salary Income: Fiesta Party Rentals	$ 1,050.00	
Salary Income: Interloper	$ 4,400.00	
Total Monthly Take Home Income:		**$ 5,450.00**
Monthly Fixed Expenses:		
Minimum Credit Card Payment	$ 100.00	
Gym Membership	$ 45.00	
Student Loan - Consolidated ($128,893 @ 5.25% / 20 years)	$ 869.00	
Cell Phone	$ 59.00	
Car Insurance	$ 83.00	
Total Fixed Monthly Expenses:		**$ 1,156.00**
Remaining Balance:		**$4,294.00**
Additional Expenses - Cash:		
Meals & Entertainment	$ 50.00	
Gas for Car	$ 300.00	
Personal / Clothes Fund	$ 50.00	
Total Additional Expenses:		**$ 400.00**
Remaining Balance:		**$3,894.00**

"I'll need a little spending money to get out to Georgetown, but I should be able to send a lump sum payment of $10,000 against my student loan principle."

"That sounds like a good plan," Oliver agreed. He then added, "You may want to consider reducing your credit card debt, rather than the student loan, since it has a higher interest rate. A good goal might be to pay off your credit card debt before you leave for Georgetown."

"Yeah, that's a good call. Thanks for that," Clayton smiled.

A woman in her early sixties entered the warehouse from the single door to the Fiesta Party Rental offices. She waved and Clayton stood and waved back. "On my way!"

"It looks like you need to leave," Oliver stood up, as well.

"Yeah, I've got that conference call. Thank you for coming out," Clayton shook Oliver's hand.

"I hope it was a little helpful?" Oliver asked, as he followed Clayton across the warehouse floor.

"Sure, it was. You made me look at my debt and think through my plan a little. I have some things to work on. It's just that...." Clayton hesitated.

"You're going to law school and your taking on even more debt?"

"Yeah. It's hard to take a stand when everything about my life is still in motion."

12

JOE FRISCO

Joe Frisco: Film & History Major, UCLA
Remaining Student Debt: $54,822.17
Current Position: Part-Time Teacher and Stunt Double,
Working on a Documentary Film
Annual Salary: $27,750

"Stunt double? Really?"

"Really," Joe said modestly. They were sitting in a beach café, sipping beers, and enjoying the late afternoon sun.

"Sounds dangerous," Oliver was intrigued.

"They take a lot of precautions. I've never been hurt. Just a little sore."

"And it pays well?" Oliver asked.

"It does for the bigger films. But not for the ones I do. But it's more money than I can make substitute teaching."

"And how often do you get these roles?"

"Not often. I'm pretty busy with teaching and my documentary project. I get the odd call."

"That's pretty cool," Oliver said approvingly, as he slid the lime wedge into the neck of the bottle and took a sip of beer.

"Thanks..."

"Did any of your friends brief you on these meetings?"

"Yeah, Kelsey gave me the run down. I have my budget and a list of my debts ready."

"How about your story?" Oliver asked.

"You mean the little plans that Nicole asked us to create?" Oliver nodded and Joe chuckled. "I missed that assignment. Didn't have anything prepared. So, I declared bankruptcy."

"I wish it was that easy," Oliver replied thoughtfully.

"It was explained to me that going bankrupt is not an option with student debt," Joe said evenly.

"I guess if it was an option, a lot of people would do it."

"Makes sense. We're young. We can go BK, wait the seven years, and then full speed ahead."

"Instead, you can pay off your debt in those same seven years, and then it's full steam ahead."

"Yeah, it could be worse. I only have $54,000 in student debt."

"Well, I want to commend you on keeping your tuition costs low. $54,000 isn't too bad."

"Thanks. My family can cover it, but I'm one of those proud people who don't ask for money. I make my own way. I worked through college, paid my own bills, and chose a state college."

"Any other debts?"

"Credit card debt and a pretty major car loan," Joe admitted.

"I'm sorry to hear that. But I will do what I can to help you out."

"Thanks. When you see my budget, you'll understand where that credit card debt is coming from."

"Got it." Oliver continued, "How are you doing with the 5 steps that I sent to you?"

"Step one is underway. We've got our accountability group going," Joe replied simply.

"Step two, then? Should we look at your list of debts?"

Joe nodded and lifted his portfolio from the chair next to him and retrieved his notes. He handed Oliver his list of debts. It felt heavy in his hand.

List of Joe's Debts	
Credit Cards	$ 9,318.00
Car Loan	$ 14,759.00
Student Loan #1	$ 44,529.00
Student Loan #2	$ 6,367.00
Student Loan #3	$ 3,926.00
Total Debt:	**$ 78,899.00**

"Pretty major..." Joe shook his head as he watched a red life-guard jeep head down the beach in front of the restaurant.

"Yes, your credit card debt is troubling, along with your car loan. Have you thought about getting rid of your current car and swapping it for a used one?"

"I guess so. Not sure how easy that will be, but I am willing to try," Joe said gamely.

"OK, let's make that assumption and have you purchase a used car for, say, $8,000, so taxes get you up to about $10,000."

"And you would want me to pay cash for it?"

"That's the idea. Before we get into your budget, did you prepare a list of goals?"

"Sure..." Joe reached into his portfolio again and pulled out another list, handing it to Oliver.

Joe Frisco's Goals

- Get Out of Debt on My Own
- Teach History in High School
- Launch My YouTube Channel with a Series of Documentary Films
- Earn my Masters in European History
- Earn my PhD
- Teach History at the College Level

"Impressive," Oliver admitted.

"Thanks. I have a lot of work to do."

"I am confident you will do all of these things, and more."

Joe nodded modestly and let Oliver continue. "That leads us to step three. Do you have your budget with you, too?"

Joe reached into his portfolio again and handed his current budget to Oliver. "It needs some work."

Annual Income of $27,750.00

Monthly Income		
Salary Income (before taxes, social security, etc.):	$ 2,312.00	
Estimated Taxes Withheld Each Month	$ 475.00	
Total Monthly Take Home Income:		**$ 1,837.00**
Monthly Fixed Expenses:		
Rent	$ 650.00	
Car Payment	$ 349.00	
Minimum Credit Card Payment	$ 250.00	
Student Loan #1: Consolidated ($44,529 @ 5.5% / 10 years)	$ 484.00	
Student Loan #2: Non-Consolidated ($6,367 @ 3.75% / 5 years)	$ 117.00	
Student Loan #3: Perkins Loan ($3,926 @ 4.5% / 10 years)	$ 41.00	
Cell Phone	$ 109.00	
Home Phone / Cable / Internet	$ 69.00	
Water / Electricity & Gas	$ 42.00	
Car Insurance	$ 68.00	
Renters Insurance	$ 33.00	
Total Fixed Monthly Expenses:		**$2,212.00**
Remaining Balance:	Negative	- $ 375.00
Additional Expenses - Cash:		
Groceries	$ 250.00	
Meals & Entertainment	$ 100.00	
Gas for Car	$ 350.00	
Personal / Clothes Fund	$ 100.00	
Total Additional Expenses:		**$ 800.00**
Remaining Balance:	Negative	-$1,175.00

"You are negative over a thousand dollars each month?"

"Some months, I am. I don't count my stunt work income in my budget."

"Why not?"

"Too unreliable," Joe replied. "When I do earn a stunt check, I treat it as found money and throw it at my credit card debt."

"Sounds reasonable," Oliver said, putting his red pen to his lips as he reviewed Joe's numbers.

"Are you opposed to living at home, just until you get out of debt?"

"It's not my first choice. Like I said, I want to make my own way. But if I had to, I could work something out."

"That's good. Then I would strongly suggest that you make that move. The $650 in rent is the biggest opportunity that you have to get out of debt. That and a weekend job."

"Max and Kelsey warned me that I would be working weekends," Joe took another sip of his beer.

"What will you do?"

"I know people in production. I can get editing projects in my spare time. It's tedious work, but the money is good."

"How much do you think you could make in a month?" Oliver asked, jotting notes.

Joe looked out over the ocean and did the calculation in his head. "$2,000, maybe. If I put my own film projects on hold."

"What do you think? Is it worth it to get out of debt?"

"Not really. I need to get my career going and these side jobs are just a distraction. I also want to go back to grad school and get my masters and PhD in history. It's hard to know what to tackle first."

"I understand. Well, let's see what the numbers look like. If we can get you through your current debt quickly, then you would be free to pursue your projects and your masters. Are you able to synergize those efforts?

"You mean my film project and my masters?'

"Yes, can the project you are working on for your historical documentary be applied to your masters?"

"I hadn't thought of that," Joe lifted his bottle and looked past it at the ocean. There was no wind, and the conditions were glassy. "Maybe. That's a cool idea."

"So, if we can get you out of debt, you could move forward with your plans?"

"Sounds like it," Joe released his eyes from the ocean and took a quick swig of beer.

"Great! We'll add the editing jobs to your monthly income, swap out your current car, and eliminate your rent and other living expenses."

"I want to help my parents with grocery costs," Joe insisted. "I'll take their free rent, but I don't want to be a total free-loader."

"That's fair. We'll plug some money in for that, too."

The revised budget follows:

Annual Income of $51,750.00

Monthly Income		
Salary Income (before taxes, social security, etc.): Teaching	$ 2,312.00	
Salary Income (before taxes, social security, etc.): Editing	$ 2,000.00	
Estimated Taxes Withheld Each Month	$ 875.00	
Total Monthly Take Home Income:		**$ 3,437.00**

Monthly Fixed Expenses:		
Rent	$ 00.00	
Car Payment	$ 00.00	
Minimum Credit Card Payment	$ 250.00	
Student Loan #1: Consolidated ($44,529 @ 5.5% / 10 years)	$ 484.00	
Student Loan #2: Non-Consolidated ($6,367 @ 3.75% / 5 years)	$ 117.00	
Student Loan #3: Perkins Loan ($3,926 @ 4.5% / 10 years)	$ 41.00	
Cell Phone	$ 109.00	
Home Phone / Cable / Internet	$ 00.00	
Water / Electricity & Gas	$ 00.00	
Car Insurance	$ 68.00	
Renters Insurance	$ 00.00	
Total Fixed Monthly Expenses:		**$1,069.00**

Remaining Balance:		**$ 2,368.00**

Additional Expenses - Cash:		
Groceries	$ 250.00	
Meals & Entertainment	$ 50.00	
Gas for Car	$ 350.00	
Personal / Clothes Fund	$ 50.00	
Total Additional Expenses:		**$ 700.00**

Remaining Balance:		**$1,668.00**

"That's better," Joe agreed. "If I applied the whole $1,668 to my debt each month, how long until I get out of debt?"

"It would look like this," Oliver took Joe's list of debts and wrote notes in the margins.

List of Joe's Debts		
Credit Cards	$ 9,318.00	Month 7 - 12
Purchase Car (price + tax and license)	$ 10,000.00	Month 1 - 6
Student Loan #1	$ 44,529.00	Month 19 - 40
Student Loan #2	$ 6,367.00	Month 15-18
Student Loan #3	$ 3,926.00	Month 12 - 14
Total Debt:	**$ 74,140.00**	**3 years and 4 months**

"I will be out of debt in under three and a half years?"

"That's what these numbers are telling us, Joe," Oliver stated evenly.

"Amazing," Joe sighed deeply. "Totally amazing."

"Is it worth moving back home? Is it worth delaying your documentary projects?"

"It is. I'll take care of this debt and then get to work on my masters."

"That's right. You could plan to start in the fall, three years from now. You'll be debt free and probably earning a lot more money by then."

"Yeah, I should be teaching high school history somewhere. Major leap in income. Then I would have summers, nights, and weekends to work on my projects and get my masters and PhD. I should be able to accomplish most of my goals by the time I'm thirty."

"And then you can pursue teaching at a university," Oliver continued.

"Exactly," Joe sighed again. "I felt so stuck before. But now I feel like I have a real plan. And not just to get out of debt, but to nail all of my goals."

"Pursue your goals, Joe. That's why you got into debt to begin with," Oliver said with a smile. "It's all going to be worth it."

"Amazing," Joe finished his beer. "Thanks, Oliver."

13

NICOLE CHEN

Nicole Chen: Computer Science and Software Engineering, San Jose State University

Remaining Student Debt: $39,412.89

Current Position: Project Manager, Enterprise Cloud Solutions, Interloper, Inc.

Annual Salary: $125,000

"I have to maintain my image," Nicole explained, checking her cell phone.

"Explain what you mean by that," Oliver countered, as he looked over the budget that she had just handed to him. They were eating lunch at a new Italian restaurant that Nicole had recommended downtown.

"I need to maintain a lifestyle that is consistent with my position at Interloper," Nicole said simply.

"I think you can choose any lifestyle you want to choose," Oliver reasoned. "It is very important to…."

Nicole held up her hand, cutting him off, "Sorry, I need to take this."

Oliver watched as Nicole excused herself from the table and stepped outside to the sidewalk to take the call. She paced back and forth in front of the restaurant, gesturing with her words, her cell phone pressed tightly to her head. She was wearing a dark business suit and high heels and carried herself as if she were a decade older than she was. While Oliver waited, he looked over Nicole's budget. It was thorough and telling. Nicole was earning an impressive salary, but her spending was equally impressive.

Annual Income of $125,000.00

Monthly Income		
Salary Income (before taxes, social security, etc.):	$10,416.00	
401K Contributions	$1,562.00	
Estimated Taxes Withheld Each Month	$ 2,950.00	
Total Monthly Take Home Income:		**$ 5,904.00**
Monthly Fixed Expenses:		
Rent	$ 2,400.00	
Car Lease Payment	$ 1,197.00	
Gym Membership	$ 125.00	
Credit Card Charges: Groceries / Clothes / Entertainment / Gas	$ 2,250.00	
Student Loan: Consolidated ($39,412.89 @ 5.5% / 10 years)	$ 428.00	
Cell Phone	$ 182.00	
Home Phone / Cable / Internet	$ 259.00	
Water / Electricity & Gas	$ 91.00	
Car Insurance	$ 115.00	
Life Insurance	$ 100.00	
Renters Insurance	$ 58.00	
Total Fixed Monthly Expenses:		**$ 7,205.00**
Remaining Balance:	Negative	-$ 1,301.00

Oliver then reviewed her list of debts.

List of Nicole's Debts	
Credit Cards	$ 19,515.00
Car Lease (plan to purchase)	$ 63,815.00
Student Loan	$ 39,412.89
Total Debt:	**$ 122,742.89**

Nicole returned a few minutes later, flustered and a little distracted. "Sorry about that. We have an issue with a major client. I'm going to need to leave a little early."

"Then we will work quickly," Oliver said calmly.

Nicole waived the waitress over. "We need to order right now."

"Of course," The waitress was warm and engaging as she took their order. Nicole quickly rejected her suggestions for appetizers and ordered a simple pasta dish. Oliver placed a similar order and they settled in to talk before their food arrived.

"So, what do you think?" Nicole asked, glancing at her cell phone and grimacing, still a little flustered from her call.

"I think I need your undivided attention," Oliver replied firmly.

"I'm sorry, what do...."

This time Oliver cut her off. "Look, Nicole, we don't have much time. You are the one who set this whole thing up. Your plan was to bring your friends to my workshop and leverage my knowledge and the concepts from my book to help you eliminate your student loan debt. In exchange for my time, I will use your stories in my new book."

Nicole sat still, carefully listening to his words. She felt like she was back in school, contending with a tough professor.

"I have reviewed your budget and you are in serious trouble," Oliver continued. Nicole started to object, but Oliver put up his hand

Wipeout!

so he could continue. "Yes, you have a nice salary, and you are clearly on the fast track. At this pace, you could be a millionaire at a very young age. But I can tell you right now that you are not going to make it. Oh, you may look wealthy, with your expensive car, professional clothes, and higher-end home, but your net worth will be far lower than it should be."

"I'm not sure I...."

"Nicole, I am not trying to be difficult here, but since we sat down, I have been competing with your cell phone for attention. I appreciate that you are extremely busy, but we are all extremely busy. So, please turn off your cell phone so we can enjoy a nice lunch and tackle your little problem here."

Nicole nodded quietly and for a second considered leaving, but instead she took a deep breath and leaned into his criticism, relying on what her parents had told her: a wise person will listen to advice, while a fool relies on his own council.

"Thank you, Oliver," Nicole sighed. "You are right. I have been distracted and rude. My work can wait. Please tell me more about the specific issues that you see in my budget."

Oliver was impressed. He had expected significant resistance from Nicole after his direct criticism, perhaps even lunch alone. It was clear that Nicole's training as an intern in the dynamic, teamwork cultures of Silicon Valley had kicked in and opened her ears to what she needed to hear.

Oliver took a deep breath and continued. "Thank you for that, Nicole. I apologize for being so direct, but I want very much to help you. You have incredible potential, and a very bright career awaits you, but you are off to a dangerous start financially. I want you to avoid the pitfalls that trap so many other young, well-paid professionals."

"I'm listening," Nicole replied, managing a thin smile. She tucked her cell phone into her purse and settled in to absorb the lesson.

"You are currently spending more money than you make. I recognize that you believe you need to live a lifestyle that is on par with your position at Interloper, but you are way over your head. You need to simplify your life, spend less money, drive a more affordable car, lower your housing costs, back off the use of your credit card and shop for clothes at discount stores. You need to adopt a lifestyle that is 180 degrees in the other direction from where you are headed now."

"Wow. Are you serious?"

"Let me ask you a question," Oliver reset the conversation. "Do you want to be financially independent?"

"I don't really care about that right now," Nicole admitted. "I'm still pretty young. I can address retirement later. You see that I am maxing my 401K contributions."

"That's certainly true, but you are also maxing your credit cards."

"I'm actually nowhere close to the limit..." Nicole began and then stopped herself.

"Let me try again, Nicole," Oliver paused. "Do you want to be a millionaire?"

"Sure. Who doesn't?"

"Well, I am telling you right now that, even though you make a high salary, and will no doubt receive stock options, bonuses and promotions that will earn you a lot of money, you will not become a millionaire if you continue to spend as you are now."

"Yes, but I am just getting started. I can worry about that later," Nicole reasoned.

"You should start now and begin a lifestyle trajectory and philosophy that attain your long-term goals. Your future spouse may have student loan debt, or similar spending habits as yours. You may have children, and you will want to provide them with a nice life, cater to their sports, maybe send them to private school. I am strongly urging you to make these adjustments now, so you have them well incorporated into your life for when greater expenses and responsibilities arrive."

"I understand," Nicole replied. "You have made some good points. And, yes, I do want to be a millionaire and, some day, I do want to be financially independent. And I want very much to eliminate my student loan debt as quickly as possible."

"I am glad to hear you say this," Oliver replied.

"I guess I am, too," Nicole said with a warm smile. "I know that I am spending too much. It's happening so fast. I get on a bit of a power trip and it is hard to stop. I need your advice to reign me in before I really get into trouble. Sorry, for the way I acted. Please show me what I need to do."

Oliver shook his head, amazed by the transformation, and not 100% certain of her sincerity. But as he pressed through the numbers, he could tell that he had captured Nicole's attention and she had bought in completely. He drafted a new budget for her, that was designed to pay off her debt quickly and then put Nicole on the solid path to becoming both a millionaire and financially independent. As they worked through the budget, their food arrived, and they enjoyed pasta and talked about what Nicole could accomplish if she mastered her finances.

She explained that she had just leased her car and still had three years to go but agreed that she would pay cash for a nice used car for her next purchase. She also agreed to several other major adjustments, like cutting her spending, quitting her gym, and moving to a more affordable apartment with a roommate. She would put cash in dedicated envelopes for food, clothing, and entertainment, so she would not overspend her budget. She would also set aside additional funds to begin investing, outside of her company 401K.

The resulting budget looked like this.

Annual Income of $125,000.00

Monthly Income		
Salary Income (before taxes, social security, etc.):	$10,416.00	
401K Contributions	$1,562.00	
Estimated Taxes Withheld Each Month	$ 2,950.00	
Total Monthly Take Home Income:		**$ 5,904.00**
Monthly Fixed Expenses:		
Rent	$ 850.00	
Car Lease Payment	$ 1,197.00	
Gym Membership	$ 00.00	
Credit Card Charges: Misc & Emergencies + Minimum	$ 300.00	
Student Loan: Consolidated ($39,412.89 @ 5.5% / 10 years)	$ 428.00	
Cell Phone	$ 89.00	
Home Phone / Cable / Internet	$ 95.00	
Water / Electricity & Gas	$ 45.00	
Car Insurance	$ 115.00	
Life Insurance	$ 100.00	
Renters Insurance	$ 58.00	
Total Fixed Monthly Expenses:		**$ 3,277.00**
Additional Expenses – Cash in Envelopes:		
Savings	$ 00.00	
Groceries	$ 250.00	
Meals & Entertainment	$ 100.00	
Gas for Car	$ 200.00	
Personal / Clothes Fund	$ 100.00	
Total Additional Expenses:		**$ 650.00**
Remaining Balance:		**$ 1,977.00**

Oliver then reviewed her list of debts and paid them off with the additional available funds.

List of Nicole's Debts		
Credit Cards	$ 19,515.00	Month 1 - 9
Save to Purchase Used Car with Cash	$ 20,000.00	Month 30 - 37
Student Loan	$ 39,412.89	Month 10 - 29
Total Debt:	**$ 78,927.00**	**3 years, 1 month**

"So, in three years I will be totally debt free, own my car outright, and be saving $3,600 per month?" Nicole was excited.

"Yes, and that does not factor in raises, promotions, and other windfalls. Now, once you get out of debt and pay cash for your new car, you may want to open up your budget a little. But, yes, you will be able to invest about $3,600 per month once you are out of debt and have purchased your used car. If you can continue to save $3,600 per month, with an average compounded interest rate of 10% per year, you will save over $1 million in 12 years."

"Really! I will only be 36 years old," Nicole beamed.

"Pretty amazing, isn't it. And that's why I wanted to get your attention today. This is important stuff, Nicole. I see how hard you work. What's the point if are not saving to become financially independent? One day you may want to be a mom, start your own business, or simply retire. By saving now, you can do those things."

"I think this might be the most important lunch I have ever had," Nicole said, almost apologetically.

"Would you describe it as a power lunch?" Oliver smiled.

"Definitely. Super-power!"

14

DOUBLING DOWN

The mid-afternoon freeway traffic was light, and they made good time getting to the airport. Kelsey took the offramp and weaved through the two-lane traffic, following taxis and shuttles as they neared the terminals. The lights at the train tracks flashed red and she pulled to a stop.

"Thanks again for the lift," Clayton said, his eyes on the rental car shuttle idling in front of them. He had a single suitcase, packed with three rented Tuxedos, a bathing suit, and a few sets of workout clothes. His wallet held $50,000 in cash and a folded boarding pass. He was flying one way to Las Vegas.

"Are you sure about this, Clayton?" Kelsey asked, as a commuter train rumbled past.

"Yeah," Clayton said with an easy smile. "You know me, Kelsey. I've got to be true to myself."

"You have always been good about that," She replied, staring ahead at the flashing red lights and the crossing barrier.

Clayton was ready to change the subject. "How's it going with you and Joe?"

Kelsey smiled and admitted, "Really great. I like Joe a lot."

"*Like*?" Clayton queried.

"Yeah… Well, you know what I mean." Kelsey flushed, feeling the warmth in her face.

"Well, I know how Joe feels about you and *like* doesn't begin to describe it," Clayton shook his head.

Kelsey kept her eyes fixed on the red lights, while her pulse quickened. The lights stopped flashing and the cross bar raised, allowing the traffic to move again. Clayton had succeeded in diverting her attention away from the most urgent topic. She drove for a while in silence, wanting to switch the conversation back to him and push a little harder, but unsure of what to say. This was crazy, right? She wanted to talk her friend off the ledge but knew he wouldn't listen. She took the ramp to Terminal One Departures and angled through the slowly moving cars, eventually navigating her way to the white curb.

"Well, good luck," Kelsey said finally. She looked over at her friend and searched his eyes. Clayton could tell that she was worried about him.

"I keep telling you, Kelsey," Clayton smiled and opened the door to get out. "This has nothing to do with luck."

"Ok, fine," Kelsey said, exasperated. "Good probabilities."

"That's more like it, Miss Sizemore," Clayton got out of her car and closed the door. He waved quickly and turned toward the departures entrance, pulling his suitcase behind him.

15

BACK TO SCHOOL

Two Years Later: Mrs. Vandamme sighed deeply when no one in her class raised their hands. She adjusted her white, cat-eyed glasses and peered through them at her high school students. "Did I mention we have a midterm on Thursday?"

The class looked back at her blankly. No one moved, their eyes were half focused on anything but her. She hated these first period classes, when her students were still half asleep. She always marveled that even her advance placement physics students were so quiet at this hour. She had thought they would be fired up and completely engaged, but she had to remind herself that these were the same kids that were staying up late every night to keep pace with the workload for all of their other AP classes, and their sports, arts and club activities. "You think you're sleepy now? Just wait until college," she warned them, turning back to the screen.

Mrs. Vandamme switched to the next slide and was about to cover the equation when the bell rang. The formerly comatose students shot out of their chairs like they had received an electric shock. Another marvel of the modern American high school student, they had so much energy and so much lethargy at the same time.

"OK, People!" She shouted over the commotion. "Don't forget to read Chapter 13 tonight and there will be 2 important worksheets posted online. All of it will be on your mid-term, so make it a priority."

Justin West grabbed his backpack and tennis bag and was the first into the hallway. He wanted to get to his AP Government class early to ask Mr. Frogly a few questions about the paper he assigned the day before. Two of his friends from the high school tennis team caught up to him by the stairs. They were all wearing their match day hoodie sweatshirts. "Hey, West!"

Justin turned at the top of the stairs and let Travis and Jonathan catch up to him.

"What's the hurry?"

"I need to talk to Frogly about a paper. His instructions aren't very clear and it's due on Friday."

"Are you going to that college thing at lunch?" Travis asked, pulling a snack out of his backpack, while checking his cell phone.

"Oh, yeah. I guess so," Justin stammered, he had completely forgotten about it. "Maybe..."

"Cool. We'll save you a seat." Jonathan fist bumped Justin and pounded down the steps. Travis and Justin followed.

"You think it's going to be crowded?" Justin asked, taking the steps two at a time.

Travis reached the bottom of the stairs just ahead of Justin and spun around. "Are you kidding? Look at these lunatics."

Justin looked around, watching the kids race from class to class, each carrying overloaded backpacks and worried expressions on their faces.

"It's about COLLEGE, Justin," Travis laughed. "EVERYONE will be there."

Justin entered the auditorium late and it was already packed. He saw Travis and Jonathan waving from the back of the room, near the rafters. They were sitting with Kaitlin and Celeste, two girls who were part of their regular group. Justin took a seat between Kaitlin and Travis, dropping his tennis bag and backpack, which weighed roughly the same as a boat anchor, on the polished cement floor in front of him. They caught up on the happenings of the day, while the auditorium echoed with a crowd of voices that competed to be heard.

One of the high school counselors, Miss Lantern, walked across the stage and up to the podium, while five or six other people followed behind her. They were young and well dressed and looked like they were on their way to important meetings after the assembly. The display screen was down, and the introduction slide of the day's presentation boldly stated, "Wipeout!".

"Thank you, Students," Miss Lantern spoke into the microphone. She was universally loved by the students, so they came to attention quickly. If it was Mrs. Vandamme or Mr. Frogly it would have taken them several minutes to quiet down the noisy auditorium.

"Thank you all for coming today. This is part three of our Consider College Workshop Series and you are all in for a treat today. Our guest is Oliver Powers. He is the author of a new book about college debt called *Wipeout!*. He is also joined today by a panel of recent college graduates who were the subject of his book. I will let Mr. Powers introduce the panel. Now, I know I can count on all of you to give Mr. Powers your undivided attention and a warm Night Owl welcome."

The high school students clapped, cheered, and gave the characteristic "HOOT! HOOT! HOOT!" of their Night Owl mascot. Kelsey, Nicole, Max, and Joe took their seats at the panel table, while Oliver took the podium and thanked Miss Lantern. Clayton was at Georgetown in his second year of law school and unable to attend.

The hoots continued to echo through the auditorium as the students poured it on. Joe laughed, "Classic."

"Does it make you want to be back in high school again?" Kelsey asked, as she settled in and popped open the ice-cold bottle of water that had been placed in front of her microphone.

"Not in a million years!" Max shouted, as the hoots died down suddenly. "These kids have no idea what's about to hit them."

His words were caught on his microphone and the auditorium went silent for a second, then all of the kids started to laugh.

Max and his friends joined in their laughter. "Just kidding," Max waived. "I loved every minute of high school."

The students cheered and started hooting again. Everyone on the panel was laughing now and Oliver had a hard time getting control of the room. Finally, when he started to tell a joke, they all settled in to hear the punch line. It was a stupid joke, so the punchline was met with pathetic groans, but it gave Oliver the opening he needed.

"The people on this panel all went to high school just a few miles from here," Oliver began. "They joined me today for one reason only, to answer your questions about college. And they will provide you with their candid, unvarnished opinions."

The students were completely focused now. They usually heard from college recruiters who tried to sell them on the various benefits of their universities. It was a breath of fresh air to hear from recent college graduates.

"I met these terrific people at a workshop I was leading, not so different from this one. When they came to me, they were all deeply in debt. Student loan debt. Because when they were your age, in a high school just like this one, they didn't really consider the cost of college. Instead, they were focused on getting into the most prestigious college that would accept them. And many of them, as well as their high school classmates, went to those expensive and prestigious colleges. And now they are trapped in terrible debt." Oliver took a sip of his water and smiled at his friends on the panel. Max saluted him and a few of them raised their water bottles in a mock toast.

Oliver moved his presentation forward from the introduction slide to a slide that listed the panel's debt after graduation and compared it to their debt now. "The average college graduate has student loan debt of about $35,000 and it will take them between 10 and 20 years to pay it off. Some college graduates have much higher debt than that. On this slide, you can see that a few members of this panel graduated with over $100,000 in debt."

A murmur of surprise spread through the auditorium as they reviewed the slide and the faces of the panel who had carried all that debt.

Name:	Debt Upon Graduation:	Debt Today:
Max Hiatt	$93,715	$42,816
Kelsey Sizemore ·	$104,812	$25,362
Clayton Moss	$128,893	$124,896
Joe Frisco	$54,822	$14,149
Nicole Chen	$39,412	$12,816

Oliver waited for it to quiet down again, grateful that they were paying attention.

"Today, approximately 70% of college graduates will borrow money to complete their four-year degrees. But that's not all. Because of the high monthly payments that each college graduate needs to make on those college loans, and the high cost of living, and their low starting salaries, many college graduates will also take on a lot of credit card debt to stay afloat…"

Max interrupted, "He's not kidding. Most of us took on huge credit card debt just to pay our bills. The debt you see on the chart is just for our college loan debts. The rest of our debt would make that number even higher. And we had to pay that credit card debt off first, before we could even think of paying off the student loan debt."

Oliver smiled and continued, "Thanks, Max. He's right. Most of this panel, and many college graduates, use their credit cards to make ends meet. The resulting combination of credit card debt and student loan debt is really terrible."

"I know that you most of you are aware of the national media discussion regarding the crushing levels of debt that today's college graduate has to carry. And we want to talk about that debt and some of your alternatives and options for avoiding it. Or, if you do decide to take on debt to attend your dream university, we want to provide you with some ways to get out of that debt quickly."

Oliver spoke for a few more minutes, hitting on the reasons why college students willingly took on the debt. He then covered some of the approaches for getting out of debt quickly, including his slide for the 5 Steps for Eliminating College Debt, without boring them with too many details.

5 Steps to Eliminate College Debt

Step 1: Form an Accountability Group

Step 2: Face Your Debt

Step 3: Set Your Goals

Step 4: Lower Your Overhead

Step 5: Create a Budget with Money Left Over to Quickly Eliminate Debt

"It is my hope that today's presentation will help you avoid graduating from college with a lot of debt," Oliver concluded the slide. "But for many of you, it will not be possible. This list is for you – or will be when you graduate."

He then transitioned to his panel with a repeat of the slide that showed their debt upon graduation and where it was today.

"Again, this is the amount of debt that each of these people had when they graduated. Now, most college graduates will carry that debt for another 10 or 20 years. But I worked with each person here and showed them how to eliminate their debts in about three years. After this exercise, I wrote my book *Wipeout!*, which takes an unusual approach to showing graduates how to eliminate their college debt quickly."

"That's enough from me. I now want to turn the remainder of the presentation over to the panel. They will each introduce themselves and then we will open it up to questions. Oliver turned the floor over to Kelsey, Joe, Nicole and Max.

Nicole leaned into her microphone. "Hi, my name is Nicole Chen and I went to San Jose State University to study computer science. I had about $40,000 in debt when I graduated."

"Hey, guys! I'm Max Hiatt. University of Texas at Austin. Hook-Em Horns! I was a business major. And I escaped college with, like, $93,000 in debt." The students cheered and Max stood and took a bow.

Kelsey waited for them to quiet down. "That's nothing. My name is Kelsey Sizemore. I studied accounting at University of Arizona and graduated with my undergraduate degree in accounting and my MBA. So, I was there for 5 years. My debt when I graduated was $104,000."

The students erupted into cheers again. When they calmed down, Joe continued.

"This feels like an AA meeting," Joe quipped, making his fellow panelists laugh, while the high school kids looked on. Joe cleared his throat and started again. "The name's Joe Frisco. UCLA film and history major. And I had about $55,000 in debt when I graduated."

The students cheered again, but not as loudly as they had for Max and Kelsey. For the first time ever, Joe was a little jealous of their bigger debt.

A student hand shot up. "Where's Clayton Moss?"

Nicole looked down the table at the rest of the panel and they nodded for her to go ahead. "He's at Georgetown getting his law degree."

The student remained standing and asked Oliver, "Um, I see that each of these graduates got their debt down really fast. But, um, why is Clayton still in so much debt?"

"Good question," Oliver motioned to the panel table. "I'll let our panel answer the questions."

Kelsey cleared her throat. "It's kind of a long story. But Clayton actually paid off the $128,000 he owed in a single weekend. He's, uh, creative that way. The debt he has now is from his law school tuition at Georgetown. So, he paid off all of his college undergraduate debt and now he is taking on new debt for law school."

Another hand shot up and a student in the third row wearing a baseball cap and black hoodie sweatshirt stood up. "How did Kelsey pay off almost $80,000 in debt, when Nicole has only paid about $25,000 in debt?"

Nicole blushed and leaned into the microphone. "That's because I had over $20,000 in credit card debt and I have lots of other expenses. Kelsey is, well…"

"I live at home now, so my only real expense is my student loan debt. I am paying it off as fast as I can. And then I will get my own apartment and all the rest of the expenses that Nicole is paying now. So, everyone's situation is a little different."

"That's the thing," Joe joined in. "We all make different incomes, we all have different living situations, and we all had different amounts of debt. So, we're paying it off at different speeds. It's been about two years. But at the end of next year, I think all of us will be debt free. It will take us about three years to pay off our college debt. But it takes a lot of people 10 or even 20 years."

Nicole pointed up to the rafters, "Yes, you have a question? Way up in the last row. The cute boy with the messy hair." The auditorium burst into laughter as Justin West stood up. He waited for the crowd to calm down and then shouted. "Would you do it again?"

"Do it again?" Nicole asked. "You mean, would we take on all of this debt, if we could start over?"

Justin listened to her reply and then raised his voice again. "Yeah! If you were like us, sitting here in a high school assembly, and you can choose your college and pick your debt and all that stuff. Would you do it again?"

"Hell no," Max whispered into his microphone. The room went silent.

Nicole leaned into her microphone. "I think I would make many of the same decisions about college. I am really happy with the choices that I made and all of the opportunities I received because of my college. But I would definitely change a few things. I would not spend as much money. I would never own a credit card. San Jose State is a good deal, so I would choose it again. But no, I would not take on all the credit card debt. No way."

Kelsey spoke up as they moved down the panel table. "Maybe I could have gone to community college for the first two years and gotten my general courses out of the way. Then I could finish my degree at a four-year school. That would have saved a lot of money. But I really enjoyed my college years. They were amazing. So, it's a decision everyone has to make for themselves. I would probably stay in state for college if I could do it again. It is so much cheaper than going to college out of state."

"I went to school in state and I worked different jobs all through college," Joe began. "I wanted to pay for college on my own, even though my parents offered to cover it. I selected an inexpensive college path, but the debts still piled up. Hard to avoid. Tuition is one thing. Meals and living expenses really add up. I agree with Kelsey. Take a good hard look at community college, shop around for scholarship opportunities, and consider going to college as a commuter student," Joe offered.

There was a rumble through the auditorium. Most of the high school kids present were dreaming of the leafy lawns, brick buildings, and college football games on Saturdays. The thought of living at home for another few years while they commuted to a local college sounded dreadful.

"I know what you are thinking," Max said into his mike. "It sucks living at home and not going off to the cool, big school. I agree with all that. Like I said, I went to University of Texas and I had an awesome time. I made tons of friends, partied, and went to football games. I also met a lot of pretty girls. They were the best days of my life, so far. But was it worth $100,000 of debt?" Max paused for effect. Then he leaped to his feet and put his arms in the air, as if he had just scored the winning touchdown. "Totally!"

The auditorium erupted with applause. This is what the kids wanted to hear.

Max loved the applause and soaked it in. Then he raised his hand and got control of the room again. Once it was quiet, he continued. "But $30,000, $50,000 or $100,000 of debt isn't for everyone. Without Oliver's help, I was totally sunk and thought about running away. So, if the idea of big debt is scary to you, you may want to choose the cheapest college that offers all those same things that you are looking for. And, like Joe says, shop around for some scholarships. But I really enjoyed the 4-year experience and would try to do something like it again. Except, this time, I would work summers and weekends to pay down the debt while I was enrolled. If I did it that way, my debt would have been a lot lower."

Questions were fired from all around the auditorium, with the high schoolers leaping to their feet and enthusiastically asking their questions. Their queries ranged from the best majors to beer pong tournaments. Miss Lantern gave Oliver the 5-minute warning and he walked up to the podium.

"You all had some great questions," Oliver said warmly. "I can tell that this is a smart group. We put together this list of ideas for lowering the cost of college for you. You can also find this list in the book and on my website." Oliver flipped the slide onto the screen so they could all review it, and quickly covered each idea. Many of the kids took notes or clicked photos with their cell phones.

Ideas for Lowering the Cost of College:

- **Apply to Small Liberal Arts Colleges Interested in Giving Scholarships**
- **Apply to In-State Universities**
- **Live at Home and Commute to College**
- **Attend Community College for 2 Years, Then Transfer**
- **Get an On-Campus Job While in College**
- **Graduate Early**
- **Go to College on the ROTC Program**
- **Take a Gap Year and Save More Money**

Oliver continued, "I understand that some of you have the money to go to any college you want. And I think that is great. And some of you will qualify for a great scholarship, which is terrific. And some of you don't care about student debt. You are determined to go to the college of your dreams, and you will worry about the debt later."

"These are all good choices and all good paths. But there are some of you who are really worried about the cost of college. You see the tuition costs of $20,000, $35,000, $50,000 and $75,000 a year and you think there is no way you can consider college. No way you can afford it. This list is for those kids. Because there is a way for everyone to go to college, and there is a way for everyone to pay for it. That's what this book is about." Oliver said, holding up the copy of *Wipeout!*.

"Let me be very clear. The idea that the government will pay for your college costs is a fantasy. It's not going to happen. I don't care if you are a Democrat or a Republican or an Independent. It is impossible for the government to pay for everyone's tuition. These are just empty political promises. The reality is that the cost of college will continue to rise, as the demand for college education rises. If demand for college drops, then, and only then, will tuition rates fall."

"Supply and demand, my friends. The leafy lawns, brick buildings, groovy professors, and winning football programs all cost a lot of money. And those costs are going to continue to rise. But don't worry! There are lots of ways to lower the cost of college and it is possible to pay off your college debt in just a few years of hard work and dedication. It is the same hard work and dedication that you will use to graduate from college."

"So, my advice is to keep working hard. In high school. In college. And after you graduate from college to pay for it all. That is how you are going to accomplish your goals. That is how you are going to reach your dreams. And that is how you will be successful in life. Keep working hard. Don't quit. Stay focused. And your hard work will carry you wherever you want to go."

Oliver paused and looked out over the youthful faces, so filled with dreams. "Thank you. We have enjoyed spending some time with you." The auditorium erupted in applause.

Many of the students came up on the platform to speak with Kelsey, Joe, Max and Nicole, while others took Oliver aside and asked more questions. High fives and cell phone numbers were exchanged, as the final bell sounded for the next class period. The auditorium emptied and the students went back to class, and back to their dreams of college.

16

YOUR TURN

It is now the reader's turn to form an accountability group, set your personal goals, make a list of your current debts, create a low-overhead lifestyle, and develop a budget that generates the extra cash needed to quickly pay off your debts. Each of these steps has been provided to you through the stories of Max, Kelsey, Clayton, Joe, and Nicole.

Review these examples as you put together your current budget, then continue to work on that budget until you can generate $1,000, $1,500, $2,000 or more each month to be applied to your student loan debt. By doing this, you should be able to pay off your college debt within just a few years.

I recognize that this will not be easy and may require some very significant sacrifices and life changes. However, these steps are probably necessary to allow you to pay off your debts in 2 to 5 years, rather than the 21 years that the average borrower needs to pay off their student loan debts.

Disclaimer: I realize that everyone has a different financial situation. Many people have dependents, disabilities, health issues, limiting factors, lower incomes, few career or housing options, additional debt, family obligations, and other very difficult life issues that will not allow them to implement some or all of the ideas within this book. This may be the case for you, as well. Additionally, life has a way of throwing curve balls at us that force us to abandon our plans to attend to more pressing and important issues. There are no guarantees that these steps, ideas, and examples will eliminate your student loan debts.

And I really want to emphasize that this is a work of fiction. I am not suggesting, endorsing, or recommending in any way that you gamble in Las Vegas (in any game, including Baccarat), seek a new identity, embezzle funds from your employer or steal anything from anyone. I am also not advocating personal bankruptcy. In fact, the opposite is true. I am suggesting that you face your personal debts, create a budget, develop a plan, and then work very hard to eliminate your debt as quickly as possible.

I personally do not gamble, have never stolen or embezzled, have no plans to create a new identity, and would not consider bankruptcy as a viable option. The stories in this book are there solely to underscore the desperation present in a life filled with debt, while proposing alternative solutions in a fun and easy to follow format. My goal for you, the reader, is simple. I want you to be able to pay off your debts and be free to pursue your dreams.

So, this disclaimer is here to state very clearly that there are no guarantees that any of the approaches within this book will eliminate your personal debts. However, if you do follow these steps in those areas where changes are possible, you should be able to pay off your debts more quickly.

A recap of these concepts follows. I appreciate your time in reading this book. I wish you every possible success on your journey to eliminate your student loan debt.

Five Steps to Eliminate Your College Debt

1. Form an Accountability Group
2. Set Your Goals
3. Face Your Debt
4. Lower Your Overhead
5. Create a Budget with Money Left Over to Quickly Eliminate Debt

Review of Additional Ideas:

Step 1: Form an Accountability Group:

- Create a group of people who are approximately your age and share your set of challenges.

- Develop a culture of honesty where everyone tells it like it is. This means that you share your amount of debt, your income, your expenses, and your personal struggles with each other.

- Meet frequently. Once a month is recommended, so you can review each other's monthly expenses, offer suggestions to save money, encourage each other to stay on your plan, and discourage each other from spending on items that are not in your budget.

- Invite an older, more experienced person to attend the group and act as a coach, mentor, or counselor. Have them work with each person individually to refine their plans and pay their debt off faster.

Step 2: Face Your Debt

- Create your list of debts. Order them with the highest rates of interest at the top.

- Include your student loans, credit card debt, car loan, mortgage, and money owed to friends.

- Pay off the debts with the highest interest rates first. These are probably your credit cards.

- Once you pay off your first debt, use the monthly payment from that debt to pay off the next one. Each time you eliminate a debt, use that former payment to tackle the rest of your debts. This cascading effect of increased monthly money will allow you to pay off your debts faster. Then focus on eliminating your long-term student loan debt.

Step 3: Set Your Goals

- Within the context of the group, develop your goals for your life and for eliminating your student loan debt. Write them down and commit them to memory. Refer to them daily.

- Review your goals with your accountability group. Then share your results for each goal. Continue to refine your goals to fast track your debt repayment and accomplish your life dreams.

- Work hard on your goals. Hard work creates unlimited opportunities for greater income and ways to save money.

Step 4: Lower Your Overhead

- Live beneath your means. Make sure you have plenty of money left over each month for tackling your student loan debt.

- Stop trying to compete with or impress others.

- Reject luxury and status items and buy only quality necessities.

- Refrain from spending money unnecessarily.

- Alter your entertainment expenses and look for free or inexpensive ways to spend your time. Take advantage of the free features of your community: parks, beaches, libraries, hiking trails, and special events.

- Focus on living very comfortably on 80% to 90% of your current after-tax income.

- Enjoy the amazing benefits or a life where you no longer worry about money.

Step 5: Create a Budget with Money Left Over to Quickly Eliminate Debt

- Include all expenses as you create your budget.

- Reduce expenses until you are saving at least 10% to 20% each month.

- Use the 10% to 20% of monthly savings to pay off your debts. Then begin saving.

- If you are unable to save 10% to 20% with your current income and expenses, it's time to make some larger adjustments. If you have car payments, consider selling your current car and buying an inexpensive used car. Consider selling your home and finding something more affordable with solid potential for appreciation. Or consider renting a less expensive home.

- Join the revolution of cord-cutters and eliminate your cable bill. Drop your gym membership and find no cost ways to exercise. Cook at home. Make your own coffee.

- To increase your income, take advantage of the gig economy. Wait tables, drive for a rideshare service on nights and weekends, deliver meals, take on a fun part-time job, or start a side business. Save this extra money and apply it to your debt.

- Pay cash for everything that you can. This will not work for your rent or your mortgage, but almost everything else can be purchased with cash. Cash is harder to spend than using a debit or a credit card. You are more likely to want to hold onto that $20 bill. Create envelopes for different expense categories like Groceries, Entertainment, Hair Care, Clothing, and Miscellaneous. Then set a budget, withdraw the cash at the beginning of each month, and place it in the envelopes in a secure lock box at home. Once you spend the money in an envelope and it is gone, do not replace it with more cash or begin using credit cards for these categories. Once the money is gone, you are done spending on that category until next month. For higher ticket items, save the cash in your envelopes for a few months until you have enough to buy what you want. Cash envelopes are incredibly effective and will help you stay on budget. You can spend the cash on these categories guilt free, knowing that this is part of your plan.

- Consider Tithing. If you honor God, He will bless you. You cannot out give God. If you tithe or give to a charity faithfully, you will be amazed at how the money you give comes right back to you, often multiplied many times over.

Ideas for Lowering the Cost of College:

- Apply to Small Liberal Arts Colleges Interested in Giving Scholarships
- Apply to In-State Universities
- Live at Home and Commute to College
- Attend Community College for 2 Years, Then Transfer
- Get an On-Campus Job While in College
- Graduate Early
- Go to College on the ROTC Program
- Take a Gap Year and Save More Money

WHO IS OLIVER POWERS?

Oliver Powers is my alter ego. I like to keep my personal life anonymous. I hide behind Oliver's identity, so I can be very public with financial advice.

My path to financial independence wound through similar experiences as those of the characters in this book. While I was never a drug smuggler, avoided gambling in casinos, and managed to stay out of prison, I did struggle with finances early in my life. Through a series of seminar speakers, books, and my own disciplined measures, I eventually developed the 5 Steps to Financial Independence and followed them carefully.

I wrote *First Million* and *Wipeout!* to help you become debt free and financially independent. These concepts really work. I am confident that you can attain your financial goals by following the steps within these books, regardless of your income and circumstances.